CW00735930

'23

THE MAGAZINE GIRLS

Linde Neuman
x

Perry Saunders

Sandie Roberie

Jan Iles-Kalinza.

Ann Carpenter   Janice Elvin

THE MAGAZINE GIRLS

(1960s–1980s)

Written by
ANN CARPENTER
JANICE COLLIER
SHIRLEY DUNMALL
JAN ILES-KALUZA
LINDA NEWMAN
SANDIE ROBBIE
PENNY SAUNDERS

Matador
Unit E2 Airfield Business Park,
Harrison Road, Market Harborough,
Leicestershire. LE16 7UL
Tel: 0116 279 2299
Email: books@troubador.co.uk
Web: www.troubador.co.uk/matador
Twitter: @matadorbooks

ISBN 978 1803136 202

British Library Cataloguing in Publication Data.
A catalogue record for this book is available from the British Library.

Cover by Richard Brookes

Printed and bound by CPI Group (UK) Ltd, Croydon, CR0 4YY
Typeset in 11pt Mionion by Troubador Publishing Ltd, Leicester, UK

Matador is an imprint of Troubador Publishing Ltd

Dedicated to the ones we love

Permissions

Many of the photographs in this book are taken from the authors' personal collections. For all others, the authors have made all reasonable efforts to contact copyright holders for permission and apologise for any omissions or errors in the form of credits given. Corrections may be made to future printings.

CONTENTS

PREFACE

By **Ann Carpenter,** who was fashion editor on publications including *Loving* magazine and the *London Evening News.*

The right place at the right time. Over the page, Maggie Koumi judiciously describes a niche in magazine publishing that not only let loose an astonishing bounty of groundbreaking ideas, images and writing, but opened a door of rich opportunity for young people who began working life as 'dogsbodies' then discovered a world of undreamed-of possibilities.

The authors of this book were among those youngsters. We came from sprawling pre-war suburbs and housing estates. Our parents, just emerging from WW2, which had scuppered so many dreams and ambitions, were mostly working to lower middle class with modest goals and cautious aspirations. We attended state schools which we left aged from 15 to 17 to earn our livings, didn't have university degrees or influential contacts, and gap years, had they been invented, would have been right off the scale. As it happened, none of that mattered. What we shared was curiosity, the ability to learn new skills, to embrace opportunities and face challenges, however scary. We cut our teeth working in the booming new wave of youth magazines before moving further into the heyday of wider publishing. This book charts our respective journeys from the late '60s to the mid '80s.

Working in journalism has always been a risky roller coaster. In our various careers, we have experienced many extremes, including sackings, redundancies, the bliss of some jobs, the misery of others, amazing pieces of good luck, the consequences of catastrophically bad decisions – all the while accepting the certainty of change and the value of 'getting on with it'.

We are one small group, one that has kept in touch and grown in friendship for around 50 years. The idea to document our journalistic experiences and memories shape-shifted for around four years while we procrastinated. Then COVID-19 emerged, leading to the lockdown which served to concentrate our minds and – get on with it. Not everyone in our group has directly contributed to this book, but they continue to be cherished as trusted and forever friends.

So here we are, five decades on, still working – although not necessarily getting paid for it – and still getting excited about our various activities and projects. There were countless others from ordinary backgrounds who 'fell' into this crazy period of journalism. Among them Maggie Koumi, who presented opportunities to a generation of youngsters as she rose through the ranks to become editor of a magazine selling over a million copies each month. Courageous, boundary-breaking women like her helped pave the way for a whole new culture that a generation not only became a part of but developed in other directions. We owe her a lot.

FOREWORD

By **Maggie Koumi**, former editor of *19* magazine
and *HELLO!* magazine

The memories that appear in this book bring back so very many for me, too. What 'The Magazine Girls' has captured so accurately and so well is that the '60s, '70s and '80s were periods of such creativity, excitement, friendships and, most of all, fun. A special period we were so lucky to have been a part of and shared friendships that remain fast to this day.

This book is not about me. Each Magazine Girl featured here has her own story to tell about that era. I hope just to give an overall glimpse of how things worked on magazines during that special time which, in my case, was magical.

A new era had begun which changed everything – from music to fashion and most of all attitudes which, in turn, changed the world of magazines. And we just happened to be in the right place at exactly the right time.

Just imagine working for a publication for readers who were the same age we were – who wore what we wore, who listened to the same music and knew exactly what it was they wanted to know about. Being lucky enough to be in the right place, whether as general dogsbody or secretary, with none of the qualifications that are required now, and learning and working your way into what, looking back, was a dream job.

I myself literally 'fell' into journalism when, at 18, I became the secretary of the editor of a teenage magazine called *Boyfriend* – which contained illustrated love stories and pop.

The very start of the '60s were heady days when the pop stars would stroll into our office for a chat and to be interviewed, from American stars like Gene Pitney to our own Billy Fury, Adam Faith, Cliff Richard.

Later came what was known as the Mersey Sound/Liverpool Beat – Gerry and the Pacemakers, Billy J Kramer, The Fourmost… all led by The Beatles, of course. One particularly memorable day was when The Beatles came to our office in London's Regent Street. Traffic had come to a standstill as the street was jammed with screaming fans. On leaving, John Lennon stuck his head out the door and said: "What's going on? The Queen must be coming along here."

The Rolling Stones, too, just starting out, would come to the office and sit about, hoping to appear in the magazine.

One day, I was told – not asked – by the editor to replace a sub-editor who had left, as well as to write some love stories, along with the then junior, whose job was also to make the tea, who pushed me to do it. (This young boy went on to edit some of the best-known young magazines and then owned his own publishing company.)

I didn't want to do it. Apart from not having a clue how a magazine was produced, I was more than happy being the secretary and having a great time with the other staff and looking at visiting pop stars.

I don't remember any of us going on holiday; we were having such fun in the office and didn't want to miss anything.

But, as always, I did as I was told and it was there, at that time, I learnt my production skills and how a magazine was put together. It was all typewriters, printers' rulers, cow gum to paste down photographs on the layout sheet, and Letraset – a kind of transfer – was used to spell out the titles of articles.

From there, I went on to become the production editor (and just a few years later, the editor) of a new young women's magazine in 1968 called *19* and created by my pal Terry Hornett, the once tea boy I had worked with!

This magazine was way ahead of its time. The fashion pages were cinematic, the articles controversial – the first being titled, 'Where Have All the Virgins Gone?'

19 covered all the subjects considered taboo at that time in young women's magazines – such as drugs and abortion. (Read more about some groundbreaking articles by our then features writer, Linda Newman, in her chapter inside.)

However tame that might sound today, and although mini skirts and 'free love' hippy style may have abounded, the really important subjects that affected and seriously worried and caused anxiety in young people were not considered suitable in a young women's magazine.

Almost each article caused a furore, and when our article on abortion appeared I was invited onto a television programme with a woman who immediately jumped across from her chair to mine shouting that I was evil and should be jailed for discussing such subjects with young girls and corrupting them. I told her it was precisely because of people like her that young women needed the unbiased information our articles were giving to allow them to make up their own minds. Gratifyingly, we received many letters of support from readers and even their mothers.

Those, too, were the days of plenty – records, make-up, invitations flowed into the office from public relations companies promoting their products. We were not only working at a job we loved, but we were enjoying free goodies, too. We were invited to travel abroad to see the latest holiday resorts and to previews in private cinemas of all the movies about to be released.

Here, too, producing the magazine was done lovingly by hand. Fashion transparencies were looked at carefully through an eye glass on a light screen. If something on a photograph, whether black and white or as a colour transparency, needed to be retouched, this too, incredibly, was done by hand.

The layouts were drawn by hand over a Grant projector, and title headings were created with Letraset or sometimes even hand drawn. Copy space was measured with an Ems rule (M being the widest letter in print) and typed to width and length – as overmatter (when copy was too long) was costly to cut.

A messenger would arrive promptly at 4pm to take the finished material to put on a train to the printers.

Then came a lengthy process of receiving proof pages, without the photographs in place, to check and, if necessary, correct the copy. Then a second set of proofs would arrive with copy corrected, but this time with photographs added, in order to check they were in the right place and that the captions were under the correct image. Finally, proofs of the colour pages were sent where colour corrections could be made. A vital check for the cover.

Tellingly, these happy days were before technology reared its ugly head and kept people glued to their computers – and chairs – with no real camaraderie. I wonder how many people now would be able to produce a magazine without the help of a computer?

We did work hard, but there were also shrieks of laughter to be heard. We were a united team, never wanting to let another department down. We actually enjoyed working with each other and away from the office too.

So, from working on a magazine at the start of the pop boom, then to one at the start of the youth culture and fashion revolution, my next job was at *HELLO!*, the very first celebrity- and news-based publication in 1988.

It was also the first colour magazine that could go to press on a Thursday and be on the bookstalls by the Tuesday (while also being printed in Spain!). At those times, women's weekly magazines went to press a month before and monthlies three months before publication – so there was not much chance of being up to the minute with news. At that time, too, newspapers were not printed in colour, so *HELLO!* was able to bring pages and pages of spectacular colour photo reportage of world events within three or four days of the events taking place.

Also, up till then, any celebrity interview was usually accompanied just by a headshot or one other photo. In *HELLO!*, celebrities were actually photographed inside their homes in many rooms – sometimes even in a luxury bathroom! Their weddings, babies, divorces, tragedies were always covered, and the ongoing trials and tribulations of major stars were followed avidly.

Once again, everything was done without computers. Photos scrutinised over a lightbox, layouts designed on a Grant machine – the only mod cons were a fax and a photocopier.

I originally worked as editor in the Madrid office with the owner and publisher of the magazine – then moved to the London office. Once again, it was messengers who took the layouts and photographs, this time straight to the airport, where they were flown to Madrid where the magazine was printed. Typed copy would follow via fax to the printer's.

Looking back, I find it quite amazing how all this was achieved – albeit frantically.

But when technology was introduced, the gloss and somewhat personal contact began to disappear. Whereas previously photo agencies would come in person to the office with photos they knew would be of interest to us in particular, with computers this practice stopped and hundreds of photographs – even irrelevant ones – would appear on screen twenty-four hours a day which, instead of helping, slowed everything down as you waded through them.

By the time I retired, staff were becoming glued to their computers, taking longer than ever to complete their work, as the easy ability to 'play' around with words and pictures became a temptation.

If only we had been able to film what took place every working day during those early days – the fun we had and the friendships we made.

We were so lucky. We really had the best of it.

ONE SUNNY DAY IN LONDON, 1965...

Ann was stacking shelves at her local supermarket where she worked part time.

Shirley was embarking on height-increase exercises, after noting she was so much shorter than her 'husband-to-be', George Harrison!

Sandie was selling shoes in a high-street chain. She had already decided she would become a journalist, and *nothing* was going to change her mind.

Penny, wearing false eyelashes and mini skirts, was walking in and out of short-lived jobs with a truculent air.

Janice was studying for her English A-Level – the only Advanced Level taken by any of the group.

Linda was firing off job applications to magazines in between kissing pop star posters on her bedroom wall.

Jan, the youngest, was in detention for breaking school uniform rules and bunching up her long frumpy skirt to wear as a mini.

A few years later, they were all to meet up and together begin their fascinating journeys through the world of mega-selling magazines. Read on to discover more in these captivating memoirs from each of the seven Magazine Girls...

OPPORTUNITIES IN IPC'S YOUNG MAGAZINES GROUP

the group that publishes

HONEY

MIRABELLE

19

PETTICOAT

HERS

VALENTINE

TRUE MAGAZINE

RAVE

NEW MUSICAL EXPRESS

FABULOUS 208

Rave/Future Publishing Ltd.

LINDA'S STORY

My treasured 'dog eared' press card

It's 1966, I'm 16 and England wins the World Cup, John Lennon says The Beatles are more popular than Jesus – and apologises the same year – 'Swinging London' is so called for the first time, David Jones changes his name to David Bowie… and I land a job on a magazine…

ONE

The Vanishing Virgins and Other Stories

I first became a Magazine Girl when I was seven years old and won a fancy dress competition dressed up as a cover girl.

But that's another story.

Fast forward to 1966 and my 16-year-old self, punching out the following on the sturdy click clack keys of my portable typewriter:

> *Dear Rave,*
>
> *I have been a regular reader of your fab magazine since your first issue. My ambition is to work on Rave. Please can I come and visit your office…*

I complimented their glossy posters (*Rave* had the best paper of any pop magazine at the time) and asked if there were any job vacancies. Then I typed out the same letter with appropriate alterations and sent to *Fabulous 208, Disc Weekly, New Musical Express* and a host of others. In truth, I was dying to work on *any* music magazine to get closer to my idols.

I was a pop-crazed fan; I loved the music and the good-looking singing boys. When I was 14, I queued all night for

Beatles tickets to get front-row seats when they appeared at the nearby Astoria. My autograph books were bursting with signatures from The Beatles, Walker Brothers, Everlys, Mick, Cliff and many more. School holidays were spent hunting down the London home addresses of my idols John Lennon and Paul McCartney. At that time Paul was living with actress Jane Asher in London and he was always friendly, chatty and happy to sign our books. We tracked down John Lennon's place in the days when he was married to Cynthia Lennon. She was very sweet and used to chat to us fans as she wheeled baby Julian in his pram. Then when the other Beatles arrived in their Cadillac to collect John, all hell broke loose as we tore after them screaming, shoes flying off our feet.

I went by the tiniest of clues. When *Disc Weekly* printed, 'Scott Walker has moved to St John's Wood', my friend Susan Rollo and I badgered every postman, newsagent and delivery man in the area for three weeks during the summer holidays till we found out where he lived. Then Scott came out looking like a Greek god, but the thrill was short-lived when he implored us to go away. Not what we wanted to hear. "Please," he pleaded, "or the fans will find me again. I've moved six times this year."

Susan and I stayed away for two whole weeks. Unfortunately,

Paul McCartney going into Abbey Road Recording Studios; Walker Brother Scott caught outside his flat – both snapped for posterity by my Instamatic!

when we returned there were hoards of fans on the pavement. But we found him first.

I like to think that tracking instinct was the beginnings of my 'nose' for journalism. Some years later, when I landed a job on magazines, I got to meet the idols of others, including Marc Bolan, David Cassidy, The Hollies, Cat Stevens and The Carpenters.

Borrowing from a magazine riff – this is how it happened to me…

I'm looking at a cover of *Woman* magazine dated 1950, the year I was born. A pretty woman dressed in pink and pearls smiles at the reader. She is holding up a plate of lickable cherry fancies matching the colour of her lipstick.

Who could resist? Not the three million women who bought *Woman*, not my mum, her friends and neighbours who swapped their women's weeklies.

The magazine world was booming. Paper rationing had been removed after the war and during that post-austerity period, consumer and domestic goods flooded the market. Sales soared as magazines burst into colour, tripling their pages with articles and lucrative advertising, feeding the desire to acquire. Editorial content revolved around the home and family, an attractive proposition after the unsettled years of war.

The 1950s was the golden age of magazine publishing.

Growing up, I read *Romeo, Marty, Mirabelle*; publications for the young teens on the block. Then the early '60s saw an explosion of more titles, magazines created by the unfettered talents of young people.

An envelope plopped onto the doormat. It was the one and only reply to my job quest. A very helpful someone at *Rave* had forwarded my letter to the company's training centre who invited me for an interview. I was *thrilled*, Mum was pleased and Dad would have been delighted if he'd been here.

Back to Beginnings

I was born on a snowy April day within the sound of Bow Bells, east London. That's where my Jewish grandparents settled when they came over in the early 1900s to escape from anti-Semitism in their respective homelands of Austria and Romania. My parents met in the 1930s in east London while working in the then fashionable fur trade.

When I was three, our family of four moved from a cramped Victorian flat in the East End to a brand-new large council estate in north London. Woodberry Down was heralded as 'a utopian estate of the future' and had several experimental firsts, including the country's very first health centre and London's first co-educational comprehensive school, which I went to. I can only remember being a happy 'princess', cherished by my loving parents and playfully teased by brother Len, 14 years my senior, until the day when all of our lives changed in the most devastating of ways.

Just before my twelfth birthday, my dad had a major heart attack and died two days later. He was only 53. The last time I saw my dear dad, I was rushing getting ready for school. He was still in bed when I left and although I couldn't remember Dad taking a day off from the workshop before that time, I don't even remember kissing him goodbye.

There was no such thing as grief counselling in those days; at least it wasn't offered to us, just two weeks of sleeping pills for Mum. I never cried about Dad in front of her or Len. I think in my own way I was trying to protect Mum from more heartbreak, and I saved all my tears for my pillow.

They say if a young child loses a parent, it shapes the rest of their life. I think that was true for me in the sense that becoming an emotionally buttoned-up adolescent may have contributed to problems of me going a bit wild later on.

CRUSHED DREAMS

Leave school at 16 and get a job, that's what I had to do. Staying on till 18 was out of the question. That's when I showed my tears. I wanted to go to university and be an English teacher. Work in a bank or insurance was the advice from Mum's loving, savvy but not scholastic sisters. I was moved from the academic stream to the commercial class and my good-natured, bookish brother bought me a portable typewriter. It turned out to be the best thing he could have done.

The magazine company George Newnes Ltd published over 30 titles with names that sounded like celebrities to me: *Flair, Honey, Woman's Own, Petticoat* and *Rave,* of course. A little shiver went through me as I stepped inside the handsome portico-stone building: Tower House, Southampton Street, London WC2. I'd seen that address printed many times before in magazines. It was just an address, just a building, but to me it was as glamorous as Hollywood. Now there I was, 16 years old and raring to go in 'Swinging London' as *Time Magazine* named it.

Disappointment number one. To my dismay, the training centre was *not f*or would-be writers as I'd hopelessly assumed, but to train girls to become secretaries. Six of us were interviewed that day. Shorthand and typing tests over, we were taken on a tour of *Woman's Own,* the company's best-selling title at the time.

All my earlier disappointment vanished. First, we were shown round the gleaming kitchens, a mini empire of stainless steel. We saw how tempting puddings and pies were lightly sprayed with water to keep them looking deliciously moist under the hot photographic lights and how fruit was polished till it shone. It was all very seductive. Next stop was the fashion department where rails of clothes were being coordinated for a photo shoot. Everyone working there looked super smart and confident, but at the same time seemed rather frazzled. Finally, the beauty department where we gazed at the exquisite contents of the wardrobe-sized cosmetics cupboard packed with products of every shade and shape and we were each given a lipstick and a copy of *Woman's Own*, still warm and smelling of piquant printer's ink.

Time to go. One of the girls pressed the wrong button and the lift dropped to the basement. Giggling, we stepped out into what looked like an empty photographic studio. There were spotlights, umbrellas, backdrops and props everywhere. One wall was covered in pictures of old magazine covers made from ceramic tiles. They were quite beautiful.

Not so the training centre, or 'sweatshop' as we trainees named the glorified typing pool where we worked – a large and characterless room over Woolworths in the Strand. Mrs W, who interviewed us, was pretty humourless, though her younger assistant Miss M was warmer and friendlier. Even so, it felt like being back at school, except that the days were much longer. On the plus side, we were being paid a trainee wage of £5 a week and I got a Saturday morning job in Woolworths to supplement my wages.

At the training centre with the girls and lovely teacher Miss M (wearing glasses). I put myself right at the front

After three tiresome months of typing in time to music and shorthand speed tests at the training centre, I was super excited when told I was going to work on *Woman's Own* for a fortnight. However, my excitement faded the moment I saw the massive typing pool several times the size of the training centre. The women there answered readers' letters and stuffed envelopes with knitting patterns and recipes, all the time watched over by two supervisors who checked the work. We hadn't been shown *that* department during our glamorous tour of *Woman's Own*. Upstairs was a small office where the agony aunt and her team answered readers' personal problems. I would much rather have worked there, but you had to be 18 to do so.

Magazines Made With Love

After six months' training, I was put forward for a vacancy as a junior on *Hers*, a brand-new fiction and practical features monthly. I was interviewed by softly spoken Scottish editor Joan Fisher, who described the job as taking care of the post and doing odd jobs generally and, "One of your tasks will be to comment on stories sent in by readers and keep the 'manny' (manuscript) book up to date. Plus, there will be articles to type, clothes and props to collect for photo sessions and..."

I must have come across as a dead keen player, because Joan offered me the job on the spot and I joined the tight-knit staff of seven. In addition, the magazine had some well-regarded freelance contributors – readers' favourite author Catherine Cookson; beauty and fashion editor, the late Arlene Usden (who became editor of *The Lady*); and the problem page was written by the late Claire Rayner, who became the doyen of agony aunts (and mother of three, including restaurant writer Jay).

A publishing company needs switched-on antennae constantly alert to potential gaps in the market. *Hers*, targeting young stay-at-home mothers, filled one such niche, but it was a million miles away from a magazine the company had launched while I was there, one that created a very big buzz when it was launched in 1965.

Nova was heralded as 'a new kind of magazine for a new kind of woman'. It ran stimulating articles and way-out fashion showcased in cutting-edge magazine design in a large format. There were great hopes for the magazine, but sadly *Nova* proved to be too far ahead of its time, or perhaps just too upmarket. Either way, it didn't survive, battered by several makeovers and changes of size. Also, it's likely the successful launch of *Cosmopolitan* magazine (by a rival publisher) sealed *Nova*'s short-lived fate and it folded ten years after its launch. (Very unlike the longevity of another George Newnes publication – *Titbits*, the first magazine launched by Sir George Newnes in 1881 – it lasted 103 years!)

Right in the centre of the third floor, our large, funky Art department serviced all of the Young Magazines Group. Magazine layouts and covers were created amid full ashtrays and sometimes feet up on desks. Work was done to blasts from the record player throbbing with The Stones' 'Satisfaction', Led Zeppelin's 'Whole Lotta Love' and Jimi Hendrix asking, 'Are You Experienced?'

Women dominated the sexes in editorial, but this was evened up in the art room where you never knew what male eye candy would be around. Freelance illustrators and long-haired photographers gathered round the lightbox, but I only had eyes for Eric, the art assistant with a sweeping side fringe that fell into dark brown eyes. But Eric didn't see me.

Not that I was bad-looking, with light blue eyes and highish cheekbones inherited from the Romanian side of my family. Heavy false eyelashes and lightened long hair completed my would-be rock chick look. Most days, I topped my outfits with a suede long-fringed navy jerkin I bought in Kensington High

Street's hippy market, still slightly pongy from its proximity to Afghan coats that smelt of wee.

For all the laid-back creative atmosphere and young people there, the group was run by some stiff older management. Approval for budgets and final say on all content came from the tall, tanned and ultimately scarily posh Patricia Lamburn, director and editor-in-chief of our group.

We were a mixed bunch at the coalface. There were quite a few posh girls who had been to private schools, as well as us kids from state schools. Some of the gals from more upper-class backgrounds swore like troopers and with their cut-glass accents they made four-letter words sound funny. However, while a few of the well-bred girls may have had a head start arriving in editorial via family links, it was hard work and talent that kept everyone there, so the Lindas, Susans, Jans and Anns (who I don't remember using such language) and the Sarahs, Suzannahs and Tillys (who did) all had equal chances.

Margaret Palfrey was Miss Lamburn's second-in-command. She had a slight schoolmarm air about her but was much more approachable than her boss. She had pretty facial features, although a starched perm did her no favours. I thought of her as old, but she was probably only in her forties.

There was a lively atmosphere and it was easy to make friends. I became good pals with Karen, Miss Palfrey's

Born to be a Magazine Girl? Seven-year-old me in a fancy dress competition

11

secretary, Magazine Girls Shirley, the general office typist, and Penny, the office junior. We became lifelong friends, joined a bit later on by Sandie, Ann and the two Jans, all co-writers in this book.

One unofficial part of my 'job training' was getting used to alcohol. So there was I, just a few months into my job and very, very drunk. Surely it couldn't have been the couple of Christmas gin and bitter lemons I'd had in the pub. More likely I was already half-drunk with amorous feelings, because I was with the art crowd and Eric was sitting opposite me. I have no memory of how I got to the station, only that once on the tube train, the mix of nausea and cigarette smoke made my retching all the more pungent. On the train, off the train, it was awful, and there was no disguising the sodden, smelly patches on my coat when I finally got home.

Revelations

Things were pretty fluid at work with people helping out if there was a crisis within the group, so when the editor's secretary on *Rave* was off sick, I JUMPED at the chance of standing in for her.

On my first day, Steve Marriott of The Small Faces came in to talk to editor Terry Hornett about a cover shoot – I knew that because my ear was pinned to the wall. And later when Cat Stevens – my idol – phoned and asked to speak to Terry, my heart was in my mouth.

My last afternoon on *Rave* in that all-too-short fortnight was spent posing for a photograph with a bunch of other girls from around the office for the launch issue of *19* magazine. We stared up at the photographer who stood at the top of a ladder. Click.

I wrote in my diary: *We got paid a pound each. The feature is going to be called, 'Where Have All the Virgins Gone?' Mum's not going to be pleased when she sees that…*

Though, in truth, Mum didn't have anything to worry about on that score yet.

On *Hers* press nights, I worked late, which led to a hugely memorable moment recorded breathlessly in my diary once again:

> *10ᵗʰ February 1967*
>
> *Something unbelievable happened tonight. On my way to the station, I passed a car at the lights and thought, that driver looks very familiar. Then it struck me – he was Mal Evans, The Beatles roadie! I used to see him when I chased The Beatles. I waved, he parked and we had a long chat about Rave. Then he offered me a lift to St John's Wood. Like an idiot, I said, "No thanks, I'm going in the opposite direction," even though St John's Wood means either Abbey Road recording studios or Paul McCartney's pad.*

I suppose at the back of my mind there had been a niggle as to what went with the car ride, although putting the record straight here and now, I cannot find a single trace of any untoward behaviour on the part of the late Malcolm Evans, only very lovely tributes to the man. He died in a tragic accident in Los Angeles when he was 40 after he threatened police officers with what turned out to be an air rifle and the police shot him.

Unfortunately, the same cannot be said about the behaviour of a certain predatory manager who worked in our office. He was probably in his late thirties, rather wide-eyed and scrubbed 'choir boy-looking'. But this chap was anything but innocent and he mentally 'groped' us young girls in our weekly meetings. He splattered his talk with creepy, crude questions… "What did you and your boyfriends get up to this weekend?" We cringed at his comments but put up with it till the day he gave us a graphic description of the contents of his wife's miscarriage. Five of us went to see Miss Palfrey. The matter was dealt with sternly and speedily, and by the end of the week a certain someone had left the building.

I think it's reassuring to think how effectively our complaint was dealt with. I hope there were other success stories like ours – there was no such thing as #MeToo then.

Time's Up

"Linda, have you finished subbing the cookery pages?" Joan called from her office. My job as editorial assistant had morphed into trainee sub-editor, and I learnt how to fit text to layouts and proof read.

"I won't be long, I'm just checking the line count," I lied. In actual fact, I was working on a feature for a different magazine. As much as I'd enjoyed my time on *Hers,* the shine was wearing off and I was desperate to work on a groovier magazine.

I went to see Miss Palfrey and asked if I could be put on the company's new journalism training scheme. I said how much I wanted to be a writer and then Miss Palfrey interrupted me, saying, "So why don't you write something?"

Now I had a real sense of purpose. I was a passionate fan of pirate radio and of those witty, swashbuckling DJs on the ships pumping out pop music 24/7. The pirate radio stations were *hugely* popular. Before they began broadcasting in 1964, our radio choices had been severely restricted, with commercial station Radio Luxembourg being the only full music choice, but the reception was sometimes poor due to pollution.

The bad news was that the pirate radio ships were in danger of being outlawed, and I decided there and then this was going to be the subject of my feature. Incredibly, just by turning up on Saturday afternoons at London's Marquee Club, saying I was from *Rave* and clutching a notebook, I got to interview a bunch of top DJs including John Peel, Kenny Everett and Tony Blackburn, who hosted Radio London's 'Road Shows'.

My feature was just about coming together when suddenly, without warning, I went off the rails, risking my job and much more besides.

One night after work, I disappeared, and no one, including me, knew where I was.

TWO

CRAZY HAZY DAYS

I am walking through the old piazza of Covent Garden's fruit and flower market in the days before it was turned into a shopping mecca for trendies and tourists.

It's April 1968 and I am 18 years old. Barrow boys pile fruit and veg into crates, getting them ready for the lorries. Something under my foot goes squelch and I slip onto the messy pavement splattered with pigeon shit. Someone shouts out, "Mind your step, love," and I walk as fast as my kitten heels will take me and nearly go over again.

I'm almost at work and the turret on the top of Tower House comes into view. It looks like something out of a fairy tale, and I can imagine Rapunzel throwing down her hair for her prince. Indeed, one morning, there was a carriage and six white horses outside the office and sitting aloft were a 'prince' and 'princess' in 17th-century finery. A photographer was taking pictures of them to illustrate a period fiction romance. I am working in an industry of dreams.

Am I really going to blow all of this?

It was Margaret Palfrey my mother turned to when I went missing one night. I don't know how my boss handled the call from my mother, who was, I was told, 'hysterical'. My poor mum.

The moment I stepped into the office, I was called in to see the boss. I got properly ticked off. "If I was knocked down by a bus tomorrow," said Miss Palfrey, "I would be replaced. No one is indispensible, Linda."

Message understood.

The facts were, I'd come to work straight from my boyfriend's flat, where I'd passed out stone cold the night before. My disappearing act came about after Miss Palfrey's secretary Karen had given me a couple of press tickets, which had landed on her desk. The invites were to a party at the famous Ronnie Scott's jazz nightclub, and when I'd finished my feature on pirate radio, I felt like celebrating and invited Gianni, my boyfriend of six months, to come with me.

My memories of that night are hazy, but I remember spinning round a lamppost after we left the club fuelled by a combination of champagne and the antibiotics I was taking for a chest infection. Then nothing at all until I woke the following morning, clothes rumpled but intact.

Miss Palfrey made arrangements for me to stay that night with my pal Karen. My diary extracts show Miss Palfrey knew *exactly* what she was doing:

When I went home the next night, Mum was quite calm. Actually, she has been fantastic, considering everything.

But shortly afterwards, I sound worried:

I've discovered that Palfrey calls Mum regularly. It seems she is a mother on her own too, and she and Mum have these long chats.

How I cringed at this collision of my two worlds, but there was nothing I could do about it. I certainly didn't consider how difficult it must have been for Mum to bring up this teenager on her own. Yet it seems incredible that someone with super managerial status like Margaret Palfrey would take time out to regularly speak to the parent of a young member of her staff.

Things settled down and I carried on as normal until my usually regular-as-clockwork period was ten days overdue and I was feverish with fear. Had I been taken advantage of that night? Gianni *said* not, he *swore* not. To this day, I do not know. To think otherwise is pretty horrific, and I prefer to put the episode down to my jangled nerves about my missing-night experience. As much as the sexual revolution happened for many, for all my 'rock chick' excesses and behaviour, I was holding on to the agony aunt values I'd grown up with of waiting for the right one.

As I was the one to sort the post on *Hers*, it was easy to slip a letter into problem page editor Claire Rayner's bag of 'sob stories' (as we nicknamed them). But Claire's no-nonsense reply, sent swiftly to my home address (I'd changed my name), shook me to the core.

Dear Miss Fishman, she wrote,

It seems to me that what you need more than anything is some good solid information and I have ticked some book titles... My insides nosedived as Claire continued. *In answer to your question about pregnancy, please let me advise you it is possible and I suggest you contact the Family Planning Association...*

Horrified, I made an appointment to see our family GP – a huge deal since he'd known all my family for many years. "Come back next month if you haven't had a period," is all he said. I wonder what he would have done if I had gone back... the controversial 1967 Abortion Act had recently been passed by then, so perhaps that was the reason for his unruffled response.

Fortunately, a return visit to the surgery was unnecessary. I sighed mountains of relief then told Gianni we were finished. He didn't seem surprised. "You have been playing with me," he said, and in a way he was right; he'd been deadly serious about me and had even proposed marriage.

A DREAM COME TRUE

Rave's editor-in-chief, Terry Hornett, liked my pirate radio saga and ideas for the magazine. He gave me a job as a sub-editor on 'Britain's most influential young magazine!' but I wouldn't be writing full features until I passed my three-month probationary period.

My story, 'Save the Pirates from Extinction,' was never published; that ship had sailed. The Marine Offences Act outlawed them, and even though Radio Caroline carried on broadcasting, my piece was considered too retrospective now. But never mind, it had got me to where I wanted to be.

We were a small core team on *Rave*, similar in size to *Hers*, plus we had our own fashion editor, beauty editor and music writer on the staff as well as regular freelancers. Terry had stepped aside to edit *Petticoat* then to launch *19* magazine, and our new editor was the genial Colin Bostock-Smith. With his thick thatch of hair, dark-rimmed specs and bemused smile, Colin reminded me of a cross between a university professor and a student. He was a bit of a rebel and used to tell us the company's directors were 'little tin gods', but he always did so with a good-natured smile on his face and I felt very much at home.

Once again, social life was taken care of by the plethora of invitations. I regularly went to plush Soho viewing theatres and saw films three months ahead of release. One very memorable review assignment involved going to a preview of the hippy musical 'Hair'; the musical summed up all the flower power vibes at the time. Notebook at the ready – I had been tipped off about the nude scene to come – I had a clear view as the cast stripped off and of one embarrassed young actor's arousal and then its fading as the audience burst into applause!

Letter writing was an important part of our culture, both to folk near and far away. One task I particularly enjoyed was going through readers' letters and photographs, pairing up those who wrote in to our pen pal column.

I want a pen pal with a beard and glasses.
He must be handsome with long hair and very tall.
She must wear mini skirts.
He must have a delicious sense of humour.
He must have eyes like Paul McCartney.

The bulk of requests came from readers in the UK, but a substantial number came from Europe, where *Rave* was distributed widely, and sometimes America. *Rave* had a fair number of male readers who liked our coverage of the music scene and the advertisements for musical instruments.

I selected several handsome writing pals for myself. There was Charles from Bordeaux, Carlo from Rome and Gunter from Stuttgart, though most correspondences faded rapidly, all apart from Hermann from Germany, who I picked out for his ice-blond hair and cool kaftan. He regaled me with lists of music he loved and his inner thoughts. I did the same, sometimes sending snapshots of those extraordinary times.

March 18ᵗʰ 1968
It's impossible to ignore the student riots in Paris, Berlin, Warsaw, Rome and of course London. This weekend, there was a massive anti-Vietnam rally in Trafalgar Square – there were 10,000 protesters and there were loads of injuries and arrests.

A couple of girls holding protest boards on their way to the American Embassy got on my train. One passenger put down their newspaper and told the girls, "Get off this train and stop wasting taxpayers' money." At least it got people talking instead of sitting in silence.

Our office hours were elastic in that lunches might stretch over several hours on non-press days, but when work required, we stayed as late as necessary.

I could be childish and certainly couldn't hold my drink. On one occasion, I rolled out of a taxi after a very liquid lunch held to launch The Move's 'Blackberry Way'. I had been at the press reception with Maureen O'Grady, who wrote all the main music interviews for *Rave*. Stone-cold sober, with the sophisticated looks of a reddish blonde, younger version of Sophia Loren, Maureen deposited me at my office and went off to her own room down the corridor, surely unimpressed with my immature behaviour.

Colin came looking for me, but I 'could not be found' for several hours. I was actually dozing behind an armchair in the corner of the room, protected by the ever-helpful Janice Collier. Magazine Girl Janice was *Rave*'s beauty editor/sub-editor and she and I became great pals, lifetime pals.

GREAT BALLS OF FUN

When an invite arrived for the first night of Jerry Lee Lewis' tour, I didn't want to go. With a plethora of press dos to choose from, we could be blasé. Besides, I was into Jimi Hendrix, and Lewis didn't seem cool to me, but when several more invites arrived, a few of us decided to go together at the last minute. The Robert Stigwood Organisation (also managers of Cream and The Bee Gees) laid on a luxury coach for the press, and we knew this freebie was going be good. And it was: champagne and canapés all the way to Peterborough, 100 miles away.

We sat at the back of the theatre. Most of the people in the row in front of us looked like 'boring 40-year-olds'; the men dressed in cavalry twill macs and the women wearing raincoats and scarves. The first act was not particularly good; we hadn't heard of the group and there was only polite applause and I sank down further into my seat.

It was pin-drop quiet when Jerry Lee Lewis came on stage; then he started his first song, a real rocker. The man in front of me stood up and shook his head and combed his hair back into a quiff. His wife took off her scarf and let down her long ponytail. Off came their coats – he was wearing a zoot suit, like those worn by jazz musicians in 1940s America.

Then, just as if a signal had gone off, everyone took off their coats. There were amazing outfits everywhere: nipped-in waists and stiff petticoats for the women, Teddy Boy outfits and 1950s paraphernalia for the men. And then we were all standing up, dancing and rocking in the aisles – when 'Great Balls of Fire' came on, the atmosphere turned electric. Lewis finished his incredible act and walked offstage; the theatre became deadly quiet again. People put on their coats and left.

Turning Point

The day finally arrived when I received my first press card (probationary). At last, I was going to write features. "I want you to interview an out-of-work hippy and a working girl, both the same age and compare their lifestyles," said Colin, "but I want a *real* hippy, not a weekend hippy."

I don't know if he knew it then, but Colin was looking straight at 'a weekend hippy'. Most weekends, I wore my kaftan, mini cowbell and put flowers in my hair and went to London. The original flower children's Summer of Love, which originated in Haight-Ashbury, San Francisco, extended to hippy gatherings in London's Hyde Park. We sat on the ground in circles, 'meditated', smoked, and someone usually had a guitar.

That's where I found my real-deal hippy in a large crowd gathered near the Serpentine. "*Krishna Toomkeyaah Karrthar*

Krishna". They chanted the words of an Indian song as a sitar played. Two hippies were getting married. Their bridesmaid was wearing a long white robe exactly like the ones worn by the bride and groom. With her wild frizzed-out hair, dark sunken eyes and flower-painted face, Cathy Schwarzenberg looked the part.

"Will I get paid?" she asked.

"Yes, three pounds."

"I suppose that will do."

"We'll take photographs too."

It was quite unusual for magazines to pay interviewees, but Colin agreed, as we thought a hippy would need the money. Cathy, 18, told me she had given up work to lead a life of meditating, burning incense, listening to music and "not much else apart from thinking." She lived with her boyfriend and they each received £6 weekly from the National Assistance, as the dole was called then.

The definition of a hippy according to the Oxford Dictionary is: 'A person in a 1960s subculture involving a rejection of conventional values and the taking of hallucinogenic drugs'. Cathy said she didn't take drugs; that she was "hooked on transcendental meditation" and would rather go without food for three days a week, so that she could buy music. Cathy's words *enraged* some of our hardworking *Rave* readers, who sent in letters to the tune of: 'People like Cathy make me sick'. There was a strong response.

God, I loved that job.

Another feature followed. This time, I was to write a story about the lives of girls in the Israeli army. Such a serious feature was not usual for *Rave* and although I relished the opportunity of writing it, whether the content was right for the readership, I'm not sure.

I was given more writing to do and my head was buzzing. At times, I may well have gone too far in my 'research', such as when I interviewed stuntwoman Cyd Charles. Cyd took on the most dangerous parts in 'The Avengers' TV series, standing in for the late Diana Rigg, who played Emma Peel. The houseboat where Cyd lived was moored near Windsor. When we arrived, there was no one to be seen on deck, so photographer Richard Sacks and I followed instructions and manoeuvred ourselves into a small rowing boat. This was linked by a thick rope and pulley to the 'mother ship'. Richard pulled the rope across the hundred feet or so to get to the main boat and we both stood up at the same time.

Everything happened very quickly. The mini boat tipped sideways. In a nanosecond, I was looking down into the depths while still standing upright (thankfully, as I couldn't swim). We shrieked as Richard held his expensive Nikon camera high above his head, and I did the same with my bag and tape recorder. Our equipment stayed dry, but our bodies and best clothes were soaked through, chest down, in the cold, murky brown Thames. We shouted like crazy till Cyd and her partner, Mark, emerged, horrified. They hauled us on board, pulling us by our arms, which was very painful and at one point I begged: "Please, *please* let me go."

Picture that didn't appear in the magazine - me interviewing Avengers stunt girl Cyd after I fell into the river! Photo: Richard Sachs

"We've had drunken parties and people leaving in the middle of the night, but no one has *ever* fallen in the river before," laughed Cyd later. Well, we did, and I have the photographs of me wrapped in towels, my muddy legs clearly visible, to prove it. The expenses I put in for cleaning were high indeed, but my Biba pink suede boots were goners. Still, I don't think I have ever laughed as much once we were back on dry land.

I think it was my piece on the launch of Blind Faith (with former Cream and Traffic band members), at one of the first-ever free concerts, which led the way to my next job writing full time about music. One sun-drenched Sunday afternoon in June 1969, a freelance photographer and I made our way to the stage, padding carefully through the rows of languid bodies, sitting or spreading themselves on the ground at Hyde Park.

One problem with working on a monthly magazine was that we couldn't compete with the speedier schedules of the weekly music papers. I wanted a different angle for my article, rather than writing a purely reportage piece. So, in the days leading up to the concert, I interviewed concert organisers Blackhill to ask why they were putting on free concerts, and basically the answer was to get exposure for the second little-known acts on the bill.

I pushed my way forward and got a direct quote from Eric Clapton as he came offstage saying why they chose Hyde Park to launch, 'The birth of a Supergroup'. I'd already interviewed Ian Anderson of Jethro Tull some days earlier, and he provided me with strong 'anti' comments regarding free concerts: "They're a dead loss… more for people to show off their clothes than about the music," he said. He definitely preferred performing when the audience paid for the gig, although others, like folk singer Donovan who was in the audience, got into the free spirit of the occasion and gave an impromptu performance. What a great day.

Missing...

Drinking too much... smoking too much... missing Dad... risking my job... missing Dad... some things went crash inside me all at once. And like many young people, I was searching for the meaning of life, and there were times when depression hit and I looked into the void. What was it all about?

Cathy the hippy's words on meditation had struck a chord, and a friend and I went to the Transcendental Meditation Centre in Chelsea. At the meeting, individual questions were asked:

"Are you a junkie?"

"No."

"What do you hope to achieve from meditation?"

"Peace and tranquillity."

I was told I would have a private half-hour with the Maharishi (not *the* one – he was in Rishikesh, India with The Beatles) and to bring fruit, flowers and a clean white handkerchief. It was stressed I must never discuss the ceremony, or the meditation would not work.

Afterwards I meditated occasionally, but not nearly enough, because I didn't have the patience to sit still and wait for the answers.

I was totally turned off taking anything stronger than occasional giggle-making hash. However, once I succumbed to the "really good stuff", as my boyfriend called the joint he passed to me. We were at a party with photographers, models and record company types and I felt in the mood. The hot, sticky joint was passed round and each time I inhaled, I felt the fruit seeds of my necklace tighten around my neck. I ran out gasping for air, hailed a black cab and it soared high above the trees for the whole 30-minute journey home.

Thankfully, Mum was asleep. I staggered to my bedroom and staring back at me from my dressing-table mirror was a pale green face. I tugged hard on the choking beads, and their clatter as they scattered all over the linoleum coincided with my head falling back hard onto the headboard on my bed.

Days I'll remember all my life, as they say.

Yes, it was a heady cocktail to be young in the '60s, but the early part of the decade also held unbelievable terrors. Many nights I went to bed afraid I would not be alive in the morning, that one of the superpowers would press the red button. During the height of the Cuban Missile crises of 1962, many Soviet missiles were being installed in Cuba and President Kennedy ordered a blockade of Soviet ships. The world was on the brink of nuclear war and I had terrible nightmares about bomb shelters and people turning yellow and dying from radiation. Perhaps that's one of the reasons we all partied so hard when the threats receded.

Never again, I swore after the green-face incident. Yet a few months later there I was swallowing purple hearts or 'decks'. Not that I knew I was taking the so-called 'club drug'. The amphetamines had been prescribed by my ever-helpful GP as slimming tablets in order to help me shift the ten pounds I'd added to my nine-stone weight. This was a side effect of taking steroids for my bronchial asthma, which in turn had been made worse by smoking. Stupid vicious circle, I know.

It was not uncommon practice in those days for doctors to prescribe stimulants as aids to weight loss. 'Speed' energised me at bedtime and I latched on quickly to the 'benefits' of the medication. Most nights I stayed up till all hours writing, reading and listening to music, turned down so Mum couldn't hear. I didn't want to waste time sleeping.

When I told beauty editor Janice I was on a diet, she asked if I would like to be one of the case histories in the before and after feature for one of the many makeovers she was doing. I would be given a beauty session for the 'after' bit and special clothes to show off my weight loss. I loved the idea, although I had no intention of following the sensible six-week diet plan Janice gave me, existing instead on meal replacement biscuits and black coffee to speed the weight loss. The feature was about fans and their pop idols, and I was going to talk about my heart-throb Scott Walker. What if he saw it! What if he liked me!

Half way through 'the diet', I went to the doctor to ask for more tablets. By now, I knew the reason for the buzz and wakefulness, but I was in for a rude awakening. "NO," he said, well, shouted really. The medical authorities had clamped down on stimulants being dished out as slimming aids – luckily for me, I think. I have since read about people who had huge problems coming off them.

When the 'after' pictures came into the office, I was so disappointed. Through no fault of the beauty makers, I looked frumpy and, to my eyes, middle-aged. I'd refused to have my long hair cut and so to make it look different from the 'before' pictures, it was piled up in quivering curls on top of my head.

"It could have looked so sleek and glossy if you'd just had a little trim," said Janice when she saw my long face. She was right, I was wrong, but I did get to keep the unsexy little black dress I wore in the photo shoot. I hoped and prayed that Scott *didn't* see that issue of *Rave*...

'Before and After' beauty feature. I much preferred myself in the 'Before' picture

It was time for some farewells. It was goodbye to editor Colin, who left to edit *Petticoat* and then to become a hugely successful TV and radio comedy scriptwriter ('Not the Nine O' Clock News',

'Spitting Image', Alas Smith & Jones' are among his list of many credits). It was farewell to Tower House when we moved to another impressive old building near Fleet Street.

And it was hello to a new job. Seduced by more money and the promise of non-stop pop interviews, I became senior feature writer on a teen pop weekly. That's where I was to discover how it felt to be mauled and pulled by 'loving fans', who lay in wait this time for *me*.

THREE

SPRINKLED WITH STARDUST

Welcome to the 1970s.

I'd arrived at the point in my career where my job focused on pop music. *Mirabelle* was a well-loved weekly teen magazine packed with star interviews, pin-up posters and picture stories. Launched in the 1950s and aimed at 14 to 17-year-olds, *Mirabelle* sold extremely well.

Feature writer Sandie Robbie and I wrote the pop interviews – sometimes two each per week, sometimes more. We'd knock out copy like dervishes possessed, fingers flying over the typewriters in between setting up more interviews. The writing style was not fancy or highfalutin, neither was it raw, rude or egoistical… it was honest, informative and connected with our readers.

As luck would have it, by the time I became a full-blown interviewer, my pop passions The Beatles and The Walker Brothers had broken up, but the array of stars appearing in *Mirabelle* was still dazzling.

I got the chance to interview some of my absolute heroes – superstar singer-songwriter Cat Stevens was at the front of the queue and DJ, comedian Kenny Everett, a quirky, I hand it to you, second. I interviewed the idols of others – Marc Bolan,

David Cassidy and pop stars with mega hits like The Tremeloes, 'There Goes My Baby', and The Hollies, 'He Ain't Heavy, He's My Brother'.

Back in the early 1970s, the record industry was mustard keen to place their artists in young magazines like ours with their power to reach record-buying teenage girls in their hundreds of thousands. Among those I interviewed were singer-songwriter Gilbert O'Sullivan, 'Nothing Rhymed', 'Alone Again (Naturally)', dressed up in schoolboy gear, glam-rock star Gary Glitter of the thumping 'I'm the Leader of the Gang (I am!)', 'bubblegum' group Edison Lighthouse of 'Love Grows (Where My Rosemary Goes)' – none of which ticked my personal music boxes, but all were huge reader favourites at the time.

As a crazed pop fan who had hollered throughout Beatles and Walker Brothers concerts only a few years earlier, you might suppose I'd be fazed at facing those others swooned over. But it wasn't like that. By the time I was meeting the stars, I was no longer a melting fan myself – one of life's ironies. Having said that, Cat Stevens was the exception. He ticked every box – talented, brilliant, *gorgeous*!

The music industry back then was a straightforward business compared to later years in my career when celebrities regularly demanded copy or photo approval, or both. I don't remember anyone asking us for anything like that when I worked on *Mirabelle,* and I can think of only two occasions when someone 'official' sat in on an interview.

One time was when I interviewed David Cassidy. The press officer from London Weekend Television 'sat guard' to ensure I asked questions to promote the TV programme David was appearing on, which was fair enough, as we'd been given the first interview with him on British shores. Plus, there was a major concern regarding whether a question about David having a girlfriend was going to come up. The star had recently been 'papped' (photographed) with a possible girlfriend, and a fuzzy image of them appeared in the newspapers. Such exposure could topple the fan base of a mega idol, so the subject was to be ignored and left to fizzle out. *Mirabelle* wasn't in the business of crushing readers' dreams.

Another time someone sat in was when I interviewed Gary Glitter. Celebrity publicist Max Clifford was present while I put questions to Gary. I wasn't a Glitter fan; his music seemed tacky to me as did his rhinestone suits and tall wig (underneath which he was plain follically challenged Paul Gadd). Anyhow, Glitter didn't need me to rate him – he was super successful, supremely confident and a huge star.

I recall Max Clifford as being a no-nonsense, sometimes tough but very good press officer. In fact, both the men I met that afternoon were at the very top of their professional trees. Years later, both went down on separate sickening charges of historic abuse, each imprisoned for a string of indecent assaults against young girls.

Sandie and I were full of energy. I was 'senior writer' based on age (19) and experience, but the two-years-younger Sandie turned out as many features as I did and sometimes more. My first impression of Sandie was that of a steely Scottish lass with spot-on journalistic instincts, who liked to be seen as a bit of a tough girl, but I sensed vulnerability underneath. I liked Sandie on all fronts, except if a temper tantrum got the better of her and high spirits went too far. Like when in a major strop, she threw her rock-heavy Remington typewriter from out of our window down to the courtyard three floors below, fortunately people-free as it was an internal window and so did not go out onto the street.But even so!

Paul Raven (real name Cohen) was our enthusiastic editor; he loved the pop business through and through. He totally understood our readers, although he could be a bit of an enigma to us at times, joining in our (often childish) jokes and japes and then swiftly switching back to boss mode, which didn't always make for harmony.

The production of *Mirabelle's* romantic picture strip stories was the work of an entirely separate department, who oversaw the scripts and artwork/production. Sandie and I thought it was an odd job for 'old' men as we viewed Sid and Jack, a couple of decades older than all of us. The lovely humorous Jack Cunningham and the quietly spoken, slightly aloof Sid Lewis no doubt thought of us as idiots.

Mostly, though, everything at work was 'groovy' as we used to say. And what's wrong with groovy? Added to which, *Mirabelle* became more than the place I worked; it was also where I met my husband... (more on that later).

18th September 1970. Jimi Hendrix died from a drug misdemeanour and we were all in bits. Plus, we had a jolly cover line about Jimi and a feature to match, which had already gone to press, so too expensive to be pulled now, for despite its success, *Mirabelle* had a low budget. On occasion, we were given surplus photographs by the company's glossier magazines *Honey* or *Petticoat*. In order to make such a feature work – if the colour 'tranny' (transparency) was good enough – we would create stories around the photos, although sometimes the stories said nothing at all as in:

IS THERE ANY TRUTH IN THE RUMOUR
ELVIS PRESLEY IS COMING TO ENGLAND?

A few pages later, we announced, 'There is absolutely no truth in the rumour that Elvis Presley is coming to England', bundled between quotes gathered from quick ring-rounds to record companies and agents. But I stress this type of thing happened only occasionally when we were in a fix and we were short of a 'sock-it-to-them' cover line.

We moved offices to Fleetway House, another old, handsome building with a long history of publishing, this time near Fleet Street. There were a whole bunch of moves during the years while the company was being restructured. This time, we were within close range of several of the Magazine Girls: Jan Iles-Kaluza, a very attractive teen, though a bit bolshy back then, had joined *Valentine* downstairs, and my 'old muckers' Penny and Janice were close by on *Loving*. They were joined by fashion editor Ann Carpenter who became a close friend and holiday pal of mine. There were many friendly comings, goings and interruptions, but the work got done and plenty of it... though admittedly sometimes things got out of hand:

One night fuelled up by too many whisky and green gingers imbibed at the nearby Hoop and Grapes was one such time. All the records sent into the office for review were muddled in great piles over the floor and we danced around them, which seemed funny until we had to sort them out to write the record reviews. Some of the demo discs had blank labels and we played one, which was absolutely fantastic, but we didn't know who it was by. We could have easily missed a trick that time, but fortunately we managed to sort things out and discovered that the fantastic nameless disc was 'Abraxas' by Santana.

Sandie and I were in perma-high spirits most of the time. Even if we moaned one day about being asked to cover a muddy music festival, we were excited the next at being sent together to Liverpool to check out the young scene there, then Birmingham, then Cornwall. *Mirabelle* was not as London-centric as some other magazines.

From time to time, we tackled serious subjects, writing up case studies of drug addicts and handing out a strong warning tone. When I had to question a gang of skinheads – a tough boy subculture of the 1970s – about their weapons culture, I was very jumpy till my photographer boyfriend was commissioned to come with me to photograph the shaven-headed 'aggro boys' in their uniform of Doc Martins, Levi's and braces. I interviewed the incredibly young-looking boys who told me, "We're always ready with our knives if there's likely to be trouble, though we don't go looking for it."

LOVING FANS

David Cassidy was HUGE, one of the biggest sway and swoon pop stars of the 1970s, though ten years too young for my fancies. It was through him I got a taste of how it felt to be a hunted pop star.

David Cassidy covers sold like hot cakes! Photo:flab/Alamy Stock Photo

It seemed such a great idea when Paul announced in his editor's letter that we would be running a David Cassidy competition. The lucky winner would come to our offices and listen to the recording of my interview with David. However, this idea wasn't mentioned to Bill Williamson, editor-in-chief of our group, and what seemed a great idea turned out to be a huge problem.

On the day the issue was published, David Cassidy fans blocked part of the Strand near our office. The police were called and threatened to close us down for 'incitement to riot'. I was mauled and pulled by fans on my way in and out of the office, which went on for several days.

Fortunately for us, a few days later, Mr Cassidy became the focus of his fans' attention elsewhere.

In my feature, Cassidy answered the questions the readers were dying to know: what could a girl expect on a date and did he like meeting his fans? "Yes, when they are alone," answered David, boosting the dreams of his fans everywhere.

On the other hand, once stars married, their coupledom was sometimes embraced, such as when we took Marmalade's Dean Ford and his wife to Paris for a special issue. Another time I visited Allan Clarke of The Hollies at home with his wife and family. It was unusual then to do 'at home with the stars' features, certainly in *Mirabelle*. Allan was charming and his wife and children sweet. I went around making notes about their new home in upmarket Hampstead, London. Most probably, anything too personal or revealing had been removed beforehand.

The next time I interviewed David Cassidy, he was very tired. He was on lockdown in a sumptuous suite in the swish Dorchester Hotel where he was giving one press interview after another. When it was finally my turn to see him, I couldn't get my new tape recorder to work and I became hot, panicky and embarrassed in equal measure. Without irritation – and in his position David could have easily been rattled – he sweetly picked up my pesky machine and got it going. While he did so, I took the opportunity to study his appearance; he was fabulously good-looking, androgynously so.

Who have you interviewed and what were they like? That's what people have always asked me.

Turn the pages of a 1970 issue of *Mirabelle* and there is Cat Stevens, as he was known before he converted to Islam and became Yusuf Islam in 1979.

I was a huge fan of Cat Stevens' wonderful songs and, let's face it, his looks. I met him in his father's Greek restaurant in London's Shaftesbury Avenue. The point of the interview was to talk about his comeback post-retiring from the pop scene after a bout of tuberculosis nearly killed him. Then about his convalescence and the songs he wrote during that time – his new album 'Mona Bone Jakon' and the wonderful 'Lady D'Arbanville' single.

His mood was reflective and introspective. Cat spoke about, 'the dark shadows, blackness and loneliness' which had dogged him and how he'd used meditation and yoga to combat his depression. He was such a sensitive, beautiful man; everything I thought he would be. I pressed my face closer to hear better, which would have been more effective if he'd been sitting next to me rather than on the opposite side of the table.

Marc Bolan had the prettiest face I'd ever seen on a male. I interviewed the T. Rex star several times at the height of his glam-rock fame. The first occasion was at his house in Putney in south west London. His wife, June, stayed with us throughout the interview, although I fear she had nothing to fear. Of course, I'd rather she hadn't been there, not for any reasons of impropriety, but simply because in a one-to-one setting it was easier to create more rapport and extract better quotes.

The last time I met Marc it was in January1972 and he was living in a flat in London's swish Maida Vale. That interview was referred to in 'Ziggyology: A Brief History of Ziggy Stardust' by author Simon Goddard, who wrote in that book, 'Readers would have been riddled with envy at Linda Newman's account of interviewing Marc at his home...'

Apparently something I said in the magazine *infuriated* Bowie, according to Goddard, who wrote, 'Ziggy Stardust read the same issue of *Mirabelle* with rapt attention. He read it again just to make sure he hadn't been hallucinating, before dropping it to the floor...'

During the interview, Marc told me about his plans to make a film, "about a cosmic messiah, a kind of intergalactic Jesus," and it was those words which apparently caused Ziggy to see stars (not nice ones – after all, Bolan's Ziggy Stardust was THE intergalactic genius).

'...If it was war Marc wanted, let the great cosmic messiah fight of 1972 commence,' wrote Goddard.'

Whether or not my article truly made a dent in the psyche of either rock god, I cannot say. However, it was something else Marc said that afternoon which stopped me in my tracks: "If I live long enough to do something else..." and he went on to talk about writing more, adding, "If I live long enough..." Those words turned out to be tragically prophetic.

Five years on, Marc's car, driven by girlfriend singer Gloria Jones, crashed into a tree. Marc, 29, died; Gloria, mother of their son, Rolan, survived.

Former pirate radio DJ Kenny Everett was so funny and as naughtily irreverent in real life as his zany radio and TV persona that I loved. He put me at ease, joked throughout our chat and broke off every now and then to go and make a cup of tea. He came back several times (minus tea), popped his head round the door and said, "You still here?" and then disappeared again. I interviewed him three times and he always gave great lines as in, 'No More Stuffed Shirts and Prunes' – the headline to my feature after he was sacked by the BBC for insinuating that the

Minister of Transport's wife had bribed someone in order to pass her driving test.

Kenny once told me about his seriously depressive episodes, but never gave any hint of the crushing guilt he was grappling with about his sexuality. Indeed, he was married for 13 years to musician and spiritual healer Lee Middleton. "I've been a much happier, more content person since Lee and I married," he said. It was more than ten years after that interview Kenny came out as homosexual. Tragically, Kenny died from an AIDS-related illness in 1995.

My spread with Lou Christie was headed, 'SHOCK INTERVIEW' in big bold letters. Lou ('Lightnin' Strikes', 'She Sold Me Magic') told me he was "not deliberately putting on a sexy act, but if that excites the audience that's nice because it excites me too," and admitted that he "gyrates all over the place". Pretty tame stuff when compared to some of the content in magazines for teen girls years later, writing graphically about 'position of the month'.

Looking back over my shoulder, I think the eclectic mix of musicians we interviewed for *Mirabelle* was incredible, considering the magazine's image of being for teenage pop fans. However, heavy rock musicians Led Zeppelin, Deep Purple and The Moody Blues – whose music I loved – all agreed to be interviewed too, as did progressive bands Juicy Lucy, Yes and Family.

We covered more than pop on Mirabelle – progressive and heavy rock bands regularly appeared.
Photo: Mirabelle © Copyright Rebellion Publishing IP Ltd. All rights reserved

Ultra-cool DJ John Peel appeared alongside the likes of heart-throbs David Cassidy, Donny Osmond *et al*. Music snobbery didn't appear to be an issue, although my interviews with the heavies always focused on their music; they were not keen on personal chat.

At times, we also cast *Mirabelle's* features net far and wide from the music scene, from praying with Hare Krishna devotees, to devouring National Youth Theatre plays, to clean-up TV campaigner Mary 'ban this filth' Whitehouse. *Who does she think she is telling viewers what to watch?* I thought, as I arrived at Mary's rose-covered front door with a smirk, thinking I would send up this 'moral do-gooder', but it was *me* who ended up with egg on my face. Mary cleverly skipped around my 'cryptic' questions, stridently putting her points across, and I didn't catch her out once. It served me right. It was a learning curve.

HERE COMES A HUSBAND

Richard. I've mentioned his name before.

We met on *Mirabelle* just over half a century ago and it was a match, but if we had wanted to get it together at work these days, we may have had to get permission first. Okay, I'm exaggerating, but that is certainly the case in many American firms where a 'no-love' clause may be written into contracts. And at home, too, the subject sometimes comes up in agreements under 'Relationship Rules'.

So there I was at *Mirabelle,* quietening down a bit, my hurly-burly days dropping behind me a little.

The very first time I noticed Richard Brookes was when a pair of emerald green velvet trousers and a paisley sweater topped by a tangle of blond hair and beard stopped by my desk to discuss pictures for one of my articles. *Mirabelle's* new designer appealed to me on several levels. He looked like an art student-cum-pop star, and he was sensitive, funny… northern, good-looking…

Richard did not ask me out and nothing happened between us until the day I received an invite to the launch of 'Make It With You', the new single by American band Bread. And however corny that sounds, it is 100 per cent true! Fab group, free drinks, free food, smoochy nightclub; everything was laid on. I didn't call it a date. I told Richard I had 'a spare invite' to the Revolution club, but I secretly *hoped* it was going to be a date.

It was very nearly a non-starter. As soon as we arrived I went straight to the loo, struggling with a false eyelash that wouldn't stay put. While I was still in there, the interviews with the band began. Richard, who had never been to a press do, remembers, "When Bread's lead singer, David Gates, came over, I couldn't think of a thing to say so I started eating the food on the table. Gates, watching me, said, "'I can see you're hungry, I'll come back when you've finished.'"

Some of 'the Mirabelle Mob' creative team.
Back row – me second from left with whistle Christmas decoration
in my mouth, boyfriend Richard fourth from left.
Front row – Sandie first on the right

I was miffed. Richard hadn't got a single quote and I might have missed my interview slot. To lighten the atmosphere, Richard went to the bar where he was charged £25 for two whiskey and Cokes – almost a week's wages. Then the girl asked if he was press. "Because they're free then," she said.

Press dos added an extra zing to our dates. One night we were at the plush La Valbonne club having a wonderful time. Singer-songwriter Peter Sarstedt was playing. We really liked him and we were right at the front. Meanwhile, many of the other journalists were knocking back the free drinks and being very noisy. Sarstedt was singing a collection of songs including his chart topper, 'Where Do You Go To (My Lovely)', and it was fantastic, but halfway through he stopped and walked offstage saying, "I'm sorry, but no one's listening."

Another time, we went to see Alan Price. That time, I thought the journalists were listening – we certainly were – but they couldn't have been because half an hour into the set he said, "F--- off and get back to your boring jobs," and walked off the stage. Perhaps Alan Price thought he was getting a bit of a cool reception, perhaps the applause wasn't loud enough, but Richard and I thought he was great.

Richard loved buying gadgets and one day he came to the office with a new acquisition: a Polaroid Swinger camera. This was something completely new at the time and Richard showed us how photographs could be developed on the spot. It wasn't a sleek object; it actually looked quite clumsy and wasn't for professional use, but it was cheap and fun.

By sheer coincidence, our staff photographer went missing that day. We couldn't find him anywhere and editor Paul went into meltdown. There was good reason for that. Clothes designer-singer Rudi Valentino – a protégé of David Bowie – had arrived for a photo shoot. Paul had managed to persuade the press officer that we would include Rudi's story as a coverline if we could have a follow-up shoot and interview with Bowie.

The make-up artist and hairdresser prepared Rudi for the shoot. Then panic stations; still no photographer. When Paul heard about Richard's new camera, he said, "You've got to do it."

So Richard and I climbed up the fire escape onto the roof where the shoot and interview were to take place. There was Rudi, hair backcombed and bouffanted, ready for action. "Where's the photographer?" asked one of his team. Enter stage left Richard, Polaroid camera swinging from his neck. Before anyone could say a word, Richard pressed the button and took a picture of Rudi. The team were gobsmacked as Richard peeled off the photo and held it under his arm to develop it. Rudi and entourage walked off swearing, and all we could do was call out "Wait, please wait."

So that was the second time I inadvertently annoyed David Bowie. Consequently, the Rudi piece never appeared and the Bowie/*Mirabelle* interview never took place either, but Rudi went on to design some of the costumes for Bowie during his Ziggy Stardust phase and beyond.

Eventually, the thrill of the stardust wore off and the speed we worked at became an unsatisfying treadmill.

I went freelance, changed track away from pop and wrote for young women's magazines on subjects that questioned the status quo: 'Open Marriage – A New Lifestyle', 'The Baby Trap; an attack on the motherhood myth', 'Women In Love With One Another' – an excursion into bisexuality. I was thrilled when *Petticoat,* one of my favourite magazines, accepted my feature 'Why are we attracted to men who are rotters?' I'd had one or two myself – who hasn't – but I wasn't interested in rotters anymore, not when going in for the long haul.

And I was going in for the long haul. By this time, Richard and I had been dating for two years and I thought it was time for commitment. I was 23 and Richard was 25 (not particularly young for those times) when we tied the knot at a very corporate-looking register office. Magazine Girls Janice, Ann and Sandie joined our jolly wedding reception held in a small 'banqueting suite' later.

I loved the variety of being freelance, but the economic woes of the early 1970s with a three- day week, miners' strikes, national strikes and soaring inflation made it risky. Some magazines vanished forever, and freelance work was much tougher to find.

As 'romantic' as it seemed writing by candlelight during power cuts, I now needed a full-time job to help pay the mortgage on our first home. The ease with which I'd walked into jobs earlier in my career had become a thing of the past. Then a stroke of luck. A friend saw an ad: 'Researcher wanted to join one of the best-selling magazines in the country...'

And that's how I came to join 'the big boys', or rather 'the big girls' of the magazine world.

FOUR

Scoop!

"Come in, Linda, and tell us what you found."
"Nothing. I didn't find anything at all."

One year into my job on *Woman's Own* and I was about to be sent on a major exclusive. But what if I didn't come back with the goods? I would be made to look a fool in front of a team of formidable editors.

That was my nightmare.

I joined *Woman's Own* magazine when I was 26, without a day's formal journalistic training behind me, but I had built up a name for myself as a pop writer in the world of young magazines. Some friends thought my new job as a researcher/writer (with the emphasis on researcher) was taking a step backwards, but I saw it as an opportunity to gain experience on one of the most well-known best-selling magazines in the country.

Most of all, I was relieved to have a full-time job again. Like most industries, magazine publishing was affected by the economic recession and unemployment was high. Much better, I thought, to be inside than out in the cold. As it happens, I joined *Woman's Own* during the sweltering summer of 1976, when UK temperatures hit a record-breaking 35.9 degrees (since surpassed by 2022's sweaty temperatures of 40 degrees).

Up till then, I'd worked on magazines with staff of just ten or 12 on each, while on *Woman's Own* over 100 people stoked a well-oiled machine. Editor Jane Reed was at the helm and she was moving *Woman's Own* in new directions, reflecting the changes taking place in women's lives in the 1970s. The magazine had also moved physically as part of a massive reorganisation and was plonked on an uninteresting site south of the River Thames. We staff called the new buildings 'The Ministry of Magazines'.

On my first day, features editor Iris Burton took me for a welcome lunch in the director's dining room on the 17th floor. *This has been a good move*, I thought.

So how come just one year into my job, I wanted o.u.t.?

Most of the people at work are horrible, I moaned to my diary. *I got told off today for being late. Only Barbara makes it bearable.*

I was referring to Barbara Rowlands, the other researcher. We did the same work, were the same age and shared the same sense of humour. We called the magazine 'Woman's Moan'.

Every morning began with us searching forensically through the national and regional press for stories and ideas to circulate round the department heads. We did research for features others were writing and most days we were back and forth to the library, fact checking, collecting and returning hefty folders, all decades before the internet, of course.

"We sweated buckets today," was our catchphrase. I even stopped seeing (Magazine Girl) Janice Collier, who worked only a corridor away in the Beauty department. No time to chat.

So it stung badly when our usually calm, friendly features editor hit the roof calling us, "Lazy, unenthusiastic, disorganised researchers", when Barbara and I asked for a rebrief on some work she'd given us. I was speechless. Perhaps Iris was having a bad day. However, she was right about our shrinking enthusiasm.

So we went to see the assistant editor and complained about

our top-heavy workload. "We're only human," I said, stating the obvious.

"Well, you should *work* like automatons," came her reply. From then on, the 'A' word was guaranteed to make Barbara and I laugh like drains.

One task I always enjoyed was searching for candidates to nominate for '*Woman's Own's* Children of Courage' awards by scouring the press, national and regional, for stories of heroism, bravery and stoicism. And it was wonderful to see those glorious children receive their awards at Westminster Abbey, regularly attended by royals and politicians.

Woman's Own could be a peculiar place to work as far as I was concerned. You could never second-guess where the next curve ball was coming from. Like the time at the office Christmas party when Barbara was scolded for "Standing in one place all the time." Or when I got my knuckles rapped by the deputy features ed. for talking to husband Richard who came by the features office with my cigarettes.

"Linda, we *cannot* allow people from other magazines to come into the office and see what we are working on."

The competition between *Woman's Own* and *Woman* was fierce, but this was ridiculous – Richard was working in the Art department of non-competitor *Mother* magazine. A raw nerve was hit and I gave a rude answer. Actually, I think I was fortunate not to be sent to one of the more senior editors for a scholarly ticking-off. There were several of these 'marms' puffed up with snobby self-importance, one or two of them quite boozy behind closed office doors (think the offices of TV's 'Mad Men'), though none of the people I've named.

Tension hit high every Thursday, conference day. Surrounded by heads of department, the editor scrutinised the planned issue. Silence was a bad sign. Jane Reed was once described by the *Guardian* (1979) as, 'The toughie at the top', but she was a passionate and gifted editor, and working for her was the best journalism training I could have had.

ALL CHANGE

Back to my scoop. What was it and why was it giving me such nightmares?

It was a royal assignment. *Woman's Own* was at the mecca of magazine royalty with flabbergasting sales of one and a half million copies a week. Much of it was down to our readers' love of royal stories.

Who is Prince Charles' latest paramour? Who will be our future queen? Sometimes, a whole bevvy of photographs were collated under, 'Who will be The One to nab a Prince?' type headings and I spent many hours researching society girls who might make the grade.

There was no shortage of royal stories, controversy and gossip for our readers to enjoy. We raised excitement for the Queen's Silver Jubilee, wrote about 18-year-old Prince Andrew's active social life and covered the stormy marriage break-up

Me (circled) nearly nose to ear with the Queen as she was shown around Woman's Own by editor Jane Reed. Photo: Phil Rudge

of Princess Margaret and Antony Armstrong-Jones, but the magazine's treatment was not salacious.

"We are sending you on an investigative assignment," said Iris, lowering her voice, "and it's *totally* confidential."

Here was my chance to shine. To be given a royal assignment which could end up on the cover was HUGE. But to come back empty-handed… well, that didn't bear thinking about. Frankly, I'd never thought of myself as a foot-in-the-door reporter; that was something I associated with newspaper hacks, but ask me to interview anyone – from a prince to a pauper – no problem… but this? I must have grimaced.

"Is something wrong?" asked my boss, standing up, her 6ft height dwarfing my 5 foot 3 inches.

"No, but I don't drive and the location is very remote," I mumbled.

"Well then, take Richard with you."

At that time, Richard was freelancing in *Woman's Own*'s Art department, so there was no conflict of interest. Iris said she would have a word with Richard's boss.

This is what happened. The magazine had been given leads by a trusted contact – someone close to the royal inner circle – saying that Princess Anne and Mark Phillips were about to move to the house of their dreams. The source had given us three addresses and said one of them was 'it'. The powers that be at work knew the newspapers would soon sniff this out; therefore, with this exclusive tip-off, *Woman's Own* would be there first.

My brief was to get full descriptions of the empty houses, so that the minute 'Buck House' confirmed news about Princess Anne's new home, my story would appear. So off we went in Richard's green VW Beetle. How great it was to be out of the office together and to be paid for it.

The first two houses were on the Queen's estate, Windsor Great Park. At one point there was great excitement; I could clearly see the Queen horse riding in the distance, sandwiched by two minders. And then just as quickly they were gone.

We followed directions. The first two houses were in paddocks – you had to drive through farmland with sheep, but the gates were locked. I called the office and Iris said it turned out the first two addresses were false leads.

After a long drive, we arrived at property number three, a grand-looking stately style pile set deep in the Gloucestershire countryside.

As we sat contemplating our next step, Richard spotted a Land Rover coming out of the drive. It had to be the gatekeeper, although, incredibly, there was no gate. "He was the only one stopping us, so let's go NOW," said Richard, and drove up to the house like lightning.

Hearts racing, we peered through one of the downstairs windows into a sitting room that was shabby, not *chic*. The room was huge with a period fireplace centrepiece. On either side were two worn-out sofas I wouldn't have given house room to. Plus, there were a few pieces of hefty brown furniture – no doubt expensive antiques – but to my taste and love of '70s Habitat newness, they were tatty, old and awful. I wasn't used to gracious living.

The tack room, however, was not at all tatty. We walked through an overgrown paddock to the barn where the horse gear, saddles, harnesses and suchlike were kept, and opened the door. It was pristine, immaculate and full of the latest gear. This was a big clue as to the future owner – equestrian competitor Princess Anne would love it.

Back at the house, we peered through a side window into the grand hallway with an open spindle staircase. I could picture Princess Anne in a lavish ball gown swishing down the steps on her way to a state occasion.

"We must look upstairs," I said – a tall order because the

only way up was via a drainpipe. Richard climbed skywards, his prized velvet green bell-bottoms nipped by lumps of rust. As he reached the top bedroom window, a reflection bounced back. The gatekeeper's Land Rover was parked at the top of the drive. Richard dropped to the ground fireman-style. We jumped into the Beetle, raced through the exit and OUT. We got away by the skin of our pants, literally.

What relief, but somehow I had to work up the scant information into a bigger story.

We drove to the nearest village and went into the post office 'to buy stamps'. The middle-aged couple were friendly enough until I started asking about royal newcomers. The postmistress' plump face froze and she said, "I don't know what you're talking about." Then, "I'm sorry, we're closing."

The shutters came down.

We walked further down the picturesque street and approached the gift shop, the teashop, the butcher's shop. One by one, down came the blinds. It was like something out of 'Village of the Damned'.

We found out later that 'Mr and Mrs Post Office' had made super quick calls alerting their neighbouring shopkeepers about us. We were shunned again when we visited an exclusive country pub where I'd been told Princess Anne had visited after a royal hunt in the area. Mouths shut tight as clams. Had the locals been pre-warned to protect the couple's privacy at all costs? Or perhaps a newspaper had promised payment for an exclusive scoop?

The next day, I went into the office glum and pretty much empty-handed. To my immense relief, Iris said she was pleased with the tenacity I'd shown, even though my material never materialised into a story. In actual fact, Princess Anne and Mark Philips moved into Gatcombe Park, 25 miles away from the address we'd been given. I wondered whether *Woman's Own* had been given 'a bum steer' to put us off the scent.

I don't remember which red top newspaper got the story – I was just relieved it wasn't *Woman*. And for a reason I never fathomed, the scoop that never was became something of a turning point and more feature writing came my way. Things were looking up. Magazine Girl Jan Iles-Kaliza, my pal from the young magazine group joined and I also became good friends with two new writers, Linda Dearsley and Ruth Brotherhood.

('Scoop' postscript: It turned out the reason Richard and I were shunned by the villagers had nothing to do with royalty. The original owner of the stately pile had committed suicide, leaving the family debt-laden. The insurance company were refusing to pay out due to 'suspicious circumstances'. The villagers loyal to the family thought Richard and I were insurance investigators!)

DECADE OF CHANGE

The 1970s saw sweeping changes and it was an interesting time to work on women's magazines. The Equal Pay Act (1970) sought to remove pay differentials between men and women, although with varying degrees of success as is still the case. The Sex Discrimination Act (1975) made it an offence to discriminate against women in terms of finance and employment (incredible to think that until 1975, women needed permission from a man to get credit and mortgages in their own right), and the Equal Opportunities Commission (1975) was set up to look for offenders.

Woman's Own ran some hugely influential campaigns. One was to change tax laws in favour of women; another pressurised bureaucrats to rewrite official documents in plain English. There were campaigns demanding a fair deal for working women and for better childcare. At the same time, the magazine was careful not to undermine the roles of those women who did not go out to work, very many of them the backbone of our readership.

In the midst of all this change, messages could be confusing. I co-wrote a peculiar story about 'hairy wild, wild women' based on a report I'd found in a medical journal. The feature, 'Is stress and work turning women into men?' listed sensational symptoms: baldness, alcoholism, excess hair, deepening voice, chest hair, even changes in the genital area. The feature began, '*Woman's Own* believes in the right of women to compete with men for the top jobs, but at the same time,

We were all doing stressful jobs ourselves on Woman's Own just as in this 'hairy women' feature. Woman's Own/Future Ltd.

we cannot ignore recent research...' The happy conclusion was that most women do *not* develop such symptoms. Just as well, I thought, since many of us on *Woman's Own* are doing such incredibly stressful jobs. Oh, the irony...

Writing probing, in-depth features became my forte and favourite. There was:

'The Great Education Debate';

'Does Marriage Guidance Work?' (Mostly 'yes');

'What Are the Alternatives to Abortion?'

Abortion was legalised in 1967, but in the mid-seventies there were calls to strengthen the existing law. I wrote a three-page feature – quite unusual at the time for a magazine like ours to go so big on the subject – explaining all the ins and out medically, morally, for and against, all with careful phrasing so as not to upset readers' sensibilities, 'Just before you get all het up about the subject again'.

Though I was writing much more, I was still billed and paid as a researcher. I suppose, why bother giving me more money and a title for a job I was already doing? I was irked.

Just before I resigned from *Woman's Own*, I was sent on a three-day 'jolly' to the film set of spy thriller 'Riddle of the Sands' to interview actors Michael York, Jenny Agutter and Simon MacCorkindale. Flying in a small plane to the Frisian Islands off the German mainland reminded me what fun magazine journalism could be. So just why I applied for a deskbound job as consumer editor on arch rival *Woman* magazine, I don't know. My interview with go-ahead editor Jo Sandilands was going well until she popped the question acceptable at the time: "Are you planning to start a family?"

"No, well, yes, but not yet," I spluttered, flustered, because indeed I was hoping to do so in the near future. I didn't get the job.

When I handed in my notice to Iris, she seemed disappointed and asked if I'd like to stay on as a full-time feature writer, with more money, etc. But it was all too little too late for me. Besides, I'd landed myself a job on one of the sassiest magazines in the country.

FIVE

19 Lives

Get stoned on the Spirit
Blow your mind on Jesus

I was on the tube after a night out, when a bunch of American hippies came onto the train. They sat on the floor playing guitars and harmonicas and sang passionate songs urging people to join and 'Get hooked on the Lord'. Interested as I was back then in hippies, bearded types and the spiritual groups swirling around in the 1970s, I went up to the lead singer.

My feature on the Children of God – or Jesus Freaks – was my first for *19* magazine and the first exposé on the sect. It was at the alpine of my ambitions to work on *19*, and having made contact with editor Margaret Koumi (of whom I was in awe), I submitted three more stories; all were accepted. I was hoping for a job, but 'no vacancies' was pinned firmly on the door.

I had looked up to *19* for a very long time, ever since the magazine's first issue when I posed for photographs with girls from other magazines to illustrate their story 'Where Have All the Virgins Gone?' ('posed' being the operative word). Some years later when I worked on *Mirabelle,* I looked up to their offices opposite, watching the glamorous, noisy folk on the balcony during their famed Friday parties.

19 magazine's first issue, March 1968, with the stonker of a cover line – 'Where Have All The Virgins Gone?'
19/Future Ltd.

19 was a glorious glossy packed with stylish fashion, quality articles and innovative, exciting design. Funny, sad, thoughtful, provocative; it was a fabulous read all for a third of the price of a pair of yellow Mary Quant tights (12 shillings) as worn by the models on the fashion pages.

A vacancy at last. My new job was to produce the main cover story each month. "I want to write meaningful features about real people," I said during the interview, then added quickly, "but I'll write about anything you want me to." Fortunately, Maggie (as I called her once I worked there) and I were on the same wavelength.

And so began a writing mélange from the Samaritans to vanishing virgins, from addictions, to sex and relationships. My erudite editor had a keen eye for strong cover lines, but the treatment had to be in-depth investigative journalism. We were exposing stories largely ignored in other young women's magazines at the time.

THE TERRORS OF SEXUAL ABUSE
BEHIND CLOSED DOORS

WHAT MAKES OUR YOUNG WOMEN TURN TO ISLAM?

WHAT KIND OF WOMEN ARE THEY
TO WALK AWAY FROM THEIR CHILDREN?

WE ARE THE KIDS IN CARE
LISTEN TO US IF YOU DARE

Incest, abortion, teenage prostitutes, schoolgirl mums, young bankrupts and gambling addicts; this was certainly not the froth of life. These subjects may appear tame these days alongside the no-holds-barred climate of what's out there today, especially online, but when *19* was launched over 50 years ago, it was unusual to write about such subjects in such an in-depth format in a young magazine. Well, that's what we did and of course there were also plenty of entertaining ingredients in the mix.

19 was never afraid to tackle controversy ever since its first issue in 1968 with the story 'Where Have All the Virgins Gone?' The radio presenter on 'Woman's Hour' at the time said *19* was raising controversy by implying that to be a virgin was out of step. Furthermore, she said the magazine was in danger of corrupting readers who happened to be younger than the target audience of 18 to 24. The editor responded by saying *19*'s articles about sex outside marriage were informing, and they trusted readers to have the intelligence to decide for themselves.

And that mindset prevailed.

Intense as the work was, there was more breathing space on a monthly than a weekly magazine and plenty of camaraderie, bonhomie and parties. Maggie created a wonderful atmosphere, but she was no pushover and everyone knew they had to pull their weight. I don't remember many fallings out; after all, staff were chosen with care. However, Maggie could not choose her bosses, 'a waste of space' as she called the publishers. There were some prickly exchanges as I remember, particularly should anyone try to interfere with editorial, or ask to see a cover. I was put in mind of my time on *Rave* magazine years before and editor Colin Bostock-Smith who told us management were 'little tin gods'. How I loved those rebel editors; both were fantastic mentors to me.

*My messy desk on 19 at 'The Ministry of Magazines'.
Insert: congratulations card illustration: Maggie Fleming*

Ironically, after all my moaning about being a researcher for other writers on *Woman's Own*, I now had a researcher of my own. This was a luxury never repeated throughout my career! First, I was reunited with my pal Magazine Girl Shirley Dunmall, who I'd worked with in the early days, and then Jane Dowdeswell who took over when Shirley left. Both were meticulous, talented, fabulous girls; both went on to have super careers.

'THE TERRIBLE TALE OF TEENAGE TRAMPS...'

Some of the girls I interviewed led raw, shocking lives. I can picture them now: Carol, 18, harrowed, homeless. Debbie, 19, pert and pretty, a prostitute. Mandy, child-like, pregnant at 14.

Stories of girls like these told the flip side of those hedonistic times.

Carol's story haunted me.

We met underneath railway arches in Manchester where Carol was living with 30 other young drifters in a hostel. Since the age of 13, Carol had been, "a street sleeper, a druggie, a thief" (her words). She lived with Hell's Angels, she lived on the streets and went one whole winter without a coat, she joined fairgrounds, she got hooked on drugs, "injecting and swallowing whatever I could get my hands on." She stole a car to fund her addictions, she was put into a remand home and finally she overdosed but lived to tell her tale.

Carol's hellish problems began before she was born. Her mother, aged 15, was "a drunken prostitute, riddled with VD and hooked on heroin." Carol was born with a form of cerebral palsy and was hospitalised for two years to correct her twisted arms and legs. When she was 15, Carol gave birth.

"I became hardened to everything," she told me, but clearly not hardened to the misery she'd caused her adoptive parents and not to son Craig, who she gave up for adoption. When she told me how she cuddled a teddy bear every night, crying for Craig, I cried too.

I contacted Carol some time after our interview. She was living alone in a bedsitter, which came with her job working for a taxi firm. When not working, she went round schools telling her story, "as a warning to others." She had ambitions to become a social worker; I hope she made it.

DEBBIE

Another teenage girl, another set of peeling railway arches, this time in north London.

Blonde, pretty, voluptuous, I didn't know whether Debbie was her real name or not, but I *did* know this young girl had spent most of her teenage years living and working as a prostitute. Her 'minder' came into the café first to suss out if I really was from a magazine; when he said okay, Debbie appeared:

"I had my first punter when I was 14. At first, it was a laugh going round the streets with friends calling out, 'Do you want a girl?' and then going clubbing with the money."

When Debbie left school, she moved in with girls she knew who were on the game. "My parents thought I worked in a punk fashion shop on the King's Road, which I did for a while, but I was also a club hostess and worked in a massage parlour too. You name it, I did it. I needed the money for rent, as well as for buying nice things."

Debbie said that she had "a few" bad experiences followed by "a terrifying one, which changed Debbie's life for good. "I was beaten up by one guy. He dragged me to the marshes and as he pulled off my clothes, I thought, 'I'm going to be raped, I'm going to die.' When I survived that, I felt completely wrecked. That's when I stopped.

"I regret it all every single day."

The stories often held a moral if you like, plus how-to-get-help info galore.

MANDY

The clatter and chatter in the dining room sounded like a school lunchtime anywhere. It was only on seeing the young girls cuddling their babies, or cradling their tummy bumps, that you knew this school in Birmingham was very different.

When I wrote my story about gymslip mums back in 1979, some local authorities treated pregnant schoolgirls as if they were 'contagious'. The girls had to leave their schools immediately, threatening their future life chances, unlike today where pregnant schoolgirls are treated equally.

Mandy was one of the lucky few in the country placed in a unit for schoolgirl mums. While her baby thrived in the onsite nursery, Mandy studied for O-levels and also learnt about budgeting, baby care and contraception. Mandy's parents were understanding. "Mum guessed when I was five months pregnant. I hadn't told her, because I wasn't sure if I was pregnant."

Ignorance was rife, as a midwife visiting that day told me. "Many young girls do not relate sex to having babies. There are some who arrive at hospital not knowing how they are going to give birth." Romantic ideas were at the heart of many problems, she said, "They think if you don't use contraceptives, it's love. If you do, it's just sex."

'The casual cocotte is not represented here', I concluded.

A Tragic Brush with Anorexia

When I wrote an article about anorexia nervosa in the late 1970s, I described the slimming disease as, 'The mysterious, totally baffling illness…' which it was then. In fact, I'd already come face to face with a tragic victim of the slimming disease several years earlier in the form of a major singing star.

When I was freelance, I'd secured a hard-to-get interview with the American brother and sister act The Carpenters. It was 1974 and, unbeknown to anyone, Karen Carpenter had already begun her deadly anorexic journey. With hindsight, it was one of the saddest celebrity interviews I ever did. The Carpenters' music may not have been cool, but their quality hits, 'We've Only Just Begun,' 'Yesterday Once More', 'Superstar', 'Killing Me Softly With His Song', 'Close To You' (I could go on) spoke for themselves. Karen's voice was all velvety smooth and silky; the arrangements by producer/writer Richard were superb. Superstars indeed.

Even so, The Carpenters were annoying me big time. My interview the previous week in London had been cancelled. "Richard isn't well," came the call on the day. *Poppycock*, I thought; *he looked well enough in the newspaper photos of them arriving in the UK.* Fast forward one week and they kept me waiting in the lobby of the Midland Hotel, Manchester for *four* hours. *This interview is never going to happen*, I thought and then the record company rang the office saying, "Absolutely no photographers," so *19* had to cancel their snapper.

Finally, I was summoned. "Karen won't be long," said Richard, "she's just with her hairdresser." Why, I wondered, when they'd cancelled our photographer?

"Photographers have no imagination," Karen said later when I asked her why they cancelled ours. "They always ask me to sit on Richard's lap."

At last, enter Karen. Same birth year, same height as myself, but actually looking smaller and can I say older – her stiff middle-aged hairstyle didn't help.

It wasn't an easy interview. A full twenty minutes passed before Karen would look directly at me, addressing her answers to my questions to Richard, but in doing so giving me the chance to look closely at her. Karen's head appeared too large for her frame; sparrow-like wrists peeped out from billowy sleeves; dark patches circled hollow eyes. The thought that Karen had an eating disorder didn't occur to me – as I said, little was known or understood about the slimming disease at that time.

I was so disappointed I'd got Karen on 'an off day'. We did not connect; there was no rapport and the fan in me so wanted to like her. Well, Karen and Richard Carpenter clearly did not like the press. In the interview, they said critics hated their fame, hated their success and their (clean-cut) image. They said how tired they were of being compared "unfairly" to "the scruffs and seedy types of the rock scene". The mood was actually quite brittle, until the interview moved on to random subjects: the tour, Richard's girlfriend, their music. "We are not the most tolerant of people," said Richard suddenly without being asked the question.

On my way out of the suite, their agent handed me two

tickets for their concert that night. Hearing her sing, I could have forgiven Karen anything. That said, my write-up did not shy away from, 'revealing another side to the Carpenters' and the headline (not written by me), played on the words of their hit saying, 'Killing *us* softly with *their* song'.

Karen was hospitalised the following year with a dramatic weight loss. By the time Karen died eight years later at the age of 32, the name anorexia nervosa had firmly entered the public consciousness.

My Carpenters interview finally appeared after several stop/go panics.
19/Future Ltd.

WHAT A DIFFERENCE A DECADE MAKES

We had the perfect idea to celebrate the new decade. *19* would run the first-ever survey on the 1980s girl. We would ask our readers what they thought about love and marriage, for their views on religion, homosexuality and other issues. And sex, of course, although I hasten to add that out of more than 50 multiple choice questions, only seven were directly related to sex.

No prizes for guessing, it was the sex story that broke all of the magazine's records in terms of publicity. 'SEX HAS NO REGRETS FOR THE 1980s GIRL' was a huge hit and was covered by all the national newspapers, the *Sun* making it their front-page story.

Our exclusive Vanishing Virgins survey broke all publicity records for the magazine
Photo: The Sun/News Licensing

The results were broadcast on the 6 o'clock news and I went on several radio shows to 'explain' what had happened to the nation's virgins, sounding shocked at the results myself.

It was a totally pucker, authoritative project – respected sociologist Robert Chester of the University of Hull devised the questionnaire. Results were fed into a computer and I wrote the article based on his 50-page report. Our readers clearly wanted to 'talk', and their views on marriage, parenthood, religion and much else turned out to be a cross between the traditional and progressive on most things. Apart from those vanishing virgin figures…

I believe we drew the largest number of readers ever for a survey of this type – incredibly, over 11,000 readers responded. We were cock-a-hoop. *Thank you very much, 19 readers – you were phenomenal!*

In 1980, my personal life changed irrevocably. I was 30 and my body clock was ticking faster... *if only I'd joined* 19 *earlier... if only I was younger... if only... if only...* but the decision had been made and baby David came along almost to order. (I was never sure whether to be flattered or upset when Maggie greeted each of my two pregnancy announcements with "OH NO!")

Two weeks after giving birth, page proofs of my feature were biked home for checking. My post-birth hormones raging and with one eye on the pages perched on my lap, the other on feeding my baby, the words jumped back and forth in front of my eyes – they might as well have been in hieroglyphics.

When things settled down, I returned to work as features editor and also to writing some celebrity interviews once more. But compromises had to be made and as much as I would have *loved* to have flown to Paris to interview Bob Geldof, baby number two, Michael, was on his way and it was out of the question. Instead, I commissioned the fluid writing and specialism that Magazine Girl pal Jan Iles-Kaluza brought to music features. Likewise, I couldn't camp out at Greenham Common myself, much to my chagrin.

After leaving the magazine, I was commissioned by *19* to organise another groundbreaking survey. The AIDS epidemic was at its height in 1987, the year Princess Diana shook gloveless hands with an HIV patient. Once again, our readers' response was astonishing. 7,000 of them took part: illustrating sympathy and awareness, this time some expressing the wish they were still virgins.

Working on *19* had upped my game and when I left to go freelance in the mid-eighties, I extended my range and repertoire further, writing on a wide spectrum of subjects for *Marie Claire, The Sunday Times Magazine, Ideal Home* and others, as well as interviewing celebrities galore for *HELLO!* magazine. Over the years, I wrote articles for various newspapers too, but I never once tired of being 'a Magazine Girl'.

It had been a mega time for magazines in the 1960s when the decade of the teenager was born, and I was lucky enough to be a part of it. These days, magazines live on in smaller numbers and with fewer readers, although there are still many stunning examples. And while digital magazines have their place in the market, to my mind, they can never replace the smell of the print, the touch of smooth pages and the kaleidoscope of surprise as you flick through a glossy copy. I loved it all then and I still do.

JANICE'S STORY

My Biba emporium Passport – lucky me.

"My fascination with looks and beauty began at an early age, watching my glam mum at her dressing table perfecting her image. By four, I was caught daubing her red lipstick round my face and draining her treasured French perfume all over myself. That earned me a good telling-off, but smelling so divine that it meant there were cuddles too!

Image is important to more people than you might imagine, as I learnt over the decades working closely with iconic image-makers, whose expertise changed the face of perceived beauty not just for celebrities but for ordinary people wanting to look more attractive."

ONE

VANDYKE 5885 –
A PHONE CALL TO REMEMBER

"Hey, Janice, do you wanna lift back into town hen?" she hollered from the kitchen, grabbing her bag and car keys. Before I knew it, we were whizzing from Hampstead Heath across Edward Heath's '70s London in her Mini (considerably posher than mine), jabbering nineteen to the dozen as besties do, about Mini cars, mascara, men and marriage (hers), comparing our ages, both 24, and our brilliant careers. All normal stuff for besties, you'd think, except she wasn't a bestie. She wasn't even a friend.

She was '60s pop icon Lulu.

I'd just finished a *Loving* 'exclusive' beauty interview with the dynamic pop star at her stylish home in Hampstead. Chatting enthusiastically about her looks and career, she said it was hard to believe she'd been in the pop business for ten years already. And now here she was, one of the UK's hottest female pop stars, driving *me* through London – I could hardly believe it.

So weaving our way through the capital, behind those smoke-filled black cabs and double-decker busses, jovial conductors swaying typically on the platforms, calling, "Fares please," I sang the praises of writing for *Rave* and *Loving* magazines while Lulu

Pop Queen Lulu was my chauffeur
Loving Magazine/Future Publishing Ltd.

beamed her sunny smile and broke into snippets of song. That fond memory still lingers on.

Only a few years earlier, in 1966, I was a typical suburban school leaver with a passion for pop stars, magazines and make-up, a flair for writing and unrecognised dreams of becoming a journalist. With occasional quirky confidence and lack of it in equal measure, I had no real game plan.

Back then, before social media and beauty influencers made everyone a 'Beauty Expert', women of all ages relied on magazines to reveal the beauty secrets of the stars, and before long it was my job to tell them.

My early fascination with cosmetics, watching Mum at her dressing table, led me into a career which saw me living the dream as a beauty journalist, getting the inside stories from experts in their fields of nutrition, dermatology, cosmetic surgery, hair, cosmetics; you get the idea. The bonus in my career was working with make-up artists, designers and photographers at the top of their game. Patrick Lichfield was a joy to work with and despite being Queen Elizabeth's cousin, never played the grandee. Patrick photographed the Royal Wedding in 1981, Barbara Daly was Diana's make-up artist (MUA) extraordinaire and the Emanuels, Elizabeth and David, designed the fairy-tale wedding gown. I was lucky enough to work with them all, as you'll hear in later chapters.

My address books, some of which I still have, were like the Little Black Book of 'Who's Who', complete with home addresses and telephone numbers!

As I flick through the well-thumbed pages now, there's *Quant*, who took the world by storm in the '60s breaking every fashion and beauty rule and who I always found warm and engaging, if a little shy. *Sassoon* is in there, confident and equally charming and *so* fit at 50 that the healthy vegetarian posed naked for a shot we used in *Woman's Own*. Here is **B** for *Brigitte Bardot* – she seldom gave interviews but in our phone chat about her life and looks at 43, the sun-worshipper revealed she tanned easily without sun cream, was proud to look good naturally without cosmetics, walked, swam and skied a lot, would never cut her hair short or use face masks or creams, "*because my lover wouldn't like it.*" Also under **B** is *Barbara Hulanicki*, who redefined the shopping experience with her iconic fashion emporium Biba in 1964.

Under **P** for *Photographers:* there's a directory of iconic lensmen including David Bailey, Roger Charity and John Swannell.

I enjoyed both Roger's sense of humour, along with his attention to detail, and John's more unusual quietness, his nose always in a book while hair and make-up was taking a lifetime. Our first beauty shoot together in the 70s was in his gloomy

Re-united with John Swannell Forty Years On
at Clarendon Fine Art Gallery
Photo: instagram.com/
piersallardycephotographer/

Victorian north London studio. The loo was down dark and creepy stairs in a place he said was haunted, which scared us all. He later declared he'd had it exorcised, much to the models' and my relief.

John's dry humour was revealed recently when we chatted about his new book 'Forty Years On' and I reminded him about this incident. The legendary photographer laughingly replied *"I've never told anyone this before, Janice, but it was all a joke. It wasn't haunted and I didn't have it exorcised!"*

It's hard to imagine how freely we gained telephone numbers and addresses for celebrities and were able to hang out in their homes for an interview. If it hadn't been the case, I would never have tinkled the ivories of actress Moira Lister's antique grand piano, shared a pot of tea with Cynthia Lennon in her lounge, sipped ice-cold ginger beer with Zandra Rhodes in her kitchen, let alone sup the finest champers while reclining in the lounge of Lord and Lady Rothermere's Belgravia pad. There's more about these encounters and a few surprises in further chapters. But it was different then and few people seemed to get in the way of a good story or a photo shoot and we got things done. Everything was so much easier, unlike today, where an entourage of PR staff – assistants, agents, advisors and the like – have to voice an opinion.

In the late '60s, we, the Magazine Girls, were all working in different capacities on magazines and were one big happy family. Despite being wet behind the ears, our opinions and ideas were soon respected and valued by our editors, who I suspect often learnt from our youthful exuberance, giving us opportunities and encouragement beyond our dreams.

I've had to pinch myself on many occasions from the day I entered the crazy world of magazines, oozing with teenage confidence and a can-do attitude while secretly fuelled with self-doubt and at times, terrified.

One minute, this 18-year-old school leaver was using sketchy shorthand as her editor on *Rave* magazine dictated letters arranging interviews with pop stars, and the next, or so it seemed, she found *herself* interviewing pop stars and actors, often at their homes.

'Pinch' moments were frequent throughout my career. Among the more memorable was another unlikely 'chauffeur' a couple of decades after Lulu, when royal photographer Lord Patrick Lichfield, drove me more than a hundred miles in his swanky limo for an exclusive celebrity interview. I sure wasn't expecting him to drive me there himself! Chatting easily along the way, he couldn't resist confiding a cheeky secret about the celeb, who he had known many years before. I promised to 'keep mum'. I can reveal, however, that during our interview in her exquisite bedroom, the glamorous lady in question also confided the same 'secret' and I looked suitably surprised. Later, the pair appeared to be having quite a friendly *tête-à-tête*. You'd like to know more, of course, but my lips are sealed – and the lady in question, a huge star, would be less than impressed!

Whether I was talking make-up with Mary Quant at the Ritz, chatting about sport with Henry Cooper or Daley Thompson, or being jetted to a dermatology conference in Paris or New York, it was hard to believe that this was now 'the norm' in my working life. That said, the dream job entailed a good deal of conscientious work, and thus ability, dedication and unsurpassed enthusiasm were key to keeping it.

In later years, working on the more 'mature' magazines *Woman's Own* and *Woman,* everything became much more serious as a multitude of schedules, conferences, planning meetings and debriefs became central to successful magazine production. New titles launched ever more frequently, so competition became increasingly stiff. Some successful editors, achieving high readerships, were popular, creative and always open to new ideas. Others were less approachable and unpredictable, and could undermine and destroy morale on a whim.

THE MADE-TO-MEASURE FAMILY

Our ordinary family of four was a happy one. Mum and Dad, both from working-class backgrounds, had full-time jobs and in the school holidays left my brother, Vic, four years my senior, in charge. Needless to say, that didn't always work for him. He was as fearless as I was sensitive, so unbeknown to them, while I was writing stories and reading *Bunty* or Enid Blyton's 'The Seaside Family', he would be off riding and wrecking Dad's bike, smoking at the end of the garden or selling apples from our tree and swearing me to secrecy. He did look out for me quite often, though, I will admit.

Mum was glamorous, confident, warm and feisty. She rather 'shielded' me from those important 'facts of life', so as a naïve 14-year-old, I was shocked to find a copy of the formerly banned 'Lady Chatterley's Lover' hidden in her dressing-table drawer, especially as I'd only ever seen her read *Woman's Own!*

She loved dancing and music – her idol being handsome crooner Frankie Vaughan. His recording 'Give Me the

Moonlight' in 1955 became his signature song and along with millions of other fans, she'd readily have shared with him some of the 'moonlight' he sang so seductively about. Mum always said I had my head in the clouds, so if I'd told her that one day I'd be chatting with 'Mr Moonlight' himself in his north London home, and writing about his special relationship with his daughter in *Woman's Own,* she'd have told me to wake up and 'knuckle down' to my schoolwork! I could have added that he would be wearing a dressing gown too!

My dad was also special to me. Despite leaving school at 14, he was well informed about politics and current affairs, always able to explain things I didn't understand. Kind and sensitive with a dry sense of humour, he was an accomplished self-taught musician and encouraged me to take piano lessons at school. I'm grateful to him, as I still play most days.

Years later in 1977 when Dad played his accordion and sang a beautiful song he'd composed for my wedding day, 'The Wedding of Robert and Jan', there wasn't a dry eye anywhere at our reception.

July 1977, newlyweds Mr. and Mrs. Taylor

Music brought our home to life and if it wasn't Dad, it was the 'wireless' or the 'gramophone'. At their many parties, Dad would sing and play piano or accordion, while Mum, looking glam, danced and chatted with their friends.

My brother wasn't so musical, but when his teenage mates came round in school holidays with guitars, playing 'Apache' like The Shadows, or Buddy Holly's 'Peggy Sue', he'd be involved, looking like their manager.

Sitting my 11+ was tricky, as my attention span was short and knowledge unpredictable. I was a 'borderline' pass. Thus in 1959 I was kitted out at great cost and ready for the learning experience that was the Comprehensive School.

No academic, I was more of a dreamer with 'attention deficit' in subjects that didn't appeal. I excelled in those that did, for example, French, English Language and Literature, inspired by my wonderful teacher Mrs Egford, who saw my writing potential and encouraged me to gain my only A-level.

By the time I left school, my love of writing and reading had led me to become focused on becoming a journalist, writing for the pop magazines I loved and related to.

So, while the crème de la crème of pupils like our head girl went off to university, and other bright girls like my best friend, Lyn, went to teacher training college, I was about to launch myself on the workforce, armed with just a handful of GCEs, A-level English, passable shorthand/typing, stubborn hope and a head full of dreams. Journalism definitely wasn't on the school leaver's job list, so no help there, but my school friend Anne Ullman knew of my dreams…

Luckily for me, she'd passed my phone number, Vandyke 5885 to her cousin, who might be able to help. He was an accountant in Fleet Street and I was soon signed into NATSOPA, a union specialising in temporary and permanent secretarial jobs in publishing.

(Area code names like Vandyke preceded numbers until around 1969, the most famous being Scotland Yard's Whitehall 1212.)

I waited in hope for a phone call…

In March 1966, Harold Wilson won a 'sweeping victory' in a snap general election and Labour was voted back in power, much to Wilson's delight. By the end of July, West Ham's 25-year-old football ace Bobby Moore had also scored a victory, as captain of the England team which beat West Germany 4-2 in the World Cup. I knew little about politics and even less about football. Dad loved boxing, having been an amateur boxer in his youth – Henry Cooper was his hero. So no real footy fans in our house, though we were all glued to the match – the nation was on fire with pride and so were we!

Imagine if I'd known that just over a decade later I'd be sitting in this national treasure Bobby Moore's home with his then wife Tina and daughter, Roberta, interviewing them for *Woman's Own!*

Still handsome and in great shape at 38, the very private man was welcoming and warm. His life had changed since his footy days, but still involved with sport, he was busy, prosperous and fanatical about fitness. Bobby Moore sadly passed away in 1993 but was to this day, as I write in 2023, the only man ever to lift the World Cup for England.

Back in 1966, I thought I knew all about life. Earning thirty shillings (£1.50) on Saturdays at Martin Ford, the 'affordable' high-street fashion shop for teens, meant I could treat myself to new skinny rib tops and mini skirts, trying like most teenagers to emulate the pop star image. Interestingly, my job was a learning curve not only in the art of 'cheap and cheerful' retail, but opening my eyes to the wider picture of other people's lives.

Dressed to impress in my 'affordable' fashion, and wide-eyed with lashings of clumpy mascara, Saturday night bopping was essential, whether slithering around to ska at the Locarno, rocking to a band in a small hall somewhere, or at a disco, jumping to 'Shout' by *Lulu*, who years later I'd be interviewing.

Here's the thing. In reality, at 18, I knew nothing. I was as green as that 'Green, Green Grass of Home', which put heart-throb Tom Jones at the top of the pop charts.

Our telephone calls were usually for Mum or from someone who'd dialled the wrong number, asking if their made-to-measure suit was ready. Dad's name, John Collier, was the same as the well-known chain of gents' outfitters, but often when he'd tired of one too many such calls, he'd just say, "Yes, friend, it's ready."

In September of '66, just as my family were preparing for my brother and his fiancée Dilwen's wedding, the phone rang and I answered: "Vandyke 5885."

This call was to change the rest of my life...

NATSOPA had a vacancy for a temp sec on a magazine in London and was I available to start on Monday, 12th September?

I most certainly was!

I was to join *Rave* magazine, a large monthly bursting with pop stars, fashion, beauty, all the things I loved. From that phone call on, sleeping and eating became secondary to dreaming about where this exciting job may lead.

So in the same year that Twiggy became the Face of '66 and George Harrison married Patti Boyd in a register office in Epsom, I sloughed off my 18-year-old schoolgirl skin and plunged excitedly headfirst into the seductive career that beckoned.

DEAR SIR...THIS IS JUST THE BEGINNING...

Monday, 12th September 1966 found me strutting my stuff along the Strand in bright sunshine, on my way to my first job as a temporary secretary to the editor and art director of my favourite monthly pop magazine, *Rave*. I wanted to tell the whole world.

Dressing the part was important, but tricky on my Saturday job money. Luckily, my great-aunt Ena had given me a snappy '40s vintage suit, and admiring my neat little fitted jacket and the kick pleat of the skirt in every shop window along the Strand, I felt the bee's knees.

That is, until an older lady stopped me and gently tucked in the huge label hanging out of my jacket collar, saying, "Don't spoil the ship for a ha'p'orth of tar, dear."

Rising in the bumpy pre-war lift to the fifth floor and feeling a bundle of nerves, I went to meet my boss, the editor, Terry Hornett. He was good-looking, young, trendy and friendly too. I was to work for him and smiley art director Roger Pinney, slightly older and married. I was also to work occasionally for a calm and encouraging lady called Miss Palfrey, who you'll hear mentioned throughout the chapters.

My little office, sandwiched between my two bosses, had connecting doors and was a real hub of activity. So many shiny, happy people popped in and out to see the 'ed.' about features or fashion or to show layouts, artwork or illustrations to the art director. Everyone seemed to love being at work, and there's no better gratification in life than having a job that you really enjoy. I loved every single minute!

It was an education to learn how ideas for features came together and which pop star would be on the front cover. Manfred Mann singer Paul Jones, a real heart-throb I'd always fancied, beamed seductively from the front cover at that time, and when he walked into my office the first time to see the editor, I was thrilled. He was so friendly and natural, I felt I knew him. I suddenly asked for his autograph – then blushed badly as I'd intended to be blasé.

Pop stars, models and photographers regularly beat a path to the ed.'s door in those days, and I soon became more chilled about meeting and greeting them and making them occasional cups of tea.

Fashion editors from other magazines, the 'influencers' of their day, sashayed in and out of the building, and most of our teenage staff were in awe of their amazing style. One of them really stood out and you couldn't take your eyes off her. Chelita just looked so cool from top to toe. Petite and sylph-like, her shiny nut brown hair, precision-cut à la Sassoon, framed her tiny heart-shaped face. Her flawless olive skin, huge dark eyes and Cupid's bow red lips drew you in. Charismatic in looks and style, she accessorised her stunning cream shearling coat, with her fluffy cream pooch nestled under her arm.

The exotic fashion editor was married at the time to Tony Secunda, manager of the Midlands group The Move. Their hit 'Flowers in the Rain' was the first record played on the new pop station that was Radio 1.

The vibe and spirit of London was on fire in the magazine offices. Fashion was central to the identity of young people, and fashion editors showed us how to get *the look* whatever our budget.

Twiggy had broken the mould for modelling and was out there with her extraordinary waif-like looks, confirming it didn't matter what background you came from. Being good at your job was all that mattered. And I, fresh from school, was right there, imbibing the enthusiasm and creativity of the movers and shakers of swinging London.

But then it was Christmas. My three-month temporary job was coming to a close and I was very sad. Determined to enjoy *Rave's* Christmas party, and what I believed was my last day in the job, I dressed to impress in my only sexy black mini dress and arrived at work for 'business as usual'.

I'd been so inspired by my editor, Terry. Starting out in 1960 as a junior on *Boyfriend* magazine, by 1966 he was already the editor of *Rave* and also associate editor of a brand-new magazine called *Model Girl*. Its content was far removed from *Rave*, but a new launch sounded so exciting and I longed to be involved!

Later at the party, when 'the boys' Terry and Roger presented me with a giant box of Black Magic and thanked me for all I'd done, I was in bits. Until Terry winked and said they weren't exactly letting me go. I hadn't the slightest idea that this was *not* the end of a job, but the start of a lifelong career. I was to join the editorial team as a trainee journalist – words cannot describe how excited I felt.

TWO

ROLE MODELS

In January 1967, with a new spring in my step and some great new clothes from Miss Selfridge, the new young wing of Selfridges, I found myself along the corridor on Terry's newly launched magazine.

Model Girl was a specialist beauty magazine with a focus on hairstyles, which were rapidly changing thanks to the innovative talents of Vidal Sassoon and Leonard. It was here I first met some of the lovely Magazine Girls you'll read about.

I was to assist the slightly older beauty editor, Kathleen Jones, doing whatever was required to get the pages up and running. At the same time, I was put on a course to train one day a week as a sub-editor, which entailed checking the writers' copy for sense and good grammar, making sure it was factually correct, the right length written in our 'house' style and delivered in the right tone for the magazine.

Part of my training involved learning how to proof read and correct the early pages, which I then took to the editor for approval. Learning about printers' marks enabled me to liaise with the printers on a daily basis, once the pages had been approved by the editors.

My baptism of fire came fairly early on when, while still on my training course, I was asked to take along some page proofs for checking and signing to our very grand editorial director, Miss Patricia Lamburn. I'd been told to knock and wait.

"Come," she responded.

Miss Lamburn was a magnificent woman, most elegantly dressed, with a well-defined jawline, immaculate hair and the most beautiful cut-glass accent, with a rather considered delivery of speech. I was quite in awe of her, as were most 'minions' at the time.

Walking tentatively across the plush carpet of her grand office, I held out the page proofs, politely requesting that she read them.

"Have you checked these pages, Janice?" she asked, peering over the top of her specs.

"No, Miss Lamburn," I said quietly, cheeks afire. (I couldn't imagine that I was supposed to!)

"Well, dear, in future, don't ever bring me page proofs to approve if you haven't checked them first yourself." With a sophisticated smile, she handed them back to me.

Great learning curve.

I never presented unread proofs again.

Since the focus of the magazine was on hair, our office was always flooded with pictures from enthusiastic crimpers hoping we'd put their salons on the map. With no model or photography fees to pay, it was cheap publishing for the magazine and free advertising for the salon.

We cherry-picked the best styles and photography, giving tips and illustrations for each style, many of which entailed roller setting. One of my jobs was to brief talented illustrator Annie Hutchison on roller size and direction.

Annie was a gentle soul with a great sense of humour and I loved her hippy style. We became good friends and worked together for years.

Despite the later emergence of short, chic styles and the genius 5-point cut with which Sassoon crowned Mary Quant, voluminous beehives, bouffants and big hairstyles were still much in demand, initiated by Jackie Kennedy and sported by Dusty Springfield, The Supremes and Marsha Hunt among many. A revival of hair pieces and fashion wigs made it possible for every girl to 'get the look', and I often wore a hair piece when the occasion called and loved trying on wigs with Annie in the office and laughing at the way we looked.

Having fun while we worked came naturally in those early days and playing the latest demo discs in the office was magical 'music while you work'. On Friday nights, a drop of warm *vino blanco* in a paper cup never tasted so good – a bowl of peanuts and a few ciggys and we were made!

Some real characters and beautiful people worked with us, among them lovely Maggie Harris, who worked in the art room designing hand-drawn layouts.

Maggie was stick-thin, with marmalade hair, ivory skin and freckles – and oh-so-cool John Lennon specs. Softly spoken with a natural warmth, she'd done some modelling in the past and would show us her catwalk moves in the office, arching her slender frame backwards with head held nonchalantly off to one side. How we loved watching her glide across the grubby office floor, draping a garment along in her wake.

When we caught up with her recently for a day of pure nostalgia, we learnt that since the '70s she has been known simply as Mangala and is both a successful make-up artist and supporting TV and film actress.

Twiggy and Me...?

In my first month at *Model Girl*, Kathleen asked if I would like a 'makeover'. The term 'makeover' was new then and I wasn't really sure what it entailed, but she said I'd get a great new look from a top hairdresser and make-up artist and the pictures would appear in the magazine. It sounded great, so I agreed.

I was to go to the posh Mayfair hair salon Antoine of Dover Street, where acclaimed crimper Mr Antoine would give me a new hairstyle. Rather like Twiggy, I had short, shiny, straight mid-brown hair with a side parting. I quite liked it actually and didn't think there was much he could do to make it look different, but I was hopeful that I would look good.

Stepping into the plush salon, all glossy with expensive décor and classy magazines, was an education in itself and a far cry from our local salons, which smelled of perm solution and bleach. The attractive staff all looked professional and well groomed. I was worried that I would let myself down with my lack of sophistication and *savoir faire*.

Mum had always said, "If you're asked something you don't know about, pretend you do." That's all well and good for some people but never seemed to work for me. While I was waiting for Mr Antoine, I was offered a *filter coffee*, the likes of which I had never encountered. As this strange-looking cup with a big plastic lidded thing on top arrived on a tray with posh biscuits, I was asked by the immaculately dressed junior if I knew about filter coffee. "Oh yes," I lied, remembering Mum's words. I gazed at it in embarrassment, not having a clue what to do. *But surely*, I thought, *it's just a cup of coffee*. So I picked up the strange plastic cup – and promptly scalded both my legs with the unfiltered coffee, which splashed everywhere! Thanks, Mum.

I'll cut to the chase with the makeover. Rather like Twiggy, who famously said she spent more than *seven hours* in Leonard's salon the day he changed her looks and life in 1966, so it was for me – except for 'the life' part.

Over many hours and cups of filter coffee, the technique of which I soon mastered, my hair was cut, shaped, permed, streaked, tweaked and twirled, and I really hadn't a clue what was going on! By the time I sat under a red-hot hood dryer in rollers, my cheeks were on fire and I longed to escape.

Emerging hours later with florid cheeks and burnt ears, I was apparently ready for part two of my exciting new look... Enter Max Factor's ace make-up artist of the day, Douglas Young, smelling mannishly divine and immaculately suited and booted.

His large cosmetics trunk housed a kaleidoscope of colours. There were shapers and shaders, foundations, fake lashes, powder puffs, brushes of every shape and size, bottles and bowls, in which he would later clean his brushes.

The Maestro began my new look with Erace, one of the first concealers for covering 'blemishes and dark under-eye circles'. Seemingly, I had both.

With the deftness of Picasso, he then swept colours over my eyes, lips and cheeks. Impressed with the result, he stood back to admire his work.

Like Twiggy, I was simply dying to see the new me. Perhaps now I'd look less like a new kid on the block and more like a model girl about town.

Unlike Twiggy, I was aghast when I saw the feathery bird's nest of short, curly tortoiseshell and blonde hair perched on top of my head, lacquered rigid.

Mr Antoine's and Mr Young's expertise was second to none, though between them, they'd transformed a shiny-haired, fresh-faced 18-year-old with clear skin, good teeth and hazel eyes into an over-coiffed, over-painted cosy-looking 30-year-old. I wanted to scream!

Shock, horror-what have they done to me?

Blonde 'streaks', as they were known, were still in their infancy, and Mr A had used breakthrough colouring techniques for the tortoiseshell effect, creatively combining colours and curls. People stopped me in the street, some of them hairdressers, for a closer look, asking which salon had created this wonderful work.

Kathleen thought the new look was brilliant – until she heard my next news.

As wash 'n' wear perms hadn't yet been invented, permed hair had to be roller set after washing, to avoid a resulting frizzy ball. Mr Antoine had a reputation to uphold, especially as my before and after pictures were in the magazine, so he insisted I went to him every Monday morning at 9am for a complimentary shampoo and set.

Reluctantly, Kathleen agreed.

Being selected for a makeover in those days was exciting for our readers, who all imagined they would emerge looking like top models. Our aim was to give ordinary girls the 'wow' factor so we could splash the images over our pages to great effect. Many did look amazing, others certainly looked different but would sometimes look disappointed, even shedding a tear if the cut, style or colour wasn't what they really wanted or if the boyfriend or husband was there and hated it.

Thinking back to Twiggy, I was also tall and slim, but Kathleen, who wasn't exactly Twiggy herself, thought I was a suitable candidate to road-test a new diet.

Dieting was a real novelty for me and I dutifully followed it to the letter, weighing my portions and literally counting out a dozen peas and one carrot at mealtimes. I lost quite a few pounds.

Impressed by what could be achieved in a short space of time, I took a much keener interest in how easy it was to control your shape and size from then on. Sadly, that interest became an issue

SLIMMER'S GUIDE TO BEAUTY

NOT LONG NOW before those summer months are with us once more! How will you shape up on the beach this year? Gorgeously sylph-like – will your figure make heads spin, eyes boggle?

There's only one way to do it – start right now! Begin your slim campaign with us – along with our slimmer's guide to beauty. Don't put off till tomorrow what you may easily begin today. Remember – everything you don't eat from this moment on counts!

First things first. Turn to the weight chart – look up your height and frame and find the weight you should be. Then step on your scales. If you're way off your ideal weight, you'll know where your target is!

Don't be put off easily. You look after the pounds, the stones will look after themselves! Concentrate on a pound at a time – they drop off very quickly.

You've weighed yourself (naked preferably, but take off 3lbs. for clothes) and checked your weight chart. You're with us all the way! Now what?

THE DIET FOR YOU

Not everybody can manage successfully with the same kind of diet. Different personalities need different approaches to slimming.

Some people find it necessary to be nibbling all the time, even though it's only good things like carrots or celery. Others, of course, feel more pleased with themselves if they only eat three calorie-controlled meals a day.

You don't have to tot up all those figures and plan your meals in advance – if you don't want to. You can simply stick to these basic rules. NO sweet stuff like cakes, biscuits

[...] potatoes, and bread. NO cooking food with fat, always grill or boil. NO eating fatty meat. You can't go far wrong.

The compulsive eaters of this world are those who will benefit from the diet that offers them about six meals a day!

They munch three average meals at the proper time, then eat three small snacks between meal times. Sounds strange – but it's all calorie-controlled! Recognise your needs, then stick to your guns!

STEER CLEAR OF TEMPTATION...
(OR three minutes in your mouth – and three months on your hips!)

Don't feast your eyes on food that is going to tempt you beyond control. Don't offer to have friends in to a slap-up dinner, knowing you'll have back in square one!

NEVER go shopping for food when you are hungry. You'll say goodbye to your money on a bar chocolate, a packet of biscuits and a huge fruit cake so quick you won't know what's hit you!

The best place to go shopping is the green grocers. You can really go to town on lettuce, tomatoes, celery, carrots, cabbage, cauliflower, mushrooms. And fresh fruits like apples, oranges, lemons, grapefruits. It's all good stuff!

Trimelts Drinking. Chocolate makes a nice meal replacement (breakfast usually) and **Bovril** makes a meaty lunchtime drink.

At the bread counter you needn't be shy. Resist those great big loaves of crispy bread. Instead, go for **Slimcea, Balance, Cambridge Formula, Nimble.**

If life isn't worth living without sweetness in your tea cup, invest in sweeteners like **Sweetex, Saxin, Sweet 'n' Low, Sugrosa.**

SLIMMING AIDS

One way to diet is to cut down or out on your normal meals and another is find a different way of eating. There are many special foods designed to be eaten instead of normal meals.

Bisks sweet biscuits make slimming for the sweet-toothed girl easy. There are milk or plain chocolate biscuits and others with cream fillings.

Many flavours on the savoury side, too (Chicken Flake tastes good!).

Complan is the meal in a cup and contains vitamins, protein and minerals. You just mix the powder in a cup and add any unsweetened flavour you like.

Limmits is another 'household' name in slimming! They offer you everything from baked beans to chocolate, cream biscuits and soup!

Trimetts have four kinds of biscuits – sweet, savoury, chocolate coated and wafers.

Ayds are those delicious-tasting caramel cubes (in vanilla or mint flavour). They contain vitamins and minerals and you'll be content to eat less. (SEE OUR SUPER AYDS

Weighing up the losing game

a couple of years down the line, when still keeping 'control', my weight plummeted by nearly a stone to Twiggy-like proportions. I was eight and a half stone and foolishly loved being told I was 'so skinny'.

During that time, my periods slowly ceased and I felt light-headed on occasion but, strange as it seems, didn't make the diet connection. Neither I nor our family GP (who dismissed the idea of pregnancy after an embarrassing interrogation about my sex life) had any idea why my periods had stopped or that I was bordering on what we now recognise as anorexia.

All things must pass, however, as George Harrison also observed on his '70s album, and happily so it was for me. After three weeks on a family camping holiday in Spain, when I ate and drank everything, the immediate spell was broken and normal functions resumed.

It would be fair to say, though, that after a lifetime of working with stick-thin models and constantly writing about diets and weight loss (more about that later), working for *Slimming* and *Successful Slimming* magazines and even running a slimming club from home, I was always diet-conscious and guess it's still in the psyche.

Magazines, models and fashion designers have long had much to answer for when it comes to our obsession with our shape and size. That said, we were not nearly as fixated about having the beauty attributes that young women seek today. It would have been inconceivable that girls in their early teens and twenties would have anti-ageing procedures or invasive cosmetic surgery to improve their looks. But in the 21st century, for many women trying to live up to images of impossible perfection on social media, these *enhancements* have become the norm. For others, however, unrealistic expectations can have a negative, demoralising impact.

THREE

SOMETHING TO RAVE ABOUT

Now it's 1968. Civil rights leader Martin Luther King Jnr was assassinated on 4th April in Memphis. The world was in shock.

At the same time, Louis Armstrong was mindfully topping the charts with 'What a Wonderful World', a sentiment confirmed a year later by another Armstrong, Neil, who took the first walk on the moon. Paul McCartney, meanwhile, was recording Mary Hopkin's debut single 'Those Were the Days'. Indeed they were, and it wasn't long before I was interviewing the Welsh talent for a *Rave* beauty special. Unruffled by her newfound fame, Mary maintained her natural image and hairstyle with trips to top London crimper Leonard and always wore barely-there make-up. Rather surprisingly, she talked about her secret love of bold colour cosmetics and really admired the bright green poster paint eyeshadows and vivid red lipsticks that Patti Boyd was wearing at that time.

By 1968, Colin Bostock-Smith was *Rave's* new editor. A fine and friendly man of integrity with a great sense of humour, it comes as no surprise that he became a much-acclaimed TV and comedy writer, even penning gags for President Reagan and Bob Hope. He recorded in later years that he once warned his teenage *Rave* readers that their parents would be offended by a particular feature on The Rolling Stones, adding, "I then suggested that another good way to offend them would be to overturn their dustbins on the front lawn. Complaints came down like thunder from the upper reaches of IPC Magazines and I was the recipient of a severe reprimand."

Rave's offices were just along the corridor and I was delighted when he offered me the job as beauty editor – writing a few general features when required. I didn't need asking twice.

I was pretty much given *carte blanche* on the beauty front, Colin having admitted he knew precious little about the subject. One of the cover lines around that time was 'Fashion and Beauty Know-How to Keep You Raving All Summer!' and I liked the sound of that.

Working alongside rock and pop writers was a real treat and a world away from the pin curls and perms at *Model Girl,* later renamed *Hairstyles.* They were such a cool bunch, hanging out with the stars at gigs and clubs and burning the candles to get that special story. I will always remember the wonderful Maureen O'Grady, a talented journalist and pop writer, who swept in and out of the office looking like a film star in her leopard print coat, glamorous hair and immaculate make-up.

And oh, the waft of the most heady perfume in her wake was divine. I'd never smelled anything quite like it and asked her repeatedly what it was called. Determined to buy some of this intoxicating fragrance, only sold at Selfridges, if you please, I took the bus there from the Strand in my lunch break, clutching the paper with the name of the fragrance on it.

Imagine now, never having heard of Estée Lauder, let alone Youth Dew!

Launched in the States in 1953 as a bath oil which doubled as a perfume, it was little known in the UK. Despite the fact that this potent perfume was very oily and its patchouli content made my neck red raw and itchy, I was hooked.

That is, until everyone's mum and granny was wearing it too!

Youth Dew seemed to resonate with older women, who were perhaps hoping to recapture their youth, and the inescapable aroma soon became abhorrent to me!

By now, when I wasn't writing general features about transcendental meditation, the stress-buster for cool cats in the '60s, or quizzing psychologists about what happens when we sleep and why we dream, I was entering a whole new world as a beauty editor.

I might be lunching across the road at the Savoy (whose car park I used daily for my little Mini), perhaps talking hair with Vidal Sassoon about his state-of-the-art salon where clients reclined over a backwash for shampooing instead of leaning forward, where trickling water ruined their make-up. Or I might be chatting with the quietly eloquent Mary Quant about her innovative beauty Vitamin B and D pills, sold in Quant pill boxes beside her skincare range.

Seemingly, this upset the chemists, who considered such products to be their serious domain. It was exciting to be among the first to reveal new concepts in hair and make-up and to be able to splash the pages with free visuals of the latest looks, styles and colours.

In a typical issue of *Rave*, while I was giving Christine Perfect a new look, celebrating her being voted Britain's Top Female Vocalist, my friend Linda Newman was busy writing about music festivals, grungy hippies and making predictions about new bands on the scene.

In the same issue, Barry Gibb might be a lead story, discussing his failed marriage and why he advised younger brother Maurice that he was too young to marry Lulu. Marry her he did and a while later I found myself interviewing her for a *Rave* Beauty Special.

Celebrity endorsement was in its infancy back then, but the principle remains the same today. Lulu had collaborated with beauty company Helene Curtis and as part of my interview would be endorsing its hair and beauty products.

SCIENCE AND THE SUN

The '60s and '70s were a golden era for sun worshippers. Drizzly holidays spent shivering on Britain's beaches were being ditched in favour of affordable sun-seeking breaks abroad, from where everyone hoped to return with a so-called 'healthy' tan. Sun protection was rarely considered, except for babies and children.

Baby boomers may recall being smothered in Ambre Solaire sun oil (first launched in the 1930s) or Piz Buin, both of which were pre-SPF and gave minimal protection from burning. Sun-sore skins were soothed and cooled with chalky calamine lotion and invariably peeled later.

Sun worshippers wanting a faster, deeper tan often used olive or baby oils, which attract more UV rays but, as we now know, also make the skin receptive to more serious sun damage.

Scientific evidence in the '70s revealed a proven link between UV radiation (sun exposure) and skin cancer.

In the many seminars I attended, the message from dermatologists was loud and clear: *There's no such thing as a healthy tan.*

This was an unwelcome message for sun worshippers.

In 1974, an Austrian chemist and founder of Piz Buin introduced the now familiar sun protector factor (SPF) rating system. Over the decades, SPFs have been further incorporated into everything from moisturisers and body lotions to cosmetics and hair products.

In 1968, however, on *Rave* magazine, my feature 'Heading For a Heatwave' necessitated a photo shoot by the sea, so off we'd go, though on our small budget it would be Brighton rather than the Bahamas, as it might be today. The poor models were usually asked to apply fake tan, like Quant Top Speed or Outdoor Girl Tanfastic, a day or so before to get the sun- kissed look. And then, looking orange and smelling of something resembling cat pee, they froze to death in their bikinis on the pebbly beach. The photography looked fairly convincing and looking back at my feature, I'm pleased to say my sun-care message even then erred on the side of 'taking care in the sun'.

Though *Rave* was based in London, we all went far and wide for stories. Jimmy Savile had been promoting a disco DJ in Leeds on his Radio One show 'Savile's Travels', calling him Irresistible Dennis and claiming that he was like a magnet to women. Colin, my editor with the great sense of humour, sent me off by train to the In Time disco in Leeds, to find out.

Savile, clad in black leather trousers, high boots and bright turquoise shirt, greeted me embarrassingly warmly, I thought, saying he'd waited all day to meet me. Eyeing my chocolate brown mini dress up and down in the murky underground nightclub, he told my photographer that he doubted he'd have got me 'safely' from London to Leeds on that three- hour train journey...

As for the rather bemused and tongue-tied Dennis, I'll leave that to your imagination! It made a fun spread in the magazine.

Notepad always at the ready...wonder what I wrote?

Keen to feature more celebrities on the beauty pages, Colin despatched me to find out what 'Beauty' meant to big names of the day. For George Lazenby (James Bond of '69), it simply meant Raquel Welch. I was wary about quizzing formidable top fashion photographer Terence Donovan, the giant of a man who rode around in a Rolls-Royce and probably ate kids like me for breakfast. The force of his strong personality came through clearly, and though bemused, he was quite gentle with me, saying a girl's face was all that mattered and personality didn't. "I mould her into whatever I want," said the playful Eastender, who reckoned Claudia Cardinale had it all.

Fitness was always a hot topic, so for one gym feature I decided to put our lovely Shrimptonesque work friend Karen through her paces at West Side Health Club. Fifty years on and fit as a fiddle, she told me she still uses similar equipment. I confess that I have lured many friends and colleagues into my beauty world to test all manner of new and sometimes bizarre beauty equipment, products or regimes. It sounds like a treat, but it wasn't always a beautiful experience! Few friends escaped model assignments or a 'new look', and my very attractive lifelong friend Lyn was often roped in to model for a beauty shoot when she was on leave from college or work.

In the late '60s, a new concept in weight loss was brought to the UK by American-born Bernice Weston. Weight Watchers (WW), a household name today, introduced fee-paying membership, weekly weigh-ins, food measuring, weight-loss goals and diamond chip reward pins. My pal Shirley was always willing to be involved with beauty features, so when she said she would like to lose a couple of pounds, I invited her to road-test Weight Watchers. With the added lure of a hair and beauty makeover at the end, she jumped at the chance. Her mum weighed and cooked her food and Shirley later wrote a good account of her slimming club experience. She said little about her 'makeover', however.

While her long hair had been beautifully cut, the curly perm that Robert Fielding of Regent Street had painstakingly created for her wasn't quite what she had in mind. We all thought she looked really good, but she wasn't convinced.

Decades later, she said, "My mum loved the new look. She'd always wanted a daughter with curly hair and had always tried to 'force' my dead straight hair into curls using curling tongs heated over the flame of the gas hob, burning my ears off in the process!"

Working for *Rave* wasn't like working at all, because we were being paid for a job we absolutely loved. We could dream up an idea, run it by the ed., then go off and do it. It was so stress-free, in fact, that I often wrote beauty features at the weekend for *Mirabelle,* where friends Sandie Robbie and Linda Newman now worked. The £5 freelance fee was more than useful.

FOUR

LOVING AND LEARNING...

In 1970, IPC launched a brand-new magazine called *Loving*, and Scottish-born journalist Bill Williamson was to be the editor. He was a lovely guy and we'd always got on very well, so I was thrilled when he asked me to be beauty editor. The offices in Farringdon Street were large and dismal but the approach to Fleetway House from Blackfriars Station meant passing the Dunkin' Donuts shop a few doors away, which lured us all with its 57 varieties of calorific jammy fillings!

The clue as to the content of *Loving* is in the title. In my 1972 issue, the ed.'s letter describes it as having *'First class real-life stories of people like you, people in love, falling out of love, marrying, breaking up, in despair, giving hope and joy'*. He claimed the readers would range from 16 to 60, and would enjoy, 'smart, budget fashion, beauty, cookery, knitting, films and showbiz'. All

We loved our early copies, this is
April 1971
Loving Magazine/Future Publishing Ltd

that for 6 pence a copy. The tag on all my beauty features was 'Loving Beauty is a Girl's Best Friend'... wince!

It was about as far removed from the free-spirited world of *Rave* as you could imagine, but with its eclectic range of contents, it seemed to work.

I was to share an office with the new fashion editor, Ann Carpenter, and her assistant, Penny Saunders – both of whom became lifelong friends.

Penny and I arrived in our huge new office first and arranged the desks for the three of us. We looked forward to meeting Ann and wondered what our new fashion editor would be like. Once she'd arrived, the first thing she did was to move her big and heavy desk to the other side of the room – declaring, "I'm not sitting there for a start." We had a little giggle about that later. Our personalities were different in many ways, but the friendship I formed with Ann extended to a most memorable holiday we had in Sicily some years later. To say that we've all been friends for 50 years and counting will tell you that we all got on a treat, and enjoyed many occasions and laughs together.

I seldom worked with Ann on combined fashion and beauty features, although we did work together on a summer shoot once, employing my then boyfriend's sailing boat on the Sussex coast. Ann was a very focused fashion editor and was as painstaking in her selection of affordable and stylish fashion as she was with her choice of models and photographers, observing the potential in new talent.

Along with most of the girls on the magazine, I loved sifting through the rails of clothes, shoes and bags that Ann and Penny would call in for a shoot. We saw the very latest samples, and the good thing was that they really were affordable. Setting aside her outfits, perfectly co-ordinated and accessorised, and deep in thought about the photography, Ann's patience was tested often as everyone dropped into our office to eye up the merchandise and ask if they could buy a particular dress or top at a discount when the shoot was over. Ann usually obliged.

The *Loving* team was small but special, from the talented art guys like Andy Harrison, Bob Reed and Pauline Dodington to lovely Sid Hayden, one of the few production guys I ever met with a sense of humour!

We were all enthusiastic and worked hard, having so much fun along the way. Some of us loved an occasional game of table tennis at lunchtimes at St Bride's Institute just round the corner from the office in Bride Lane, and most of us enjoyed a Friday night drink before the train home.

When it came to a photo shoot with all our staff for *Loving*'s first Christmas card, Bill asked Ann if she would kit us all out in festive clothes from her fashion cupboard. Well, what a nightmare! She did it, though, and everyone loved it – slimline shirts with butterflies and motifs for the chaps, a touch of tartan, black crepe dresses and cosy jumpers for the girls. We all looked great – and yes, we raised our Babycham glasses for the photo – then drank the contents!

Thirty years after that iconic picture was taken in 1971, our *Loving* team met up and it all seemed like only yesterday. Another 20 years has since passed, though happily many of us are still in touch.

I spent five happy years on *Loving* covering every popular and topical beauty subject, reporting on hypo-allergenic and natural products – you may remember Almay, Alo and Weleda – and witnessing the emergence of companies who campaigned against animal testing. Beauty Without Cruelty had first appeared in 1960, pioneered and developed by a woman dedicated to animal rights. Lady Muriel Dowding had paved the way for ingredient-consciousness and the scores of cruelty-free beauty brands we have today.

For photo shoots, if I worked with make-up artists from

beauty houses rather than agencies, it was free publicity for them and didn't cost the magazine anything, which pleased the editor. At that time, the better-known beauty companies like Max Factor and Miners had in-house make-up artists and more interesting colour palettes.

So for a feature on make-up for different skin colours and types, I worked with four different companies.

Our black model Tammara from Guyana was delighted that colours in Biba's new Black cosmetics range really reflected the beauty of her complexion and didn't disappear into her skin like most others had done. Similarly, Liz, our sensitive-skinned redhead was impressed when her skin didn't react to ingredients in Almay's hypo-allergenic products.

With interest in health, fitness and diets gaining ground and Weight Watchers growing ever more popular, I researched and wrote many features on the subject. Every week, another new product caught the imagination of would-be slimmers.

Beauty advice for all skin types and colours
Photo: Mike Gilchrist. Loving Magazine/Future Publishing Ltd

Among them were meal replacement Limmits biscuits, Bisks and chocolate bars for the sweeter tooth. Sandwich lovers could use guilt-free Slimcea and Nimble, bread so light you needed another sandwich to feel satisfied.

So in the hope that I would do a good write-up about a new slimming experience, I was invited for five days to Ragdale Hall in Leicestershire. The former Victorian mansion had been converted to a health hydro in 1973 by the co-founder of *Slimming* magazine, Audrey Eyton. A decade later, she was best known for her revolutionary high-fibre F-Plan diet.

I wasn't overweight but keen to gain the experience, which included lectures, fitness activities, daily massage and a strict diet of 900–1,000 calories per day. I didn't cheat once, felt hungry a lot and my clothes felt looser. And yet when it came to the weigh-in on the last day, Matron declared I had lost only two pounds! I was fuming, certain I'd lost much more. That said, it was all good experience and, as predicted, it made a three-page Health and Beauty Special in *Loving*.

Loving and Leaving...

Back on the job at the office I'd be booking models and photographers, running photo shoots and planning features. One of the models I worked with several times was Lorraine Chase, whose glossy waist-length hair was perfect for hair features and whose sylph-like figure looked great in fitness shoots. Putting a spin on fitness was more fun, so for one feature, 'Man-Made Exercises', we told readers to work out with their man, following the energetic exercises Lorraine and a bare-chested male model were doing. The visual impact had the desired effect and made a great double-page spread.

The years I spent on *Loving*, working and socialising with so many special people, were exceptional, and I was deeply

Fitness and fun -all in a day's work
Photo: John Wheble

saddened when told I had to take redundancy. It was 1974, Ann had left the magazine and a lovely girl called Sheila Bridgeman had taken over as fashion editor and we got on like a house on fire. By now, it had become a luxury for magazines to have both a fashion and a beauty editor, and the powers that be decided one of us had to go. It turned out to be me. Sheila was in tears, as she didn't want to take my job, but it wasn't her fault and we remained good friends. The colleague who delivered the bad news was less than tactful, but every cloud has a silver lining and I did receive a very handsome redundancy settlement!

On the strength of that, the first thing I did was to treat my family and boyfriend to a slap-up dressy dinner and dance. Aperitifs were followed by the very '70s menu of prawn cocktails, pepper steaks and Black Forest gateau, washed down with Mateus rosé.

With my new glowing bank balance, I was now able to look at life differently. I banked the money and eighteen months later was able to buy a flat in Wimbledon. The caretaker of the refurbished ex-council flats showed me several that would be for sale when redecoration and fittings were complete. I chose one, gave him 50 quid as a deposit and, pending the mortgage, the flat, complete with avocado green bathroom suite, was mine. Imagine that now. Life was so simple then.

A few months after leaving *Loving,* I was back in business, having been headhunted to work on the top-selling women's weekly magazine.

Prior to that, however, there were some darker days…

FIVE

As Luck Would Have It...

Once the novelty of having money in the bank and a life of leisure had worn off, I became anxious about the future. I was unemployed and my self-esteem plummeted.

I knew my savings wouldn't last without an income, so I had to leave my happy flatshare and move back to my parents' house, which was empty while they lived in an apartment which came with Mum's job. I'm a natural optimist and usually up-beat, so I wasn't expecting to feel so isolated and depressed at times. I began to wonder if I would ever return to the fabulous world I loved on magazines.

Jobs in beauty journalism were seldom advertised and any that were had usually been taken. Luckily, I was able to write some freelance beauty features, but even though the work was required instantly, as was always the case, it could take weeks for payment by cheque, which then had to be cleared by your bank.

Press invitations arrived daily, but after a few months of unemployment I didn't feel confident enough to go to any of the events. Many people have both a professional and private persona, which was certainly true for me, and at times I didn't feel at all like a beauty journalist. (Interesting that during the coronavirus lockdowns of 2020/21, people obliged to work from home were advised not to work in pyjamas or lounge wear but to dress as if they were going to work, which helped boost confidence and put them in a working frame of mind.)

But back in 1974, eight months after my redundancy, something exceptional happened. Out of the blue, I received a press invite for a beauty launch at the Orangery in Holland Park, London. I suddenly decided to shake myself up and go. I don't know why, but I do know that this random turn in the road was meant to be.

At the Orangery, my former persona slowly emerged as I confidently chatted over lunch with another journo who introduced herself as Jo Foley, assistant beauty editor on *Woman's Own*. She asked my name then said, "Yes! Janice Collier, we've been looking for you! You MUST come and work for us, we need you. Can you come and see the beauty editor tomorrow?"

The rest, as they say… Within days of that chance encounter with Jo, I was showing my portfolio to the beauty editor and a week later was the new beauty writer on *Woman's Own*, the magazine selling 1.5 million copies every week!

Once again, chance had played a hand.

Beauty features were divided between three of us, but the *pièce de rsistance* was our awesome beauty salon with backwash, hair dryers, huge mirrors and heaving with the latest beauty products of every type from budget to luxury brands. Before writing about new products, we tried and tested everything from perfumes to body creams, fake tans to hair colourants and hair removers. Then later we held regular in-house sales so other staff could benefit too. And yes, you're right, we had first pick – wouldn't you?

Senior editors regularly popped in to see what was new – and at the end of the day to get a blow-dry and make-up fix, often with a G&T and ciggy in hand.

In earlier years, on the young magazines, we were used to

having our name credited by every feature we had written: a 'byline'. And very proud of it we were too. On *Woman's Own* when I first joined, all beauty writers used one pseudonym: *Diana Day*. Readers believed she wrote every beauty feature and sent her letters and regularly phoned the office asking for her. My humorous dad made me laugh saying he couldn't remember if I was now singer and actress Doris Day or Diana Dors, the voluptuous 'blonde bombshell'. (Some years later when chatting with the popular actress Diana Dors, I found she also had a great sense of humour.)

Woman's Own, to my amazement, employed an army of around 80 to 100 people at that time. In the Knitting department, needles clickety-clacked all day as our experts transformed multiple balls of wool into magical garments and checked the patterns for accuracy. A team of seven in Fashion were permanently calling in and shuffling clothes on rails, teaming them with accessories and preparing for shoots. Further down the corridor, another team of master chefs were testing, tasting and cooking up new recipes in the kitchen. The golden rule was *never eat the photographed food* – it will have been sprayed and glossed with all kinds of inedibles to look great in the pictures!

While those in Fiction studied endless short stories and serialised work from renowned authors, the all-important Features dept, where Jan Iles-Kaluza and Linda Newman worked, was a bustling world of its own at the end of a very long corridor. Features were very serious business at WO, and you could sense the intensity as soon as you entered.

On the rare occasions I popped in, probably asking something frivolous like, "Who wants to test a new depilatory cream?" I felt like a rude interruption! I was always pleased to see my friends Linda and Jan, though we seldom had time to chat.

In the art room, while the talented designers, then called

layout artists, were busy creating fabulous pages, the permanently harassed Production guys took no prisoners, always berating us for lateness of copy and rising printers' costs.

My first feature for *Woman's Own* was a fun fitness piece called 'Rock Away the Pounds' – which entailed a hoot of a shoot with a girl and guy demonstrating the latest dance crazes –the Bump and the Hustle. We had a ball! We shot on black and white film rather than colour, for more of a late-night feel, and I'm sure we had a drop of something alcoholic to get us all in the mood as The Bay City Rollers boomed out, urging everyone to do the bump and the giggling barefoot models in jeans and t-shirts bumped high bottoms, low bottoms, hips and shoulders.

We knew men often took a sneaky peek at the family copy of *Woman's Own*, usually at the problem page, so we decided to encourage them and hoped it might boost sales. My brief was to find four men in different age groups who were up for a new look, and quickly roped in my brother, Vic, and my boyfriend, Rob. I lured them with a promise of a free haircut in a top London salon and their pictures in the magazine. They might also get a sandwich lunch – and bus and train fares would be paid, of course! Enthusiastic crimper Alan, at Vidal Sassoon, cropped Rob's long dark curly locks with a vengeance, then reduced his friendly wayward beard to stubble. Shock, horror – I hardly recognised him!

One unhappy reader wrote in saying, 'What have you done to poor Rob? He looked great before, just like Cat Stevens, but now he looks more like Rolf Harris!' Whoops…

Readers often phoned in at the end of the day, just when we were about to leave. Some started with a simple query about a beauty product or to ask for advice on improving their looks, then went on to say how unattractive they felt, how their husbands didn't love them and how depressed they were. On occasion, some became emotional. I was never quite sure whether it was their G&T time, but I never had the heart to cut them short, so consequently had many late nights at the office.

DIETS MAKE ME FAT

'Dear Beauty Editor' letters poured in constantly. Standard queries were answered by our Correspondence department, suitably armed with charts, specialist info and press releases. More serious topics were referred to us, as we had the hotline to experts in all fields, among them, dermatologists, nutritionists, cosmetic surgeons and trichologists such as Philip Kingsley, whom I met many times and who taught us that hair responds to everything that touches our lives, including sex, or lack of it.

Dieting was a major issue for many readers who said being fat had affected their whole lives. They sent photographs and confided personal details, including how desperately unhappy and unattractive they felt. Some blamed excess weight on their 'big bones'; others believed they had a 'slow metabolism'. Marriage, children, separation, divorce, work overload, cheating partners and no partners were also blamed. Many said they were yo-yo dieters who would systematically lose and regain weight, blaming diets for making them heavier each time.

Women's magazines have always embraced the slimming culture, and since the late '40s and '50s, *Woman's Own* had been dispensing well-received diet features on a regular basis. Opinions and diets constantly evolve and the '70s and '80s were no exception. In fact, in those years, there were more diets, theories and quirky fads than you could shake a celery stick at. Eating half a grapefruit before a meal was one, the theory being the citrus fruit's special enzyme was a fast fat burner.

I have a friend who still inflicts the '80s Cabbage Soup diet on herself a couple of times a year for guaranteed pre-holiday weight loss.

Our search for Britain's Most Deserving Slimmers saw 3,000 women and many men send a cry for help. Heart-rending letters arrived from women whose marriages were on the rocks because of their size, others who feared never finding a partner. One 23-year-old described herself as, 'fat, aggressive and lonely'. Another said she loathed her layers of blubber. Many people said that diets made them fat because after each diet they would gain even more weight than before. One young man, who at nearly 22 stone found it hard moving around, was unemployed and had no friends.

We read every letter and selected 50 people, monitoring their progress with tailor-made diets and phone calls for three months, encouraging our slimmers every step of the way. Their losses ranged from a stone and a half up to nearly 4 stones over the three months, and many of their stories were featured in the magazine.

In 1979, American cardiologist Dr Herman Tarnower first hit the headlines with his book 'The Complete Scarsdale Medical Diet'. With exceptional rapid weight loss claims of 20lbs (9.072 kg) in two weeks, the strict 14-day high-protein plan was questionably low-calorie at only 1,000 per day. Despite grapefruit and other fruits featuring heavily, it claimed not to be a fad diet.

Woman's Own was first in the UK to publish extracts from America's best-seller, and we invited a cross section of sceptical people to test the regime. It worked for some, who then continued with Tarnower's low-fat, low-carb Keep Trim diet, but others found it miserable and unsustainable.

Only a year later in 1980, Tarnower hit the headlines again when his former lover, headmistress Jean Harris, was reportedly jailed for his murder.

By contrast to our regular slimming features, including interesting angles such as 'Diets that Defied the Experts', in 1978, the magazine simultaneously embraced the groundbreaking work of Susie Orbach in her much-acclaimed book 'Fat is a Feminist Issue'. Far from offering keep-slim diets, the book resonated with the emerging Women's Movement, exploring not only the psychology behind women's relationships with food and body image, but the whole subject of inequality.

Lose weight or change your job...
Woman's Own/Future Publishing Ltd.

When my friend Jo Foley left our department to launch *Successful Slimming* magazine, I was delighted to be offered her job as deputy beauty editor, working closely with our beauty editor, Willa Beatty. An experienced journalist, she was witty, humorous and always open to new beauty angles, giving me free rein to develop my ideas.

Invitations arrived daily for posh lunches, events and beauty launches. On a couple of occasions, I was invited to be a judge in the Glamorous Grandmother competition which Butlin's held every year. Billy Butlin (later Sir Billy) launched the idea in 1955 after discovering to his amazement that the glamorous Marlene Dietrich was a grandmother.

By the '70s, the holiday camp competitions attracted 10,000 grannies every year. Many reapplied annually, hoping to win.

The grand final was a posh black-tie affair, with grannies dressed to kill. In 1976, when I was at the Brighton semi-final, long gowns, long earrings, dazzling smiles and bouffant hairstyles predominated. Two years later in Blackpool, hemlines were shorter; it was all about legs and, surprisingly, stilettos.

Most contestants were aged 50 to 70, 'well preserved' and

Top left: I'm judging sparkle, stilletos, dazzling smiles and serious bouffants
Photo: Courtesy of Butlin's

looking good, without any help from surgeons. We were all surprised, though, to see one finalist was only in her thirties. She was a gran, to be fair, but the goalposts had moved and age didn't preclude her from entering. It did seem a little unfair to those youthful-looking more senior grannies.

Beauty, viewed as frivolous by some, was good for business, with the ability to attract advertisers and hopefully increase readership. Money-off coupons encouraged readers to buy their own copy of the magazine, rather than share someone else's (it was estimated there were four readers of every copy sold). Free beauty gifts on the cover (cover-mounts) and inserts, which might be perfume, moisturiser or small cosmetic samples, attracted readers, though with rising production costs, they were eventually phased out.

Regular reader events, shopping weekends and foreign holidays were popular, as were our Beauty Roadshows with hair and make-up demos and live makeovers.

In 1978, the magazine's involvement with Jumbly, 'The World's Biggest Jumble Sale', held at Olympia, was a huge success. Our fashion team staged a catwalk show, auctioning celebrity cast-offs, including a dress from Sophia Loren, a silk scarf from then MP Margaret Thatcher and an Ossie Clark number to die for. Proceeds went to Save the Children, and WO gained invaluable free publicity.

Reader identification was hugely important. In 1979, at a weekend seminar with senior staff, *reader image* was discussed in some depth and later an in-house report concluded that words which came to mind about a *typical Woman's Own reader* were: 'In her twenties, probably married, possibly working, lively, occasionally sophisticated, a little more adventurous than Mrs Average; interested in what's going on in the world; needing greater self-confidence; changeable; bright; friendly; informative; concerned'.

When I dreamed up the idea of giving a *typical reader* an extra-ordinary 'My Fair Lady' lifestyle for a week, I searched high and wide and finally found Lesley, a super girl from Bridge of Allen, just outside Stirling.

Lesley was curious and loved the idea. She would be introduced to London's top society hostess and former '60s debutante Liz Brewer, who would teach her everything she needed to know about behaviour, posture and etiquette when mixing with 'upper-crust' jet-setters and aristocrats.

Following her week of beauty pampering and a brand-new look, the grand finale saw us sipping champagne with society 'playboy' Dai Llewellyn at Mayfair's exclusive Clermont Club, prior to us all heading off to a late-night party as guests of Lord and Lady Rothermere, at their Belgravia mansion. There we chatted and mingled with the guests, among whom was the then young Marquess of Blandford. Despite a reputation as a wild child and subsequently troubled life for many years, the now 12th Duke of Marlborough was charming and amused by the idea of our magazine feature.

Although my seven years on *Woman's Own*, ultimately as beauty editor, could be challenging at times, there were so many memorable moments. Watching glamorous Joan Collins pore over her photographs on the art room lightbox was fun, as she discarded any with a bad angle or suspicion of a wrinkle!

Waiting in anticipation for our royal visitor in 1978 was special. Lining the magazine's long corridors, we waited patiently for HM The Queen to arrive, marvelling at our Art and Production guys all suited and booted – the likes of which we'd never seen before!

The Queen beamed throughout her visit. Her interest in the production of the magazine seemed genuine as she, too, studied front covers and selected pictures on the lightbox. She was much more petite than I'd imagined, with a flawless porcelain complexion, just a hint of make-up and soft brown hair, which years later we learnt was probably enhanced with 'Chocolate Kiss' hair colour.

Being able to travel as part of my job had its memorable moments.

I was lucky enough to work in Paris with world-famous make-up artist Olivier Echaudemaison. Elegant and welcoming, the legendary genius counted not only the *crème de la crème* of celebrities but royalty among his clientele. I was also delighted to work with him on several occasions in London.

It was in Milan that I met and worked with Richard Sharah, one of the world's most influential make-up artists and famous at that time for his innovative *Italian Vogue* covers.

Two decades later during my interview for the *Daily Mail* with fashion icon Zandra Rhodes, she remembered Richard Sharah fondly, saying he 'broke the boundaries' of what women could and would use on their faces. She had the highest respect

Olivier Echaudemaison with model Marianne Lah Swannell
Photo: John Swannell

for him as an artist, a friend and an 'amazing human being'. It was he, she said, who had helped shape her own identity.

Zandra, sociable and down-to-earth, with a tendency to drift, arrived in her Mini car an hour late for our interview, meeting me on her doorstep one scorching summer evening. Apologetic, hot and tired, she offered me a cold drink, and I was so ready for a glass of chilled white *vino*, but was amused when she handed me ginger beer! We talked about her younger self and how she hated being bridesmaid at her sister Beverley's wedding, even though she loved her. It was in Zandra's Sassoon days, she said. "I had jet-black hair and very black eye make-up. Beverley was horrified and told me to take all that make-up off, which I did very grudgingly, then refused to look in the camera," she laughed.

Ours was a memorable interview, not least because halfway through she nodded off momentarily, so I waited, sipping my ginger beer, then opening one eye warily, she said, "Run that one by me again."

It was fascinating going into the stars' homes and not something which would happen often, if at all, now.

In 1979, singer and showman Frankie Vaughan and wife Stella welcomed me warmly into their London home with tea and biscuits, before our interview for a Father's Day special feature.

Having released a new LP, the charismatic 50-year-old had lost none of his sparkle or charm. Bearing the same dazzling smile, his 22-year-old daughter Susan was studying to become an actress. Confirming that he was a loving family man and caring dad, she said, "I know he's famous and performs in top hat and tails, but to me he's just Dad. He's very neat and tidy and relaxes at home in a dressing gown, as he hates creasing his clothes!" (And yes, he slipped into a dressing gown for our photo!)

Actress Moira Lister's elegant home housed a beautiful gilded antique grand piano, which she was kind enough to let me play. At 54, she was stripping off onstage for 'Murder Among Friends' and was proud of her figure, saying, "It would be stupid and prudish not to strip off in a natural love scene."

SIX

Woman's Own Seeks Beauty Editor...

In 1977, having been the department's deputy for a couple of years, I was encouraged by colleagues to apply for the newly vacant beauty editor's job. Although I was excited at the prospect, I was about to get married and I'd heard that the editor thought I'd now be off home early every night 'with a shopping basket on my arm'. She was mistaken and must have been persuaded differently, as ultimately I was promoted and introduced in her editor's letter as 'one of the most highly respected names in the business'.

My new rite of passage meant attending all meetings with the editor and entourage of deputy and assistant editors, art, production, and so on. Every issue necessitated weekly Pre-Plan, where department heads, armed with great ideas for features and photography, enthusiastically pitched to the editor – a bit like 'Dragons' Den'. When ed. was bubbly and liked what was in front of her, it was sighs of relief all round. When she didn't and made it clear in no uncertain terms, a kind of hush descended and 'twas a brave colleague indeed who defended the pitch, though some often tried their best.

When a couple of years later, in 1979, I fell pregnant, my

friend, a senior on the magazine, said she'd have to play it carefully when telling the ed. "If conference goes well, I'll say you have some exciting news for her, but if it doesn't, then we'll have to keep it under wraps for now," she said.

The weekly conference was always angst-ridden in case the ed. was unimpressed and things got heated. On this occasion, it had gone well and later on I was allowed to reveal my *exciting* news. It was a frosty reception and I think the first question from the very *unexcited* editor was whether or not I'd be returning after the birth.

Sadly, some months later, half an hour before one of those nerve-racking conferences, I started to miscarry. Seemingly, a 'colleague' had visited me in hospital while I slept and from her description sounded like someone who might have been feeling more sympathetic than I'd imagined about her attitude towards new mums on her staff.

By the following year, we were all delighted to have a new editor at the helm. Iris Burton had been with the magazine for many years, latterly as features editor. A brilliant and popular journalist, she had a fresh and receptive approach to her staff, combining the magical qualities of professionalism and friendliness.

At the start of 1980, the fashion editor and I organised a combined trip to Miami for the great WO summer fashion and beauty shoot. Foreign shoots were a mammoth undertaking, entailing not only trunks full of paraphernalia but strategic planning and dossiers full of paper work permits and visas necessary for working abroad.

We hired top photographer Tony McGee, who by the age of 21 was already established, his work gracing every prestigious glossy front cover. That year, he won Best British Fashion Photographer.

Shooting on location with an entourage of models and

make-up artists necessitated a people carrier, and photographers would usually do the driving. But we soon established that Tony would not be doubling as chauffeur. Mild panic set in, before my husband offered to step in as a freebie chauffeur, taking time off from his day job at IBM. How kind of him!

We stayed at the Miami Beach Hilton Fontainebleu Hotel in Collins Avenue. The iconic '50s hotel, whose guests had included Elvis and Judy Garland, was frequently used as a movie location. The grandeur was awesome; the photography was brilliant and very well received back at the office, filling pages cost-effectively for many issues.

The trip was a great success in more ways than one, since we discovered on our return that my 'chauffeur' husband and I were now expecting a baby –and yes, he was *Made in Miami!*

When I announced my *exciting* news this time, our editor, Iris, couldn't have been warmer and was delighted for me. It seemed, though, that I had started a baby boom, as my deputy, Jimi, then fell pregnant, as did the fashion and the home editors, but Iris embraced us all with warmth and sincerity, while at the same time quietly hoping we'd all return post-baby!

SEVEN

ALL CHANGE PLEASE, IT'S THE '80S

The crazy '80s were simultaneously dark, colourful, sweet and sour, like a bag of Liquorice Allsorts! Alongside a new affluence, contrast and exaggeration in all its forms, the troubled decade saw riots, shootings, war, strikes and disasters, among them Brixton, Toxteth, Falklands, Miners, Lockerbie, Hillsborough and Chernobyl. I am reminded, now that we have experienced COVID in all its forms, that mad cow disease (later vCJD in humans) was prevalent in the UK. The Government insisted it posed no threat to humans, until, that is, the first man died in 1995.

1980 witnessed John Lennon's murder outside his home in NYC on 8th December, and four decades on, the loss of a legend is still mourned. I'd never met him, though in 1963 I saw him on stage at my first 'pop concert' – a Beatles gig at Wimbledon Palais, just a mile from my home. Dizzy and faint with excitement, breathless from screaming, I couldn't hear a word and, to be honest, was so far away I could barely see the Fab Four, but it was awesome!

So… never having met John Lennon, I was lucky enough a few years on to meet both his first and second wives.

In 1988, having landed the job of assistant editor at *Woman* magazine, I went out to interview Cynthia Lennon at her home on the Isle of Man. Unassuming, warm and still bearing her trademark smile and blonde hair, she welcomed me into her home.

I was there to talk about the launch of her perfume, 'Woman', which interestingly she told me she'd named as a 'tribute to John's beautiful song'.

It's thought by many to have been written for Yoko, but a closer look at the lyrics suggested to me it could be interpreted differently. So I was delighted more recently (Oct 2020) to hear a recording of John talking about the song on the BBC Radio 2 tribute show, John Lennon At The BBC, as part of their John Lennon At 80 season.

Lennon explains his thoughts while he was in Bermuda:'It suddenly dawned on me,' he said '… what women represent to us, not just the sex object or the mother, but just their contribution…that it is the other half… without each other there ain't nothing…It was a different viewpoint of what I'd felt about women and I can't express it better than I said in the song.'

By the time Cynthia and I met, she'd had two further failed marriages and declared openly that she could never seem to marry the right man – but was currently in a very happy relationship with Jim Christie, her partner and business manager.

She talked a little about her early life at Liverpool College of Art, where she first met John, saying how she'd admired his innovative work from the start, although wasn't initially attracted to him because their characters were very different. While she was a realist, calm and down-to-earth, John, she explained, was a dreamer and could be outrageous and a bit scary at times, which unsettled some people. Their friendship grew and later when the pair started dating, she fell pregnant with Julian. It was John, she said, who first mentioned marriage.

The couple divorced six years later.

Cynthia named her perfume Woman as a tribute to John's song

Talking enthusiastically about her new venture into the world of fragrance, she was very proud that 'Woman' was created and produced locally at Tynwald Mills on the Isle of Man. Being an artist herself, she had designed the psychedelic red and black packaging for the perfume's striking crystal bottle, and was excited about the launch party, to be held at London nightclub Stringfellows.

The launch was a glitzy affair and well attended, but sadly as editorial mentions decreased, so did sales of the fragrance.

By chance, many years later, I also had the pleasure of meeting and chatting, off the record, with Yoko Ono at a vintage fashion fair in Chelsea Town Hall. Softly-spoken and quietly polite, her tiny frame was birdlike, and there was a peaceful aura about her.

Back In 1981, only seven months after Lennon's untimely death, Royal Wedding Fever swept the globe, following the six-month engagement of Prince Charles and Lady Diana Spencer.

The grand and glorious *wedding of the century* was watched on TV by 750 million people and became known as the fairy-tale wedding. David and Elizabeth Emanuel designed the wedding dress, Patrick Lichfield was the official photographer and Diana's make-up was created by Barbara Daly. I was privileged to have worked with them all.

For models previously used to doing their own make-up and hair, the gradual emergence of make-up artists and session hairdressers was a revelation. Some, like Barbara, who I caught up with recently, excelled with sheer imagination, skill and creativity. She was destined from the start to gain her reputation as one of Britain's first superstar *visagistes*.

"When I started out, there was a limited choice of skin products, eye colours and lip shades. Theatrical make-up was brighter and more varied but, of course, it was 'greasepaint'. So I started to create the colours that I wanted by mixing Caran d'Ache crayons with foundation and, in fact, these inspired one large cosmetic company to create the first make-up crayons. I went on to create the first powder pencils with them when I started my first make-up range."

Her work graced British, American and Italian *Vogue* beauty pages and covers, and she admits she did some 'serious face painting' with extravagant designs in the '70s and '80s, including silver zig-zag lightning bolts over the eyes for *Italian Vogue*, surreal painted eyes on closed lids for *British Vogue* and other magazines. "Not really something to try at home, although I did see other people copying the look for themselves," she said.

Her clientele included Hollywood stars, supermodels, royalty and a British prime minister who was definitely *not for turning*, but whom Barbara found friendly and approachable. "I worked with Margaret Thatcher for years and liked her a lot. She'd always sit still, no fuss and let me get on with it."

A few months before Charles and Diana became engaged in February 1981, Barbara and I were working together on a Bridal Beauty Special for *Woman's Own*. One of our models was fair-skinned and blue-eyed, while the other had a 'black coffee'

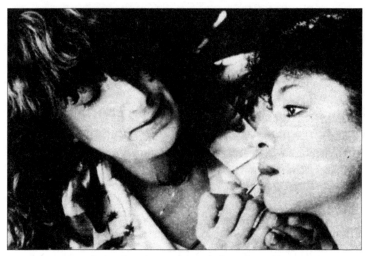

Barbara's work was celebrated all over the world

complexion and dark brown eyes. Barbara's work was stunning and the make-up tips she gave to both models were invaluable to them.

Not long after that feature appeared, Barbara received a phone call from her friend Felicity Clark, beauty editor of *British Vogue*, asking her to meet the shy teenager, Lady Diana Spencer. It was for a make-up trial for her forthcoming marriage to Prince Charles.

Forty years on, I asked Barbara if she was nervous at the prospect of working with the future princess. "I was not exactly nervous, but with new people I would worry about certain aspects of the job, since putting make-up on someone brings you very close to them – it is quite intimate. Part of my job was getting on well with and listening to people. Diana was only 19 and flushed a lot. I had to stay calm and gain her confidence. I involved her completely so that we could experiment with colours and ideas. She had lovely skin and beautiful blue eyes, which she always lined with a blue pencil. I managed to wean her off that eventually."

Not surprisingly, Barbara was given the royal assignment.

"Diana was a really lovely person, friendly and humorous. I worked with her many times, whether it was for a magazine or Christmas card or she was going somewhere special. We built up a rapport and became friends."

On 29th July 1981, all eyes were glued to screens big and small as onlookers waited for the marriage of Prince Charles and Lady Diana, and especially for the 'big reveal' of the fairy-tale wedding dress by British designers David and Elizabeth Emanuel. The show-stopping gown did not disappoint, with 10,000 pearls and sequins intricately embroidered into layers and ruffles of ivory silk taffeta and antique lace. At Diana's request, the designer duo created an eye-popping train trailing 25 feet, the longest ever seen at that time.

When later interviewing the legendary designers at their Brook Street atelier, I found them engaging and happy to share a secret or two about their iconic design, including well-documented creases and 'wardrobe malfunctions'. During the discreet little insight into their most famous client, I learnt that after the wedding, the princess phoned them from her honeymoon to thank them again.

Following publication of my feature in *Woman* magazine, Elizabeth sent me a hand-written letter of thanks and a specially designed greeting card adorned with an exquisite 3D lace and pearl dress.

In the '80s, your style defined your personality. Punk, spawned in the late '70s, was still expressed in music and fashion, though keenly contrasted with both a return to glamour for some and a lycra and leggings love affair for others.

Hairdressing legend Trevor Sorbie, who I've enjoyed working with for several decades, was as happy giving our readers stunning new looks as he was playing showman on stage at the annual hairdressing event Salon International. Hairdressers worldwide flocked there, hungry for cutting-edge inspiration.

Showcasing his uniquely creative thinking and technical ability, he proved repeatedly why he was four times awarded British Hairdresser of the Year.

Thinking back to those heady days as we chat over coffee, Trevor describes the '80s as the new '60s: "It was a new decade in which you could break away from the norm, something I have always enjoyed doing. The punk era of anti-establishment and aggressive safety-pin fashion really inspired me. And to this day for me the most important thing in life is to be inspired – it helps you get up in the morning!

"I was first to jump in breaking the rules – with hair! I took inspiration from the streets, turning technique on its head. I wanted to capture the spirit of the time, applying bad colour and creating rigid stand-out hair to make an aggressive statement. I wanted something shocking.

"In 1980, breaking with tradition, I used razors rather than scissors to achieve the wild look I wanted. Razors really did the job, creating great texture with that punk edginess. It needed edgy colour, so I experimented by bleaching just the ends of the hair, to give that grown-out look. I'm sure I was the first to do that! Then rather than drying the hair downwards as was normal, I dried it upwards, and the result was just what I wanted: shocking! And that's how 'the Wolfman' was born. I was very happy and so were many of my clients."

The go-to crimper for punks Siouxie and the Banshees and Toyah Willcox, Trevor regularly collaborated with Vivienne Westwood and Zandra Rhodes on new season fashion extravaganzas and styled many of Zandra's iconic posters. The first hairdresser ever to be awarded an MBE by the Queen, for Services to Hairdressing, he says, "Knowing I was doing something I'd never seen before, using inventive materials from art to architecture, has always excited me."

Hairdressing has evolved over the decades since the '60s,

when Vidal Sassoon and Trevor, who was Sassoon's artistic director, changed the face of what was achievable. "It continues to evolve and I find it exciting and am always inspired by creative and technical innovation."

Two decades on from the punk era, the ever-creative crimper launched the national charity 'mynewhair', which offers advice, support and details of a bespoke wig-cutting service for women with medical hair loss.

"I was inspired by the psychological effect that a customised wig had on my late sister-in-law Jacky when she was undergoing chemo," he says.

Punk fashion and beauty didn't feature much in *Woman's Own*, though some aspects of razor hair cutting and safety-pin or tartan fashion did percolate down to more wearable high-street style.

For those hooked on the fitness craze, leggings, leotards and gym membership were the new must-have accessories, regardless of whether or not you actually went to the gym!

Headbands tamed unruly locks, and nude colour cosmetics were key. Back then, make-up guru Barbara Daly expounded the virtues of natural looking make-up.

Her constant bywords: 'Less is more' and 'Blend, blend, blend' – which she did with real hair make-up brushes from a vast selection in her scrupulously clean fishing tackle box!

She confesses, however, that some of those 'natural' looks she perfected so deftly, back in the day, required an artistic sleight of hand, gentle brushstrokes and a shedload of cosmetics!

Even Diana's wedding make-up, which she described as 'strong but subtle', involved layer after layer, a great deal of time and much 'TLC', with only two chances to retouch when the camera wasn't on her.

Full of admiration for today's very skilful make-up artists, she says, "I find the evolution of make-up intriguing, and some of the modern techniques require so much dexterity and artistry."

MOTHERHOOD AND MAGAZINES

Today, many people can work from home, as proven in the recent COVID lockdowns, but for many in the early '80s, it wasn't necessarily so. That said, I returned to my role as beauty editor five months after our son was born at the end of 1980, but not being with him was painful, as it is for many new mums, and I subsequently resigned. My editor, Iris, was totally understanding and I was lucky enough to be able to pitch, produce and submit my features for *Woman's Own* and many other magazines from home, using just a telephone, typewriter and post box – I was a familiar sight bolting down the road to catch the 4pm post to meet the editors' deadlines!

Petsa, my creative friend at Woman's Own beautifully captures my pregnancy
Illustration: Petsa Kaffens

Freelance work is unpredictable –there's always either too much, or too little, it's equally stressful, and working hours are frequently bizarre. Having grown up watching me perpetually chasing multiple deadlines and permanently attached to a 'great ideas' notepad, our son, Oliver, now married with two sons himself, has been a constant source of joy and inspiration. His support and enthusiasm always made my full-on working life more bearable, and yes, I am very proud of him.

Towards the end of 1982, our work and home life going well, we moved house and entertained our parents every weekend, whether with Saturday night dinners or Sunday roasts. Life was good.

Everything changed in the summer of 1983.

Mum was abroad with friends and Dad was coming to dinner with us. Racing against the clock with yet another deadline, I didn't mind when he hadn't arrived on time. But then I decided to ring him. When he didn't answer his phone (no mobiles then), panic struck and I sped to his home a few miles away… and found him 'life extinct' on the kitchen floor.

Despite later confirmation that a medical condition was his cause of sudden death, I longed for answers which would make sense of things. It was the saddest day of my life.

A leading newspaper columnist wrote recently that she was still unable to remove her dad's recorded message on her phone even though he'd died two years earlier.

Phone Calls that Mattered

Later in 1983, I received an unexpected phone call from the editor's office of *Woman & Home*, inviting me to attend an interview with editor Sue Dobson, as there was a vacancy for a regular freelance beauty editor.

One of the leading monthly titles at the time and aimed at women of 40+, the perfect cocktail of 'grown-up' fashion, food, home, family, features and celebrities was bright, informative and stylish.

Quietly spoken and a popular editor, Sue Dobson knew how to steer her magazine to success without any histrionics. Much to my delight, she offered me the job.

I relished the prospect of their larger page size with acres of space for glossy, colour-laden beauty features and interviews. One of many I enjoyed was with acclaimed British actress Susannah York and another with the poised and sylph-like former Royal Ballet dancer Jackie Elliott, who on marrying later became Jackie Kennedy, a name guaranteed to turn heads.

I enjoyed the more leisurely pace of the monthly magazine for five years, during which time I was also able to do a variety of other freelance work, including the production of in-store beauty booklets and press releases for beauty companies. I also wrote the 'Supersoft Hair Care Book', detailing everything from structure, growth patterns and health to colour, treatment and style for all hair types. London's top black hairdresser of the day, Winston Isaacs from Splinters, guided me through a chapter on Asian, Oriental and Afro hair, saying he'd spent 15 years educating people on the amazing potential of Afro hair, which he said was, 'really quite remarkable in the hands of qualified people'.

But then in 1988, I found myself unexpectedly working full time for *Woman*. The new editor, David Durman, was looking for an assistant editor to head up the practical departments, i.e., Fashion, Beauty, Home, Cookery and Knitting. I was invited for interview.

My first thought was thank you but it's not for me! I enjoyed working freelance and was also a wife and mother of an eight-year-old, with a balanced home, work and social life. But then my friend Linda Newman encouraged me to go for 'the experience' so I wouldn't have later regrets, which I knew was true.

Have you noticed that when you're desperate for something, like a job, things don't always turn out, but when you're not even looking, offers come your way?

I went to meet David, purely for 'the experience'. Friendly, witty with a dry sense of humour, he seemed to like my quirky humour. We vaguely remembered each other from years earlier while working on *Woman's Own*, though our paths didn't actually cross.

Despite being published by the same house, IPC, *Woman* and *Woman's Own* were fiercely competitive, though readers probably assumed we were one big happy family. In a serious attempt to help readers distinguish between the two titles, and to gain more readers, of course, *Woman* was given a new identity, redesigned with a practical emphasis. The head of Practicals role required confidence, stamina, people skills and the ability to be a caring 'conduit' when certain things hit the fan – aside from being a creative journalist at the drop of a hat! It was a scary prospect and although flattered and excited by it, I *definitely* didn't want to take on that responsibility.

All I will say is that he was pretty persuasive when he called a few days later, insisting that I was perfect for the job.

Happily, before this new rite of passage began, I was off to celebrate my 40th birthday in France, where copious amounts of rather good champagne inspired me to think more positively about my suitability for the role – and our mortgage!

My welcoming editor and I bonded almost daily over our concerns about the big job that lay ahead for us both. He confessed to being as nervous in his new role as me.

I admired my Practicals team for their enthusiasm and knowledge of their subject. One minute I'd be discussing how best to fillet and photograph a fish with the cookery editor, the next I'd be studying a knitting pattern (as though I understood it!) and choosing vibrant colours for a quick-knit chunky mohair sweater. Or I might be with our Home editor, deliberating interior design trends like vertical blinds or Laura Ashley's rather over-floral bedding. Then again I might be consoling one of the team about the editor's vociferous rejection of their fabulous photo shoot or breaking bad news to the cookery editor that her mouth-watering cakes were deemed 'burned' and needed to be reshot.

It was a roller coaster of a ride during my two years at *Woman,* some of it creative, lively and productive, some of it less so. Actually, it was insane on many occasions. Imagine being told to ask highly acclaimed actress Felicity Kendal to return to the studio for a reshoot with her hairdresser, what a true star she proved to be! Or having to ask Patrick Lichfield if he would reshoot his beautiful soft focus pictures. The royal snapper was so generous when I couched the blow tactfully and I was delighted to work with him again on the reshoot!

Luckily, when I joined the magazine, I had bonded almost instantly with our new deputy editor, Sally, who together with our features editor June lightened many a difficult day at our local tapas bar lunches.

The story that makes my friend Linda laugh most (the Magazine Girl who thought I should take the job for the *experience)* is the time I was tasked by the editor, at very short notice, to organise a traditional family Christmas photo shoot. David wanted Granny playing an old piano, Grandad in a comfy fireside chair with the family dog at his feet, teenagers dressed to impress, old-fashioned decorations, lots of glitter and balloons, kids ripping presents open, Christmas wrappings everywhere – you get the idea.

It proved mission impossible, as high costs for room hire with pianos were beyond our budget and I couldn't hire a dog or a granny for love nor money. David insisted I made it happen somehow, which I did.

In fact, I converted my own home, complete with piano and log fire, giving my family and friends parts to play: My teenage niece Vikki sparkled in her strapless dress, my good friend, Lyn, was the glam mum with my hubby, Rob, in his Christmas jumper, while my dear mum posed playing piano. Someone's grandad patted someone's dog, and my son, Oliver, and little friend Amelia pulled crackers and littered the floor with wrapping paper and toys. What could possibly go wrong…?

I will simply say that on viewing the pictures at conference, and without knowing that I had used my own house, family and friends to produce the setting, down to his last instruction, the furious editor bellowed, "What is this load of…sh*t!?" then took aim and decorated the walls and floor of the conference room with 50 sets of festive photos!

Cringing but standing my ground, I told him it was *exactly* what he had asked for…

The sympathetic looks from my lovely colleagues, all knowing it was my home and willing friends, soon turned to sheer horror with accompanying gasps when he retorted: "I didn't ask for shi*ty photography in a shi*ty studio with naff decorations, fake family models and a dead dog, did I?"

Few experiences are wasted in life, and I'm glad I took the job on such an iconic magazine. I had a rather humorous rapport with the editor and I both learnt a lot and gave a lot; it was an interesting time. It's always good to know when a thing has run its course and thus I left after a couple of years to preserve my sanity, but still freelancing for them and producing a *Woman* 'New You' Health and Beauty video.

I resumed freelancing across many titles including *Hello!*, *Ideal Home* and *Yours,* on a variety of subjects including celebrity interviews, health, beauty trends and family relationships. I also enjoyed the immediacy of writing for newspapers, which included *The Sunday Times,* the *Daily Mirror,* where I was a regular contributor, and the *Daily Mail* for whom I did many memorable interviews, including one with the wonderful actress and wildlife campaigner Virginia McKenna.

We met at her cottage in the heart of the Surrey woodlands, way up, at 750ft, above the town of Dorking, her happy haven for several decades. The star of the silver screen and founder of the Born Free Foundation was welcoming and, at 65, still beautiful and passionate about animal conservation. Her youngest son, Dan Travers, greatly admired her stamina but revealed that her frail looks belied a strength and determination which saw her always rushing around on very little sleep. Showing concern for his mother, grandmother to six, he felt it was time for her to slow down a little.

Fast forward to 2020, when at 89 years old the 'Born Free' star joined campaigners for part of a charity walk across Hampstead Heath, still raising funds for the animal conservation charity, and who in 2022 opened a 'Born Free' outdoor exhibition of life-size bronze lions in London. A true star.

And that just about wraps up this Magazine Girl's story; so many happy memories, particularly of the early years when we were young, excited, learning on the job and raring to go! I'm lucky to have had a long career I loved and the love and support of my husband Rob and family.

Perhaps one day my memoir might just be a useful slice of family history, should our much- loved little grandsons, George and Freddie, ever wonder what Nanny Jan did when she was young.

SHIRLEY'S STORY

Bowie had my telephone number and on occasions he would ring me and play a specific record down the line to see what I thought of it. It was clear from what he said to me that he was never happy being pigeonholed into one specific genre of music, he always wanted to go on to something new, explore and experiment all he could, with music and life. And so it proved in later years, when he moved from one persona to another, and from one life experience to another.

ONE

1965

A BATTLE OF WILLS

Voices were raised! My mum was adamant – but so was I. I would not be deterred. Cinderella would go to the ball. My mum and I were arguing about my desire and determination to work in London. I was nearly 16-years-old and stood 4'10" in my stockinged feet.

An opportunity had arisen for me to work at George Newnes Publishing in Long Acre, Covent Garden. They were looking for junior clerks, and my friend Avril, who already worked there, had put me forward.

Mum was totally against it, and for the life of me, I couldn't see why. This was my future! However, with the help of a little bit of persuasion from my dad, she relented. She didn't want to ruin my job prospects; she was just always overprotective and quite strict. London, to her, was a million miles away.

Looking back now, as an adult with my own grown-up kids and grandchild, I can understand how the protective element comes into parenting. Add to this the fact that as a five-year-old, I trotted along behind my brother to follow the Salvation Army band (I have no idea why we did that!) and, not paying attention, I

My 5-year-old self, in hospital after my road accident

ran across the road and was hit by a car before I could reach the other side. If that happened today, I would probably have not survived, but cars didn't speed back then so I 'got away' with two broken legs. I was taken to hospital and spent the following few months with both legs hooked up to a pulley. I remember my hospital stay fondly, with visitors bearing treats and me getting lots of attention, although I am sure it wasn't all a bed of roses. Once my legs mended, it would appear there was no lasting damage – or so I thought…

VERTICALLY CHALLENGED

I never recall my height bothering me at school. Sure, I was called 'titch' and 'shorty', but it was never an issue for me and it was never said in a nasty manner. There really was no escaping the fact that I was vertically challenged – and at 4'10" still am. However, the light-bulb moment came in 1964 when I decided I was going to marry George Harrison, yes, the Beatle. I had already '*met*' his mum. Well, on paper at least. I had written to her twice in 1963 and both times she replied, the first time enclosing a signed picture of The Beatles, with a series of kisses and her name written on the back.

The second letter mentioned that The Beatles were working on a new song titled 'Eight Arms to Hold You', which was later changed to 'Eight Days a Week'. So I felt I was already a part of the family. However, George was 5'10" and if we were going to

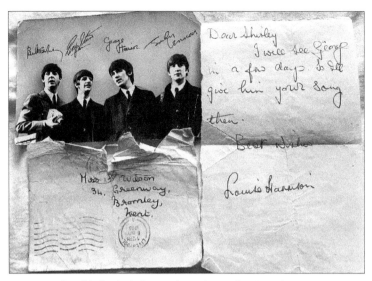

Part of the family: the letter and signed picture from Louise Harrison

make a good match, I needed to grow! I marked on my bedroom wall George's height and beside it, my height. Yes, I definitely needed a few more inches.

I invested in a book I saw advertised: 'The Safe System of Height Increase' – it was clearly talking directly to me. It cost around eight-shillings and six-pence and had 14-pages imparting little gems such as, 'Shortness in the legs is responsible for lack of height in many cases'. (You don't say!) And it gave useful exercise tips: 'Lie across a kitchen chair and perform the movements of swimming the breaststroke. Start slowly and work up speed. Attach something heavy to each foot after two weeks' and 'Sit on the ground with hands on hips and feet kept in position by some article of furniture. Revolve the trunk so that it describes a large circle. Omit this if you have a weak heart'. However, the *crème de la crème* had to be: 'Exercise preferably first thing in the morning near an open window and wearing only a jockstrap or anti-strain body belt, so that you secure a

THE SAFE SYSTEM OF **HEIGHT INCREASE**

The simple, safe and natural Method of Height Increase, perfected after years of research, which has increased the height of hundreds of grateful men and women to an extent varying from two to three, four and more inches.

Established 1928

PRACTICAL COURSES 26, DEAN ROAD, LONDON, N.W.2.

Trying to grow – and the book that didn't quite live up to its promise!

health-giving air-bath at the same time.' People passing my open window would have a field day, I thought. Did I try any of it? Of course! Did any of it work? No, it did not. I was still 4'10"!

My back-up plan was to pester my family doctor, a lovely man who had helped bring me into the world and my siblings too. In the 1950s and 1960s, the first doctor you had was one who you would usually see throughout your childhood and teenage years. There wasn't a lot they didn't know about you or your family. I convinced myself – beyond any doubt – that the culprit for my lack of inches was the accident in childhood: two broken legs. The bones had simply failed to grow. It was blatantly obvious to me. I had read somewhere that you could have bone added to your legs to make you taller. Yes, I truly did read that! I was sure therefore that my lovely, patient, calm doctor could help me with this. Give him his due, he didn't laugh. He kept a straight face and told me that the accident was not the reason I was short. It was to do with ancestry and my genes.

Not one to be fobbed off once I had the bit between my teeth, I probably mentioned it to him again a further God knows how many times. He would not budge on his stance. Sad to say, I had to let go of my idea of a union with George H. With the height difference, it just wasn't going to work – oh, if only I had been blessed with the gift of foresight and known that platform shoes were going to be the big fashion item of the decade, maybe I could have stalled. However, without being privy to the future, it was what it was. I'm sure George was as disappointed as me –

well, would have been had he known about my marriage plans. Pattie Boyd, however, was no doubt relieved. The way was now clear for her to marry him, which she did in 1966.

I was always a little envious of Pattie Boyd, for obvious reasons, until sometime in the summer of 2005, a mere 35+ years later, I was working in Public Relations with a top salon in Mayfair. One day, while having my hair done, I glanced in the mirror and to my astonishment Pattie Boyd was sat at another styling station with her back to me. I could see her very clearly in my mirror, and the face I saw was, of course, a much older Pattie. Now let's face it, no one looks good sitting in a hairdressing chair, with aluminium foil and tint covering their head, but, in that moment, I noted that she had aged (of course she had) and that the picture I had of her in my head of the young model from 'A Hard Day's Night', who, metaphorically speaking, 'stole my man', wasn't the reality. The envy I had harboured in the deepest furrows of my mind completely melted away.

My Early Job Aspirations

When I was around 12-years-old, I started reading a series of books: 'Sue Barton'. Each book focused on her nursing journey, from student nurse through to staff nurse. Her work sounded such fun, and I always liked the idea of being part of a team. I also remembered, with rose-coloured spectacles, the few months I spent as a five-year-old in hospital. The seed was sown and watered. Nursing would be my vocation.

School leaving age was 15-years-old at that time, but I was determined to apply for a trainee nurse position, which meant staying on at school until I was 17-years-old. The teachers explained to my mum that I was certainly bright enough to pass my exams and that they were keen for me to progress my education further. Mum, however, wanted me to leave school and get a job. She needed the extra wage coming in. It was how it was then; most of my weekly earnings went to my mum, and she gave me back enough money to get to work and some pocket money. I was extremely disappointed that my chosen vocation was thwarted, but the decision was made. I would be leaving school at 15-years of age, and any thoughts of a nursing career would be shelved. Looking back, she was completely right. She knew the first sight of blood would have me reaching for the nearest bucket.

I wasn't tall enough to follow my second full-time career choice: telephonist. "What's height got to do with it?" I wailed. A lot, as it happened. You had to be tall enough to sit on a chair and insert the connecting peg to the highest point on the large telephone exchange system – no standing allowed. I just could not manage it, even with the chair raised to its highest level and my legs dangling eight inches off the floor. The person who interviewed me broke the news in a very brusque manner. No sweetening the pill here. My dad had taken me to the interview and did his best to cheer me up, but good Lord, if I wasn't tall enough for that job, what job *would* I be tall enough for!

My Brief Flirtation with Fashion and Casserole Dishes

Our local department store, Medhurst, was advertising for shop assistants to work on the fashion floor. It really was just like 'Are You Being Served?' – and equally as hilarious. I was often taken for someone's child, rather than someone who worked there, which was extremely embarrassing. I marvelled at the way everything was neatly stacked away in large pull-out display drawers. Gloves, underwear, jumpers and every other type of apparel. It was an elegant way to shop.

I loved helping the ladies choose an outfit for a special occasion, standing outside the changing room, handing clothes in and then giving them the benefit of my *vast* fashion experience! Some ladies were regulars and often asked for me specifically to look after them. The assistants were on commission, although I was too young to be on commission (not quite sure where age came into it) so they weren't overjoyed for me to be constantly asked for. One or two would ask me to sign over the customer to them at the point of paying so that their name would be on the sales receipt, and they'd get the commission. I was quite happy to do that. If I couldn't have it, someone else might as well. I enjoyed this little dalliance with fashion, such as it was, and it helped my confidence no end to know that customers trusted my judgement.

I stayed at Medhurst for quite a few months before progressing in my career – to the local supermarket, Caters. It was the first and only supermarket in Bromley at the time. Working there was somewhat of a family tradition. My grandad, my brother, my sister and my aunties all worked there at some stage. The pay was better too. I went to work in the accounts department, also helping on the shop floor when they were short-staffed.

I loved looking around at the kitchen appliances and utensils, daydreaming of a time I would be buying them for my own home. I remember saving up a lot of my wages for two or three months, the first Christmas I worked there. I wanted to buy my mum a Pyrex casserole dish I'd seen. It was on a stand and had a small tea light candle under it to keep the food warm. *How sophisticated*, I thought. *Ingenious*, I thought. *She'll just love it*, I thought. You're right; she did not love it. She did not think it was the height of sophisticated kitchenware, and even today I can feel the disappointment of her disappointment – and who could blame her? Come on, people, is that a gift that would float your boat? Candle or no candle!

Department stores and supermarket jobs didn't pay a big wage, so to earn a little bit of extra cash I got a job in the evenings working at the local cinema as an usherette. It was called the Embassy Cinema and was built in Art Deco style. How I wish I had appreciated the architectural design then. Sadly, it's now a supermarket! There was a café on the upper floor, where I also remember working, although waitressing wasn't to be my future! I often managed to muddle the orders up. It wasn't a big café, but it could be very busy. I did learn how to cook a mean omelette and the perfect scrambled egg from the chef, though!

These were in the days when usherettes, with torches, showed you to your seat. Watching a TV programme recently, where a cinema, very much like the Embassy, was central to the plot, brought the memories flooding back. I wore a uniform that was miles too big, virtually down to my ankles – I wasn't one of those slim, glamorous cinema usherettes that we so often see in old films. Unbeknown to me at that time, I was actually following in my mum's footsteps. She had also been a cinema usherette and kiosk girl, but she did fit the 'Hollywood-style' glamour of an usherette, with her beautiful dark curly hair and tiny waist!

At intermission time, I had to carry a huge ice cream tray and stand at the front of the screen, for people to buy their Kia-Ora drinks and choc ices. An abiding memory I have is that just

My Mum in her cinema usherette uniform (far right)

before the intermission, we had to go backstage, behind the screen, where the fridges were kept, and fill our trays in readiness. However, as young girls we chatted and giggled, not realising that everything we said could be heard by the cinema audience – eek!

We were also allowed into the projection room at the top of the building, and I can recall many a time when the film reel snapped in half and had to be soldered back together before resuming the film, albeit with a big chunk missing! Plus, other shenanigans between projectionists and usherettes – what, *moi*?

I really loved my time there, and I met some great people. It was where I made an enduring friendship with my best friend, Linda Garner (née Harris). We still keep in touch.

Funnily enough, before I had ever met my husband, I met his sister-in-law Winnie – who was one of the cashiers at the cinema – and Margaret Rusk, another who became a good friend. I developed a love for Westerns such as 'The Good, the Bad and the Ugly', 'For a Few Dollars More' and 'The Magnificent Seven'. I must have seen 'The Sound of Music' 30 times at least, and never got tired of it, and what a joy, too, to be working in the cinema when 'Yellow Submarine' and 'Magical Mystery Tour' were released. When you think of special times in your life, this period was certainly one of mine.

Then came the call from my friend Avril and a whole new chapter in my life was to begin.

And the Winner Is...!

1966 heralded a new beginning for me! I had won the battle of my mum's reluctance to let me take the job that Avril had lined up for me in London. In the mid-nineteen-sixties, it wasn't always necessary to have an interview. If a friend recommended you, then you were in. Jobs were easy to come by, even those in publishing. A far cry from the last few decades when it has become almost impossible to secure a job on a magazine without a degree in journalism or a few years at university under your belt. I don't remember ever being fazed or nervous about starting this new job – the confidence of youth! I *was* excited, though.

1966 was also the year England won the most coveted prize in football – the World Cup. I loved football (and still do). I remember watching this very important game at home, on our small TV screen, in black and white. I'm sure the whole family were there. We prayed that England would win, but I don't think in our hearts we thought they would. Brazil were the team expected to win, as it would have been a hat-trick of World Cup titles for them had they clinched it. But they went out to Portugal earlier in the tournament.

So there we were: England v West Germany. The excitement was palpable. Streets were deserted. Union Jacks were flying high everywhere you looked. Even people who wouldn't usually watch football were glued to their small screens, and the shops that sold television sets had the game on in their shopfront windows, so passers-by could stop to watch. I can't honestly remember how I felt at the time, although I do recall the anticipation and hope everyone had. But it was a nail-biting match. Finishing at 90 minutes a 2-2 draw, the match went into extra time. Geoff Hurst (now Sir Geoff Hurst) scored two more goals (he had already scored one before extra time), bringing the score to 4-2 to England.

Never had I known such elation over a game of football – although Terry Venables' 1996 England team provoked a similar kind of excitement, but sadly we went out to penalties in the semi-final of the Euros. In my opinion, Terry rates as one of the best English football managers we've had, and I was lucky enough to be working with him during this time. Such a lovely man, with an engaging, 'Jack the Lad' personality!

So, here was I, working in England's capital city, at one of the most thrilling times in football history, where everyone was on a high and London was the place to be. It was magic!

Unlike most of my co-writers, I have no idea what I wore on that first day (although I feel sure my attire would have involved a cardigan) or where my ambitions laid. I remember I took the train from Bromley North Station to Charing Cross with Avril, and we walked to the building at 15 Long Acre, WC2. I took my place in the large office among other junior and senior clerks and my life in publishing began. There were about 15 to 20 women of varying ages and status. They were all friendly and helpful.

Wages were paid each week – cash in a little brown envelope. I loved Fridays and that magical moment when I opened the envelope to reveal my weekly wage of around four pounds and six shillings – not that there was much left by the time I'd paid for my lunch, train fare and given housekeeping money to my mum. But it didn't matter. I was working in London, and it didn't get much better than that.

For a naïve teenager, this first proper job was something else altogether. Long Acre mostly housed the clerical side of the publishing company, such as the Accounts, Post and Filing departments. However, the exception was *New Musical Express*, on the 4th floor. *New Musical Express* is an iconic music magazine that has stood the test of time, and is still being published today. One of my tasks as a junior clerk was to nip down to the postroom, pick up the mail and deliver it to each floor. This meant going up in the lift to the *New Musical Express* offices. I was pretty self-conscious – and my confidence zero. I handed over the post to the nearest person and fled, blushing like crazy, back into the safety of the lift.

This music magazine was the one all teenagers read. It had one real competitor, *Melody Maker,* which to me seemed more 'highbrow' with an emphasis on jazz and serious interviews. I was a huge NME fan, however, because it was all about pop music and the UK pop charts of the time – and its annual NME Poll Winners' Concert, which I was so lucky to go to on several occasions. The Beatles and Rolling Stones were always featured heavily. In the mid-sixties, I remember a guy called Andy Gray was the editor and Jeremy Pascall (who, coincidentally, I later worked with in Tower House) was a young writer. He went on in later life to become a much-respected author and broadcaster but sadly died, far too early, of throat cancer, in 2001. He was only 55 years old.

Like every other teenager of the time, I was madly into pop music and pop stars – I used to listen to Radio Caroline with my little transistor radio late at night under the bed sheets so my mum couldn't hear. I had a little torch (it was dark under there) – Simon Dee and Tony Blackburn were two of the DJs I remember. Radio Luxemburg was another favourite. 'Black is Black' by Los Bravos was a big hit along with 'Concrete and Clay' by Unit 4 + 2, so imagine my excitement bumping into both these bands in the lift (at different times, of course, the lifts were only small – thank goodness I was too) while doing my daily post delivery to *NME*!

Pop musicians would make their way to meet journalists who were going to interview them. There were no entourages, just the pop idols themselves. *NME* was a huge influence in the music industry and therefore had the power to truly help the careers of budding, and established, stars of the time.

The daily post run became a joy, as I regularly bumped into a pop singer or two. I felt really lucky to have landed such a job. So, imagine my devastation when the company decided to 'promote' me – to the role of filing clerk! My days of meeting my pop idols in a cranky old lift were over – or so I thought!

THE ART OF FILING

There was quite a community of filing clerks. In the 1960s and 1970s, filing clerks were trained individuals, who, without the benefit of computers, were responsible for every bit of paperwork in that building. Each document had to be filed in the right category, ordered and cross-referenced. It was good training and held me in great stead throughout my career and personal life. Filing skills were not to be sniffed at!

It was during my tenure in the department that I made great friends with Sandra Gibling and Violet Neal. We were pretty much the same age and spent a lot of time chatting about pop groups and teen things. Then one Friday they mentioned that a singer called David Bowie was playing at the Marquee Club in Wardour Street on Sunday afternoon and did I want to go along. They'd seen him once before and thought he was fab (as well as good-looking). I didn't think my mum would be keen for me to go, but I guess because it was the afternoon, she was fine. What an eye-opener. The only live acts I had seen previously in a theatre setting were the likes of Pearl Carr and Teddy Johnson and the Ted Heath Band, neither of whom could be described as pop music!

It was so exciting to see the singers and pop groups of the time – The Yardbirds, Spencer Davis Group, Unit 4 + 2, Small Faces, The Move, Episode Six, Graham Bonney and many more… There were no bodyguards keeping fans at arm's length, so you really could interact with them on a personal level. Then onto the stage came someone whom I recognised. It was Bowie, but I knew him as Davie Jones, a boy who lived in Bromley, where I also lived.

As Davie Jones, Bowie used to play with bands around Bromley's local schools and colleges but being a couple of years younger than him, I didn't know him personally. I do remember that his mode of dress, even then, was somewhat 'different': high boots, truly tight trousers, bohemian clothes – in contrast to what the general youth in Bromley were wearing anyway. A friend of mine, whose husband had a local pop group, recalls Bowie asking if he could join their band. They turned him away. A decision based purely on how he looked. I bet they regretted that a few years later. Never judge a book by its cover is a favourite mantra of mine.

When I went to see him at the Marquee Club, he was with a band called The Lower Third and I fell instantly in love with the music and the band. More of Bowie in Chapter 2!

MOVING INTO TOWER HOUSE

Back in 1961, George Newnes had been bought by Fleetway Publications (previously known as The Mirror Group) and was renamed IPC Magazines. For those who worked at George Newnes, this eventually meant a new job and new contract. We were offered positions in a building in Southampton Street, Covent Garden: Tower House. Sandra and Violet decided to leave and work elsewhere, as did many others, but we kept in touch and made regular trips to see Bowie wherever he happened to be playing. I, however, decided to go with the new regime, possibly the best career decision I ever made!

I was given a job in the Accounts department. It was in the basement of Tower House, and to be honest, very boring, but I did what I was asked to do and made the best of it. Soon, I was singled out as being very helpful and smiley, by a lady who *seemed* to run the whole company. She was known as Mrs Mills and was quite a remarkable person. I shall always be grateful to her for rescuing me and insisting I join her team across the road in the Weldons building (same company, different building) to be her junior. The Weldons building was where the comics and a couple of other music magazines of the time were. I became Mrs Mill's run-around, a job I loved. I was working with others of my age. Everyone was young and vibrant, and focused on fashion, beauty and pop. Pure Bliss.

The lovely Mrs Mills was like a mum. She really looked after *her* girls. She was the boss, full stop. Even top management wouldn't argue with Mrs Mills. She was a bit of an enigma. She came from the East End and hadn't had the easiest of lives, as I recall, but she was very fair and very generous. Some found her a little intimidating, but I can't say that I ever did. She would treat us all to presents at Christmas, buy the Christmas tree to put up in the building and bring us the most delicious mince pies, cakes and sandwiches. If you had a problem, she would help. She was always on your side.

Mrs Mills was a larger-than-life character who nobody really knew too much about. We were in awe of her but never in a scary way. It seemed there wasn't anything she couldn't do, fix or resolve. It seems inconceivable now that one woman, who wasn't management, could rule the roost in the way she did and from the top down. They certainly broke the mould when they made her.

Living the Life!

The Weldons building was a world away from the Accounts department; pop stars would come for interviews with our music writer, the rooms were always full of clothes for fashion photo shoots and the cupboards groaning under the weight of the many beauty products that were sent to the beauty editor to be featured in the magazines – it was seventh heaven for a teenage girl. One of my jobs was to take clothes back to fashion houses once they were finished with. I remember trying to hail a black taxi in the Strand, with two armfuls of dresses by top designers of the 1960s, terrified that I would lose a few on the way. I never did, thank goodness.

The clothes had to be delivered back, in one piece, to fashion shops of the time: Bazaar or Biba – Bazaar was the creation of iconic dress designer Mary Quant and her husband, Alexander Plunket Greene, while Biba was the brainchild of Barbara

Hulanicki and husband Stephen Fitz-Simon. Both were the names on every fashionista's lips in the '60s and beyond.

I would drop off my armfuls of clothes and watch top models and the fashionable London set trying on mini skirts and shift dresses, wishing I earned enough to buy one of the fabulous Biba or Quant outfits that were on display. I consoled myself with the promise that one day I would!

MY FIRST-EVER POP CONCERT – AND THE BEATLES TOP THE BILL!

New Musical Express held a Poll Winners' Concert every year, where all the big pop idols of the day would appear. One of the music journalists, I believe her name was Julie Webb, asked me if I'd like to go with her to the concert – this must have been around 1966/7. She was a lovely girl, only a few years older than me, but she had taken me under her wing. I could hardly contain my joy. The Beatles were topping the bill. As a music writer, she had secured seats in the front row. It was one of the most amazing things that could have happened. A pop-mad teenager, getting

The Beatles on stage at the New Musical Express Poll Winners Concert. I was watching in the front row! Photo: Trinity Mirror / Mirrorpix / Alamy Stock Photo

front-row seats, watching her idols a few feet away performing their hits of the day. I swear that George smiled at me! I believe it was the last live stage performance by The Beatles. I will forever be grateful to Julie for that opportunity.

It was while working in the Weldons building that I hit on the idea of getting David Bowie an interview with our teen magazine, *Mirabelle*. So I approached our music writer and waxed lyrical about this amazing singer who was bound for huge stardom and how lucky he would be to be one of the first to interview him. It worked, and he agreed. I remember Bowie coming to the building with his manager, but I don't know to this day if the interview was ever published!

TWO

1966

THE DAVID BOWIE YEARS!

I was thoroughly enjoying my job and the weekends at the Marquee but feeling a little guilty about the occasional white lie I had to tell my mum in order to stay out a little later than she would allow. To get around that, I would tell her I was staying at Sandra's, Sandra would tell her mum that she was staying at Violet's, and Violet... well, you get the gist. What we were doing was going to a music gig to see Bowie and then staying up all night wandering the streets of London and sipping coffee in Lyons Corner House opposite Charing Cross Station.

One time, we went with Bowie and the band he now played with, The Buzz, to a gig out in Cambridge. The band used to travel in what was once an ambulance, looking a bit sorry for itself at this stage. Sandra, Violet and I jumped in for the trip through London and out to the venue. It was late afternoon and we pulled up alongside a coach of elderly people who seemed fascinated with the old ambulance. The windows were blacked out so they couldn't actually see in. Bowie did no more than allow his thin white arm (he was very pale-skinned) to flop out of the side window – needless to say, they looked horrified.

After the gig, the band dropped us back into London and we proceeded to walk around until the trains started running. On one occasion, we were stopped by a policeman on the beat who asked us what we were doing at that hour of the morning and proceeded to berate us. I am ashamed to say that I was extremely cheeky back to him, but he let us go on our way (although not before calling me a young reprobate), telling us to go straight home. As it happens, he did have good cause to be concerned for us. There had been a stabbing in the area and the knifeman was still on the loose. We never felt in danger or threatened at any time. I certainly know I wouldn't feel quite as relaxed about it today.

By this time, we had become pals with Bowie and asked his co-manager, Ken Pitt, if we could run his first fan club. Ken said yes and we were thrilled. I had my address for fan letters. I was surprised at how many came in. David clearly had quite a following even in the early days; such was his charisma and talent. The letters mostly wanted to know where he was going to appear next, some expressed their undying love for him, and others were asking for a signed photograph. We answered every letter and, where necessary, got the information and signed photographs from Ken Pitt to pass on to his loyal fans.

David invited us to his home around his birthday time. I remember the house so well. It was a small, very pretty terraced house in Plaistow Grove, Sundridge Park, about 15 minutes from where I

Ken Pitt and David Bowie circa 1967.

lived. There were flowers around the door, which David's mum, Peggy, nurtured. We sat in the small front room and his mum brought us in tea. She was lovely to us. Inside, the décor was of its time and although I can't recall the pattern of the wallpaper, my abiding memory is of a very neat and cosy room. Homely. Bowie, I believe, played his guitar and we all felt totally relaxed and at ease. I wish I could remember what we discussed, but the years dim the memory!

David was a thinker; he soaked up everything that was going on around him. He was well spoken, articulate, caring and sincere. Absolutely no ego or pretentions. There was absolutely nothing to dislike about him.

Bowie had my telephone number and on occasion he would ring me and play a specific record down the phone to see what I thought of it. I remember particularly he loved Marc Bolan's music. We used to have some great chats, mainly about music and what was happening in our lives, and when he would be next performing. Living in Bromley, we had a lot in common.

One thing that was always obvious to me, which I believe he alluded to during one conversation, was how he was never happy being pigeonholed into one specific genre of music. He always wanted to go on to something new, explore and experiment all he could, with music and life. I guess this was at a time when he was trying to break into mainstream music, and I could totally understand what he was saying – and so it proved in later years, when he moved from one persona to another, and from one life experience to another. His mind was always full of the next opportunity, the next thing he wanted to do.

In 1967, Bowie's career briefly took a different direction. He had met mime artist Lindsay Kemp in 1966, and in 1967 appeared in one of Kemp's productions, 'Pierrot in Turquoise', in which he played Cloud. Sandra and I, along with Bowie's parents, went to see him at the Mercury Theatre in London. We then

Picture of David Bowie 1968. Photo: Tracksimages.com / Alamy Stock Photo

saw it again, at the Intimate Theatre in Palmers Green, where Sandra remembers: "This time, we went backstage before the performance just to say hello to David, and I remember that he felt very awkward and hustled us outside to talk, and the reason for this was because all the guys in the production were partly undressed and very camp. He didn't want us to feel awkward." I guess he was protecting our innocence!

Fascinating as these Lindsay Kemp productions were, it really wasn't something that excited me. As David himself is quoted as saying: "Mime is limited when you start, but I think it's a marvellous medium which requires a lot of concentration on the part of the audience." Maybe it was my concentration that was limited. If I'm truly honest, I wasn't keen, at that time, on the direction Bowie seemed to be taking. However, I know the

Lindsay Kemp era was a formative time in Bowie's career and, from reading comments Bowie made later, it opened a whole new world of image transformation and interpretive dance for him.

There is no doubt Lindsay Kemp was a huge influence on many of Bowie's alter egos. This quote by Lindsay Kemp says a lot: "In improvisations, I tell people to listen to the music, to abandon themselves and become totally transported to other places, therefore becoming other characters. David was always very good at that. God knows, he was a chameleon." (Quote taken from 'Bowie Unseen' by Gerald Fearnley.)

David's first album, simply called 'David Bowie', was a collection of songs, written by him, which drew on his experiences and influences from his surroundings at the time. I still play that album and am always particularly drawn to 'Rubber Band', which features the Library Gardens in Bromley and evokes images of the band that used to play on the bandstand every Sunday afternoon, and the people that would be there, sitting around the bandstand and listening to the music while munching on their freshly made sandwiches. David was there on many occasions, as was I.

He had never really ventured far from south London and was a real Bromley boy (albeit born in Brixton)! His singles, released prior to the album – 'London Boys' and 'The Laughing Gnome' – couldn't be more different, the former being a rather dismal observation of the London scene at the time, and the latter, as you might guess from the title, being more of a novelty record, showcasing his sense of humour. Apparently, however, I read that it involved a technique to create a very specific sound, which he would use in a more serious fashion in some of his later music. He was always experimenting with different sounds and instruments.

When he first started being more widely recognised, his voice was likened to that of Anthony Newley – which didn't upset him at all, why should it? Anthony Newley was an entertainer – and a successful one at that – and David was never a 'rock singer' per se. He never put himself in that genre. His aim was to be an all-round entertainer. In his book 'The Pitt Report', David's former manager, Ken Pitt, said: "David never was a devotee or exponent of rock and roll. Whenever he rocked and rolled, he did so in the context of theatre, as an actor. He himself has said: 'Rock does not play an important part of my life. Music for me is something I use to put down my thoughts – like paint.'" David was, at heart, an artist first and foremost!

By 1969, David had moved into the neighbouring town of Beckenham, sharing a house with his friend Mary Finnegan. He was dating Hermione Farthingale, had met Angie Barnett (who later became his first wife) and 'Space Oddity' was released.

Bowie had moved on and was much in demand. Our little relationship, such as it was, sadly petered out. After Bowie died, and many clips were shown of him in the last few years before his passing, the Bowie I knew when he was just 18 or 19 was still there. Listening to him speak took me right back to those early days. He was always so informed on many subjects, and his voice was very distinctive and soft, with his throaty laugh, and an ironic smile never far from his lips.

In the early 1980s, Ken Pitt was writing a book about Bowie called 'The Pitt Report'. He wrote to me, asking if he could ring me to chat about it. I of course said yes. I was flattered that he remembered me, when I was such a very small part of the big picture. He asked if there was anything I would like to contribute, any old photos or fan club stories. I told him that my folder of memorabilia consisting of fan club letters, personal photos and my written thoughts of David Bowie 'went missing' after I naively lent them to Angie Bowie. Her agent, back in the 1970s, said Angie would love to see it and wanted to show it to David. I handed it over, foolishly in hindsight, and never saw it again – although not from want of trying.

Ken was upset about it, on my behalf. He wasn't in touch with David or Angie at that stage so there wasn't anything he could personally do. He did however call me a couple of times after that, once to tell me that he had seen some pictures in an article on Bowie in *The Times* newspaper and they looked like ones that I had described to him, taken behind the Marquee Club. He suggested I get in touch with the newspaper and see if I could find out more. I tried, but to no avail. Ken still mentioned Sandra, Violet and me in his book, though, just a little paragraph, but I thought how sweet that was of him.

While writing this, I had the urge to speak to Ken, so I googled him, only to discover that he had died just a couple of months before. He was such a lovely man and very generous with his time. He commented in his book that I must have been one of David's very earliest fans!

Having read Angie Bowie's book 'Backstage Passes' and her reference to him as the 'ghastly Ken Pitt', I really couldn't reconcile it with being the same man. She has been quoted as saying: "…I brought in Tony Defries to get rid of Ken Pitt…" [source: www.loudersound.com by Ian Fortnam (Classic Rock) published 15th May 2017] which is exactly what happened. After that, Ken and David of course drifted apart. But I did read that a couple of years before David died, he visited Ken and they had a long chat, putting the past to rest. I was so heartened to hear that.

Ken Pitt was undoubtedly a huge early influence and the driving force at a very formative time in Bowie's life. He shaped and prepared Bowie for stardom! Sadly, he rarely got the credit he so surely deserved. If you want an authentic account of Bowie from his childhood through to the early 1970s, without the sex, drugs and intimate detail of 'Backstage Passes', you should try and get hold of a copy of Ken's book 'The Pitt Report'. A must-read for Bowie fans.

GROWING UP IN THE '50S AND '60S

I know when looking back to our early formative years, there is a tendency to remember those times fondly and nostalgically. But I can truly say that they were good, innocent times to grow up in. I had a happy childhood, with my three siblings: my older brother, Glenn, and two younger sisters, Pam and Dawn. My brother and I were very close in age, and for the first six years, it was just the two of us. The first house I ever remember living in was a huge detached property in my hometown of Bromley, Kent, where many happy childhood memories were made. We had the ground floor: three bedrooms, a large living room, a kitchen and a cellar, where the coal was kept for the open fire. We had a huge garden and the train line from Bromley North to London ran along the back of our garden. My maternal nan and grandad lived close by.

My brother and I would spend hours in the garden. I used to make mud pies and put them into a pretend oven, deep under some bush, to cook, and then give them to my brother to 'eat'. We had a beloved pet tortoise who we called Sputnik (I think we named him after the Soviet Union's Sputnik satellite). I don't remember what age he was when he died. I don't think we'd had him very long, but I do remember my brother and I taking him to the vet, as we hadn't seen him move for a while! We had to walk across a bridge that went over the railway line. It was also the way we walked to visit my nan and grandad, who lived just the other side of the railway track. The vet pronounced Sputnik dead – in the kindest way.

My brother and I returned home, back over the bridge, still clutching Sputnik, tears streaming down our cheeks for our lost pal. We gave him a good send-off with a nice burial spot in the large garden, under the trees. When we got our second tortoise, we called him Sputnik 2.

When I was ten, we had at last been given a council house. Another spacious garden. Three bedrooms. A dining room and a living room. There was a big walk-in larder in the kitchen and a small scullery, which housed the washing machine and clothes wringer, plus a large cupboard for the coal. Every weekend, something would be happening. Most Sundays we would drive to Camber Sands with our aunts, uncles and cousins, taking along a picnic lunch of sandwiches and hard-boiled eggs. Other times we'd go to the Bluebell Woods, and come back with armfuls of bluebells, or go fruit picking at local farms. Simple pleasures.

But then along came a demon that worked its way into our lives, causing us all a tremendous amount of worry and angst for a number of years!

BATTLE OF THE BARBITURATES!

It was sometime around the early 1960s when my grandad died. My mum was devastated, and it affected her greatly. She was very close to him and had sat beside him, night after night, during his illness. On the evening he died, however, she wasn't there. I don't think she ever got over that. A couple of years later, when I was 13, my little sister Dawn was born. I remember going to school in the morning and when I got home in the afternoon there she was, this beautiful baby. My younger sister, Pam, was seven years old and my brother was 15.

A few years after Dawn was born, Mum had trouble sleeping. The doctor prescribed sleeping tablets (barbiturates), which treated insomnia, anxiety and depression. For the first number of years, it helped her tremendously. However, it was a drug that could be addictive and, as time went on, she came to rely on them.

When I think back to those times, I realise that my mum

wasn't alone in trying to deal with issues of depression and anxiety. It could have been several things: post-natal depression, my grandad dying or even the early onset of the menopause, which was something women never talked about, or maybe even knew much about. The only option for many housewives was turning to alcohol or relying on prescriptive drugs handed out freely by doctors – who probably weren't equipped to deal with such problems themselves.

The first inkling we had that something was wrong was when we noticed Mum's speech was slightly slurred, and she couldn't walk a straight line. We used to have a giggle about it at the beginning – that is, until it became a big concern. It got worse after she'd had an accident on her bike. We were told by the doctors that she'd had an epileptic fit. We felt it was the tablets and not a fit that caused the accident, because when she took too many it was akin to being drunk. Anyway, they knew better and prescribed Phenobarbitone to combat the fits. Combining those with the barbiturates spelt disaster.

Unfortunately, Mum became totally reliant on both prescribed medicines. I noticed sometimes she would take more than the suggested dose and it would affect her mood and sense of balance. She would take her month's supply in two weeks and have to wait for the next prescription. This resulted in two weeks of mood swings and erratic behaviour, but then two weeks of having my mum back again. It became so bad that she would occasionally overdose on them – not intentionally – but she would forget she had taken them and so take some more. I came home from work on many occasions and found her out cold on the floor.

My brother and I had to call an ambulance a couple of times and they would take her into hospital and pump her stomach. My dad did his best to wean her off, sometimes emptying the tablets down the drain. This of course caused untold arguments.

Out of desperation, I made an appointment to see our family doctor and told him how the drugs he prescribed were affecting my mum, and how she was misusing them. My hope was that he would agree to reduce the dose he was giving her. But I was told that it wasn't something he was prepared to discuss with me and that was the end of the conversation. It was a very upsetting and worrying few years.

My dad threw in the towel when my little sister was eight years old. I know that must have been so awful for her, but the family were always around to help. If it got really bad, my brother would pick Dawn up from home and take her back to stay with him and my sister-in-law, Yvonne. I guess it affected me insofar as I declined invitations to go out with my pals after work. I always came straight home, never quite knowing what state my mum would be in. I often got irrational telephone calls from her when I was at work, as did my brother. I gave up my job in London for those couple of years so that it didn't take me so long to get home.

Mum always seemed to be able to take care of Dawn, though – and I guess Dawn learnt to take care of her, but there's no doubt it was a difficult time. When my dad left, I guess I understood why he found it difficult, but I did wonder if he should have done more, rather than walk away, but it wasn't an easy situation, and really, who was I to judge?

That glitch in my mum's life, however, does not overshadow or affect how much we loved her, nor diminish the memories of the very happy childhood we all had, and the life she made for us, making sure we wanted for nothing, and this she continued to do until her death. It was just a few years of malfunction in an otherwise exemplary life. In the end, she won the battle of the tablets, shook herself down, got herself a job and, while there would never be another man in her life – not for want of offers, she was a very attractive woman – she took her joy from her children and then her grandchildren, whom she adored.

My mum's favourite perfume was Chanel No. 5 and she loved champagne. These were things we were able to treat her to as we got older and earned our own money. I still have one of her bottles of Chanel No. 5 in my bathroom cabinet. I sometimes take it out of the cabinet just to smell it, evoking only good memories of her.

It was rather a paradox that here was my mum, on the one hand abusing prescriptive drugs, while on the other drumming into us the dangers of recreational drugs of the time, such as cannabis, LSD and purple hearts. Working, as I was, in the fashion and music industry, it was commonplace to see someone smoking a joint and passing it around, and inevitable that at some point I would be offered them. However, having witnessed the misuse of drugs first-hand in my own home, there wasn't any way I was going to be drawn into that scene, tempting as it sometimes was to be 'part of the crowd'.

It was around this time that I met my husband, Eric. His marriage had recently broken up and he was devastated about it. I had left home and was lodging with his brother Bob and sister-in-law, Mary. They threw a party and that's when I met Eric. He was older than me by nearly nine years and he was drinking a lot at that time, depressed about the breakdown of his marriage. He had two young sons, Paul and Andrew, whom he missed terribly – although he saw them every weekend.

We just hit it off and I think having a relationship eventually helped him get over his broken marriage. Eric was adamant that he didn't want any more children, and I guess when you're young and in love, you go along with that. I totally understood. However, best-laid plans! I was just 20 when we met, and we married when I was 25. Five years on from our wedding, when I was 30, our son James was born. He was a little love, always full

My three wonderful children who are now 42yrs, 34yrs and 36yrs respectively

of smiles – and a daredevil! Nothing seemed to scare him, and jumping from the top of a climbing frame was just one occasion when my heart was in my mouth! But, goodness, did he hate to sleep!

Six years later, we had our beautiful daughter, Amy. Having a girl brought us different joys. She was a confident, artistic child who loved dressing up. She was an avid reader and always had a book in her hand. Michael, our lovely youngest, was born 19 months after Amy. He was quieter than the other two, not surprising when you have two older siblings hell-bent on running your life for you – he would often appear in our living room dressed in some outlandish attire that Amy had decided to put on him. He and Amy were close in age, so it was rather like having twins. We counted our blessings that we had three healthy, happy and caring children.

Amy made us grandparents in 2009, to our gorgeous grandson, Michael, who is the apple of our eye – and we looked forward to many more happy years. Unfortunately, fate had

My dear husband Eric and me, just a few months before covid caught up with him.

other ideas, and before this book was finished, when Covid had us all in its clutches and the pandemic was at its height, my dear husband sadly died of this horrific disease. We had 50 years together, so a big chunk of my life was taken as well. He is greatly missed, and loved, by us all, and always will be.

THREE

1967–1973

Working on the New Wave of Fashion & Beauty Magazines

It's 1967 and my days at the Weldons building were numbered. Across the road, in Tower House, exciting things were afoot, and they were looking for junior assistants to work on a magazine called *Rave* and, a soon-to-be-launched, *Model Girl* magazine. I had really enjoyed working with Mrs Mills and all the team, but it was time for new challenges. I loved the idea of moving back to the main building and working directly with the two new publications.

I was soon ensconced in a small office alongside two other teens: Penny Saunders and Karen Clark. Both gorgeous-looking girls, either could have been a model, and in fact did do some modelling for the magazines we worked on. We got on so well that going into work every day was a pleasure. We were on the same wavelength and enjoyed the same things. We chatted non-stop – but I guess some work got done in between. We got up to mischief and often laughed uncontrollably at nothing in particular. It could be something as simple as a hiccup, or a sneeze!

I also met Linda Newman, who was to become a lifelong friend, along with Penny and Karen. She was working in a nearby office on *Hers* magazine. She was the same age and had started at a similar time. Linda was a very lovable character, and still is. She was also extremely ambitious. I envied the fact that she knew exactly where she wanted her career to go, whereas I just didn't. I certainly didn't think I had it in me to make my way as a journalist. Regardless, we all became firm friends and, to this day, 50-plus years later, we still have regular lunch dates and the friendships have never waned. It was a good time to be young.

The magazines we worked on were all staffed by young, keen, ambitious and budding journalists – with the exception, of course, of those who were there to run the company and keep us in line! Two of these wonderful women were Margaret Palfrey and Joan Felton. They really couldn't have been more than 40 themselves but, to us 17-year-olds, seemed older. They were so caring, though, and really looked after us.

Back in the 1960s and 1970s, we were all great letter writers, what with the absence of computers and mobile phones. When Linda went on holiday, for example, I would write and keep her informed of what was happening in the office. It was, after all, our second home, and we were like family. Linda kept a few of the letters and returned them to me recently. They show how well we were looked after. In one extract, written in August 1968, I tell Linda:

I had to go to Brighton today – well, not exactly Brighton – Burgess Hill actually. I had to take a £25 cash prize to a Rave winner, 'cos Penny wasn't in. I left the office at 11am and got back at 5.10pm. Miss Felton told me to have my lunch at Burgess Hill and charge it to Petty Cash, also Miss Palfrey said to buy a magazine or book to read on

the train, as it is such a long journey, and charge that also
to Petty Cash – so… I had great fun.

In an extract from another letter to her written in 1967, Linda had gone on holiday, and I asked her an *extremely important* question: 'Did you remember to take your bell with you?' referring to the bells we used to hang around our necks during the hippy period.

Janice Collier, our charismatic beauty editor, who is also still a good friend and one of the co-writers of this book, was looking for someone to try out a revolutionary new weight-loss programme that had swept into the UK from America. It was

My Weight Watchers weight loss makeover for Model Girl Magazine in my 60s Quant mini dress. Circa 1967

called Weight Watchers – which we all know today is now WW! Originally conceived in New York in 1961 by housewife and mother Jean Nidetch, it took another six years before the UK arm was founded by Bernice Weston and London was alerted. I duly went on the diet – cooked by my mum, who was very keen for me to lose weight. She had always had a lovely figure, unlike her plump eldest daughter. All I can really remember is having plates of boiled/baked cod and vegetables served up to me. I wasn't allowed near the larder myself. I'm sure there was far more to it than that, but it's what sticks in my mind and is probably the reason it took me until middle age to make my peace with a fillet of fish!

I lost a good few pounds and as a reward I had my hair and make-up done by the top professionals of the day. I was kitted out in a lovely turquoise and black Mary Quant dress and matching coat. The before and after pictures, and the story of my weight-loss journey, appeared in an edition of *Model Girl* magazine. Looking back at the picture today, the hairstyle made me look a lot older than the 17-year-old I was. I did so love the outfit, though – but sadly, I wasn't allowed to keep it!

It's 1968 and London is swinging. Twiggy was the name on everyone's lips and The Beatles were top pop gods. Carnaby Street and the King's Road were the places to hang out and be seen. The song 'San Francisco' became the anthem of the times, with talk of free love and flowers in your hair. As a young girl, I soaked it all up. I desperately wanted to go to San Francisco; it sounded such a happy place. Travel to America at that time was a million miles away from my wildest dreams, but dream I did, nevertheless!

I remember wearing the obligatory bell – everyone could hear me coming. Not sure why but I think it was to do with Peace, Love and Music. I adored the hippy era and the fashions that came out of it. I wasn't confident enough to wear it all, but I did brave very short skirts – much to my mum's horror – and the hippy accessories. I also vividly remember the group of Hare Krishna disciples who would walk along the Strand, singing and chanting their message of peace and love. I was fascinated by their very short cropped and shaven heads, and the Indian robes they dressed in were distinctive and enticing.

In the '60s, films such as 'Blow Up' and 'The Italian Job' were big influences on fashion, and by the mid-sixties, British fashion had successfully usurped its French and Italian counterparts. Hip designers and shops such as Biba and Quant had set the style revolution, and hippy fashion such as kaftans, psychedelic prints and short skirts led the way. What a perfect era for dedicated followers of fashion!

THE GRASS IS NEVER GREENER

The old saying 'You don't know what you have until it's gone' was very apt in 1969 when I decided to change jobs, mainly because of problems at home with my mum. I sought a more local position – in a typing pool at the local town hall.

Typing pools were commonplace in the late '60s and '70s! A large room housed about 15 desks with a typist at each! The various bosses recorded documents they wanted typed onto a Dictaphone (a small tape recorder) and left the fully loaded tapes in trays at the front of the office to be picked up by whichever typist was available. It could be hard to decipher the tapes depending on the voice clarity of the person dictating. It was sometimes hit and miss, although a lot of common sense and a good understanding of grammar went a long way to producing an accurate result! I lasted in the typing pool for about eight months. It just became so boring and monotonous. I handed in my notice and started looking for another job.

A week later, I was in a smaller office but doing much the same thing. This was more secretarial, though, and I worked with just one other girl. Chatting in the office was heavily discouraged by our boss, but he was out quite a bit, being involved with the RNLI, so we made the most of his absences, playing music and swapping stories. Boredom, however, set in once again. I handed in my notice and moved on to what I hoped would be a more exciting prospect at the Mobil Oil Company in Kent. It turned out to be the same old same old. By the time I left this, my third job, almost two years had passed since my time with the publishing industry – although it felt like a lifetime.

BACK WHERE I BELONG

I had kept in touch with friends at IPC Magazines and decided, as I was in between jobs, to drop into Tower House and say hello to my pals. A fortuitous decision as it turned out.

A new magazine, *19*, had launched before I left IPC, under the editorship of Terry Hornett, but by the time I went back to visit, Maggie Koumi, who I had worked with prior to leaving, had taken over the role.

Maggie was such a very warm and attractive personality, and we had always gotten along well. So, there I was, trotting along the corridors of Tower House (how I had missed that building), and coming towards me was the exquisite Maggie Koumi. Maggie is of Greek Cypriot heritage and beautiful. She had long dark hair and the most fabulous eyes. In later years, Maggie's hair turned completely white. It really suited her and became her trademark, as it still is today.

We stopped to chat, and she asked me where I was working. I explained that I was between 'options' and she immediately said: "Do you want to come back and work on *19*?" I was gobsmacked and delighted.

"I'd love to," was my instant reply. She was just popping out so asked me to come and have a chat in her office in an hour. To say I was excited would be an understatement. I asked her, as a by-the-way, what the job would be, and her reply was: "I'll find you something to do," or words to that effect. It takes my breath away whenever I recall that meeting. If only it was so easy for the kids today. But it's how it was. There were plenty of jobs and opportunities. However, people like Maggie Koumi were in short supply. She was to play a pivotal role in my life and my career, and still does to this day.

The job she found me was answering the sackfuls of readers' letters that were delivered daily. The previous person had let them pile up so here was certainly *something for me to do* and I loved it. The day I was due to start back at the Tower happened to be my birthday. When Maggie realised that, she told me I shouldn't have to work on my birthday, so to start the day after. That is how she was. I took her words to heart and still, to this day, try to make it a rule never to work on my birthday.

Being back at Tower House felt like coming home. The working environment was such fun. I believe we (myself and my co-authors) were so lucky to have worked in publishing when we did. It was so relaxed. We got to meet fabulous people, including our pop heroes, and go to great events.

Maggie was a fantastic editor who had very little time for hierarchy and was completely unfazed by the rules set out by them. Fridays were of particular irreverence. We went to the pub at lunchtime and returned to the office laden with bottles of red wine (Bull's Blood, if I remember rightly) and beer. The weekend, for us, had begun. The afternoon was spent playing darts, drinking red wine and generally having fun. This never interfered with the work that had to be done, though. Deadlines for all writing, sub-editing and production would have to be met. Maggie was a relaxed boss, but the magazine was her priority, her passion and her baby. It always came first.

During my time answering readers' letters, I shared an office with fashion editor Norma Moriceau. Norma was Australian and as glamorous and interesting as her name suggests. She was a very confident person, and a little bit mysterious in my eyes. I wasn't at all surprised that she went on to become a famous film costume and production designer; her style was very eclectic, exotic and innovative. I could see how she would fit into the film world. Sadly, I heard that she died of cancer in 2016, aged 72. How I would have loved to have seen her again.

Then there was the enchanting Jo Dingemans, Norma's assistant and a former model. Jo was as beautiful as she was kind. She was extremely easy-going and a fantastic creative fashion journalist. I worked with Jo for many years, both in and out of journalism, and I am pleased to say that we are still in touch today and our paths cross on many occasions. The other person in the office was Hilary Smith, who kept both Norma and Jo organised – not the easiest job in the world, but Hilary was perfect for the job. She had long dark curly hair and a lovely personality. She and I got on extremely well. We had our children about the same time, except she stopped at two!

Models would waft in and out of the office hoping to be chosen for fashion shoots and to grace the pages of *19* magazine. What always fascinated me was that the plainest-looking of them all turned out to be the most amazing model. They would turn up with no make-up on and their hair scraped back. Jo and Norma, along with the photographer of the moment, would decide which ones fitted the bill for whatever the shoot was. I learnt a lot just from watching them, and it held me in good stead when, many years later, I became a PR and had to organise photographic sessions for my clients.

From the Fashion department I was moved to the Features department, and it's where I met and worked with the features and music writer, Mick Brown. He was tall, with lots of charisma – and good-looking. All the girls were mad about him. He clearly put his faith in me and sent me on a couple of interviews for the pieces he was writing. My first one, with the head of the students' union at the London College of Art, was a total disaster. I went back to the office with very little on my tape recorder for Mick to work with, but he didn't make me feel awkward or a failure.

Actually, writing this reminded me of another time I felt my height was a bit bothersome. It was when I was sharing an office with Mick. He was a good 6ft tall – and I wasn't. I would get off the train at Charing Cross and join the throng of people hurrying down the Strand, all trying to get to work on time – and so would Mick. I tried to spot him on the station concourse – before he spotted me – which allowed me to hide until he had gone past. Why? I was convinced that he wouldn't want to be seen walking along with a little shorty like me. However, one sunny weekday morning, I was making my usual mad dash along the Strand to Tower House and heard my name being called. I turned around and Mick was striding towards me. "I saw you ahead and have been trying to catch up," he said. We then proceeded to chat for the rest of the walk to the office, and did so many times after. I guess it was all in my head (and not his) about the height difference.

He was always very supportive. I learnt a lot from him in both practical and constructive terms, which helped my writing skills. I recall he suggested I should open the dictionary daily to a random page, find a new word and use it in a sentence, essentially broadening my vocabulary. This might sound a simple bit of advice, but it instilled in me a real love of words. It is something I still practise to this day. So, when the super-encouraging Maggie Koumi gave me my first writing assignment, I thought Mick's advice would hold me in good stead.

My prose was to be featured on the Looks and Talks page of the magazine, which showcased new and interesting products and happenings. I was so excited! Then I discovered what I had to write about. A glue stick! Yep, you read it right. It was for the Christmas issue. How to master the art of homemade decorations using said glue stick.

I rolled two clean sheets of copy paper (separated by carbon paper) into my trusty typewriter. I then proceeded to stare at that paper for hours, not once hitting down on a letter key. I gazed into space hoping for inspiration. I checked my nails. I stared back at the typewriter. I opened the dictionary, just as Mick had instructed (but there wasn't much I could do with the word 'hallelujah' in this context – except maybe 'praise be to God' when I finally had it nailed). I concluded right there and then that my lofty ambitions to become a magazine writer would have to be shelved, but that would be after I had written

The 19 Magazine Team circa 1973/74. Mick Brown at the back peeping over everyone else's head, me in the front standing next to our lovely Editor Maggie Koumi

this small piece. I couldn't give up; I wouldn't give up. Maggie had put her faith in me. Mick had put his faith in me. After about three days, I managed to put together enough words and ideas to pass muster, and to give our readers one happy – and sticky – Christmas.

FOUR

1974

ALBERT AND I

It was at the beginning of 1974 that my early mentor, Mick Brown, left *19* magazine to go and live in America, and while I felt a little sad, I also realised it was such an exciting thing to do. Since the mid-sixties, I had hankered after going to America, particularly San Francisco, but it all seemed so out of reach – and here was Mick off to New York on a one-way ticket. His role as features writer was filled by a friend of his, Albert Gayol. Mick remembers: "Albert was an old friend, teenage sidekick and fellow miscreant! I introduced him to Maggie, and he got the job."

On his return from America, Mick went on to have an enviable career as a much-respected and lauded author and serious journalist. He has written for several British broadsheets and international publications and is still a contributor to the *Daily Telegraph*. I was certainly blessed to have been coached by two wonderful people in my very early and tentative days in magazine publishing: Mick Brown and Maggie Koumi. I may have ended up in a totally different, and boring, job if it hadn't been for these two glorious beings.

Albert, as it turned out, was like Mick in so many ways, and just as loveable. He was my age but far more experienced in journalism, having started his career at the age of 16. Mick had a rudimentary fanzine called *Soulbeat*. A fanzine was usually a one-page newssheet that was written by, and for, people who were fans of a particular person or group. I guess it was a precursor to what is today a social media blog.

The fanzine was created to share the best fan art, commentary and clips with like-minded friends. Albert would also write for the fanzine. Mick's parents had a small business and owned a duplicating machine; they were able to run off multiple copies, so each copy would look fresh. The newssheet would reach its audience via hand-to-hand distribution. Its print run was somewhere in the region of 50 to 60 copies, so didn't pose too much of a threat to the ever-popular music magazine *New Musical Express*!

From One Tower To Another!

Soon after Albert started at *19* magazine, the company moved us all out of Tower House, to a new building at Waterloo called King's Reach Tower. It was an unimpressive high-rise modern office block, and *19* magazine was put on the 13th floor. The surrounding area was totally undeveloped in terms of shops and restaurants. We were all a bit despondent, having been moved from the fabulous Covent Garden area, with its buzzy atmosphere and abundance of restaurants and cafés, theatres and hotels along the Strand. There was even a small department store – the Civil Service Stores – and shops aplenty. Waterloo, in contrast, was desolate. Fast forward a few years and the area was totally transformed, with restaurants, cafés and sandwich bars popping up – even a hair salon – but for now, it was what it was: a 30-storey building, with brand-new open-plan offices and views over Waterloo rooftops.

When we first moved to King's Reach Tower, I was still in the Fashion office with Jo and Hilary. Norma, by this time, had moved on to pastures new and the start of her journey to becoming a highly respected name in the world of film costume design.

Models and photographers were always popping in, sometimes just to hang out, other times they were there for specific fashion shoots. One of my favourite photographers at that time was a guy called David Anthony. He had dark hair, was good-looking and had a slightly bad- boy look about him.

I remember one time he came into the office with a friend of his, an American singer-songwriter called Tim Hardin; dark brooding good looks and definitely bad-boy status! I was tasked with the job of entertaining Tim while Jo, and David Anthony, went off to audition models for an upcoming fashion feature.

Here was a guy I didn't know, a little the worse for wear (drugs or alcohol, I had no idea at that time), and I had to keep him amused. It was all a bit daunting, and I wasn't looking forward to the next few hours. What on earth would I talk to him about? What common ground could we possibly have? I needn't have worried. Tim was absolutely delightful. We found lots to talk about. He was interesting, amusing and somehow or other seemed to like me, serenading me at one point with one of his songs. We got on like a house on fire and the afternoon passed quickly – too quickly, in fact.

Before leaving, Tim drew me a lovely picture with a little note thanking me for being such good company. I so wish I hadn't lost that precious piece of paper. I discovered later from Jo that Tim Hardin was a successful song writer and musician. He wrote 'If I Were a Carpenter', 'Reason to Believe' and one of my personal favourites, 'Simple Song of Freedom', among many others. He was, however, a heroin addict, and I was so sad when

I heard that he died a few years after our afternoon together. He was just 39 years old. A wicked waste of such a talent, and a good guy. Drugs have taken so many lives over the years. It's heartbreaking.

On the inside, King's Reach Tower was a rather soulless building. But, as usual with Maggie at the helm, there was a real buzz about the *19* magazine office. We were a team of about 14 people, and we all got on amazingly well. After a few months, I was given the role of researcher, charged with assisting Albert. With a desk in his office, it was my job, as much as anything else, to keep him organised!

I remember a time when he was going off to an important celebrity interview. Albert was never in a hurry, and I usually had to push him out of the door! This particular day I asked him the usual questions that were totally necessary: "Do you have the address of where you're going?"

"Yes," he said.

"Do you have your notebook and tape recorder?"

"Yes," said a little more impatiently –

"And what about your camera?"

"Of course I have my camera," he growled.

"What about film for the camera and batteries for the tape recorder?"

"Err, yea, umm, let me check, err, no, I don't think I have," came his sheepish reply.

It was the kind of ritual that had to be done most days. It became a joke between us and was always said in fun, but he would be the first to admit that he needed to be kept on track.

Albert was a brilliant journalist and writer, but just not the most practical person. One thing that always fascinated me was how he wrote and edited his features. I would usually transcribe the taped interviews and type them up for him. He would then set about what in today's computer talk would be 'cut and paste', by literally doing just that. He would take a pair of scissors to my neatly typed manuscript and start cutting out paragraphs and sentences. He would then jigsaw them back together with Sellotape until he had created his feature in exactly the way he wanted it to read. Genius!

When I saw him recently, he reminded me of the time he went to interview the famous opera star Demis Roussos, whose music style would not have been top of Albert's hit list. However, after just a few minutes into the interview, Albert was asked to leave. Albert recalls, "It was Demis Roussos in person who threw me out of the Chelsea Hotel. He didn't feel that I had expressed sufficient respect for who he was, so just a few questions into the interview, he stood up and began shouting at me, 'I am a star all over the world,' while pointing to the door." I have to say, that did make me laugh. One of the most inoffensive people you could meet thrown out of the hotel by one of the biggest stars of that time.

As Albert's assistant, and researcher, I would often be sent to interview people or companies for a feature that was being written. One that sticks out in my memory was for a feature Albert was writing about battered women: 'Behind Closed Doors'. Erin Pizzey had opened the first domestic violence shelter for women and their children in Chiswick in 1971. I was tasked with going to the refuge and talking to the women there about their experiences and to those who worked there about Erin Pizzey's pioneering work. Albert did ask me if I wanted him to come along (for support), but I was determined to do this one on my own.

Mrs Pizzey had not been a newcomer to the cause of women's rights, having attended her first meeting of the UK Women's Liberation Movement in 1959. Fast forward to the 1960s and early 1970s, when the issue of women being abused in their own home was largely ignored by the establishment; Erin Pizzey was one of the first to highlight the seriousness of the problem – and do something about it. She didn't just voice her concerns; she actually did something to help by setting up the Chiswick Women's Aid Centre. There was no government funding at this time and very little support from local authorities.

However, she was a formidable and determined character, and ran afoul of 'militant' feminists when she stated that domestic violence wasn't only man against woman, but that women could also be equally as violent. She was reported as saying, "...having experienced my mother's violence, I always knew that women can be as vicious and irresponsible as men."

She put on record that she 'never saw Women's Aid as a movement that was hostile to men'. To her, it was about removing the abused from their abuser. With still no public funding, she went on to open more shelters using the only avenue available to her – squatting. That certainly did not go down well with local authorities – who regularly took her to court, prompting Lord Hailsham to state: "This appellant, and the registered charity of which she is the agent, is providing a service... which is in fact provided by no other organ of our much-vaunted system of public welfare... When people come to her door... in desperate straits and at all hours... the appellant does not turn them away... but takes them in and gives them shelter... And what happens to her when she does so? She finds herself the defendant in criminal proceedings at the suit of the local authority..."

Erin Pizzey clearly had many friends and supporters, but she also made enemies, too, in pursuit of her work.

So, it was armed with all this background information and research that I found myself outside the Chiswick Women's Aid Shelter. While I had conducted many interviews – some successfully, some not so – this task scared the life out of me. What was I expecting to find behind those locked doors? I had no idea. I had no experience of battered women, and although, as always, I had done my research and had my questions ready, I just didn't know what sort of reception I would get. I actually walked past the door three times, before taking a deep breath and knocking firmly and loudly – more to give myself confidence than to alert those inside!

The door was duly answered by one of the lovely ladies who worked there, and I soon realised that security was very tight indeed. They were always vigilant to the fact that men, looking for their partners and their children, could be waiting for the right moment to ambush. It was a real concern that terrified many of the women housed there. I remember being very saddened by what I saw: women who had literally run away from home to shelter in the refuge, leaving everything behind. Children were playing, but cautious. It hurt my heart to think what they may have witnessed in their young lives.

What I did recognise at that time, though, was that Erin Pizzey was a saviour to these women. Her dogged determination not to give in, to forge ahead with more shelters, even though there was no money available to help, and be regularly hauled up before the courts. She was thwarted at nearly every turn by agencies that could not, or did not want to, grasp the seriousness of what had been going on behind closed doors – and sadly still does today.

While writing these chapters, we are in the grip of COVID-19 and government lockdowns. Statistics that were released show that the number of women killed by domestic abuse since lockdown is three a week, although the Police and Crime Commissioner, David Jamieson, believes the real figure could be even higher. Erin Pizzey knew that she couldn't put an end to domestic abuse full stop, but that she could do everything in her power to try and give some dignity, confidence and shelter to as many women as it was in her limited power to do so. To my mind, then and now, Erin Pizzey was not perfect, but of the fact she was a pioneer, there is no doubt. I don't believe she was an idealist; she was, though, a realist. She herself was verbally battered and abused by many who should have been rallying to her cause.

I recall another time going along to interview men whose wives had left them and their children, usually to pursue another relationship in which the kiddies didn't figure. I found many of those cases incredibly sad, for the men who were not necessarily equipped to care for their brood as a mother would be, and for the children who were clearly missing their mums. I could not imagine any situation where I would leave my children behind while I sought a different life elsewhere.

19 magazine was always balanced, never one-sided in favour of the female. Maggie was not afraid to tackle subjects that were not openly talked about in the 1970s either – such as battered men, racism, drugs, mental health, abortion, incest and adoption. These types of features wouldn't raise an eyebrow now, but back in the 1960s and 1970s, eyebrows were raised. *19* was a magazine ahead of the times, however, and Maggie Koumi an editor who never shied away from difficult subjects.

Working with Albert was always fun, and while he loved tackling the social issues of the time, he was never happier than when he was pursuing interviews with the good and the great of the music industry. Music was a passion of his and it allowed both him and me to attend many record and album launches. In the day, these were lavish affairs with champagne flowing, plenty to eat and goody bags to take home. They would go on all afternoon and often into the evening.

There are a couple of these that stand out in my mind. The first was when Johnny Bristol released his record 'Hang On In There Baby'. While I loved the music and the guy, the reason it stands out is that I ended up going back to the office with my arms full of bottles of champagne. Every press reception was bigger and better than the previous one – and whether it was for a record release or a beauty product, there were gifts galore for the press.

The second press event that I remember very well was a lunch for the launch of a new perfume. Joanna Lumley was guest of honour. Most of the invited press were beauty editors (not assistants), and I felt a little bit intimidated. I had not expected it to be such a big affair and I didn't feel 'dressed for the part'. I did sense (maybe imagined) a few slightly disapproving glances. I felt completely out of my depth, my confidence ebbing away.

I was seated at the same table as the delightful Joanna Lumley. I remember it was a large round table and Joanna was seated opposite me. Questions were being fired at her from all sides by the beauty editors. I sat quietly, not wanting to draw attention to myself by asking a question. It must have been

The beautiful Joanna Lumley, my 'champagne buddy'!
Photo: Gemma Levine

evident because I looked up to find Joanna Lumley locking eyes with me; she smiled and winked. Such a small gesture, but it immediately lifted me. She could clearly sense my discomfort and tried to put me at my ease. I thought that was such a kind thing to do, and in my mind's eye, she was saying, *Aren't these ladies a bore – let's go drink champagne!*

When I met up recently with Albert and Maggie, we were, of course, reminiscing about what a great time we had during those many years working together at *19*. Albert recalled the time he upset Brian Ferry, who banned him from further interviews and concerts for knocking Roxy Music's 'Country Life' album: "I just didn't realise my opinion was so important to him! In retrospect, though, I regret what I said about the album because I got to actually really like it."

There was also the time he came back to the office rather starry-eyed after interviewing Debbie Harry. He had been backstage with her and her band as they were getting ready to play a gig at the Hammersmith Odeon: "Blondie was getting ready to go on stage," remembered Albert. "There I was, one of the million Debbie Harry admirers, in a unique and privileged

My dear Albert Gayol and Maggie Koumi, circa 2019

situation, acting as if I wasn't looking, open-mouthed, as Debbie rushed about half naked, getting dressed for the show. She was obviously used to dressing in front of anybody backstage so it wasn't a big deal for her – but for me…"

Albert's career as a music journalist was most definitely an eventful one, from the Demis Roussos episode to having coffee served to him by Omar Sharif in his Park Lane hotel suite – and so much more in between. It soon became clear to me that here was another person who would be influential in my life. Albert taught me so much, and I was so pleased he trusted me enough, as his assistant, to carry out some difficult interviews on his behalf.

It Wasn't All Serious Reporting!

In addition to keeping Albert organised, my job as researcher was to trawl through the daily papers to identify any stories that could make relevant feature copy for the magazines. You learn very quickly to skim-read, looking for words that drew you in rather than whole paragraphs. I enjoyed that part of research, and the latent detective in me loved digging much deeper to find out more. Bearing in mind there was no Google or Yahoo to take you there in seconds, it really was a matter of one lead taking you to another lead – usually by phone, occasionally by letter, often by foot or via the library.

Even now, I still enjoy solving the impossible, except today I have search engines on my side, but I somehow feel like I am cheating. I also find, due to the constant skim-reading of my past professional life, that I rarely read a complete article. I find myself jumping from one part to another in no particular order. I very often start at the end of an article and work backwards to the beginning, a few paragraphs at a time.

One of the more bizarre pieces I reported on was after

picking up on a small article in one of the national papers about how bad the toilets were in London department stores. I came to wish I hadn't brought it to anyone's attention after I was given the assignment of going around London, checking out the public toilet facilities. The aim: to find which were the best, how well signposted they were in the store, and which really did not stand up to scrutiny. I believe we published our Top Ten Guide to London Loos after I had completed my 'undercover' work.

There was one other feature I researched and for this I called in the help of some friends from my local pub. Tom and Popsy Grehan, a delightful Irish couple, had taken over the pub. They had two sons, John and Paul, and a daughter Mandy. We all became like family very quickly and still are, more than 40 years later. They moved back to Ireland a few years after we met but always stayed in contact. Popsy became my best friend and confidante.

Taken at the Three Degrees Concert at The Dome in Brighton with Paul Grehan and John Grehan either side of Valerie Holiday, and me on the end. Circa 1979

I sometimes worked behind the bar, because I enjoyed it, and on occasion would send John, the younger of the two brothers, to attend press events on my behalf and I would do his bar shift. Sarah Brightman was one of the record launches he went to – and he was born to it. He loved to chat and was never daunted by any situation. He was about 19 at the time. I was also given tickets to go and see The Three Degrees, at the Dome in Brighton, by their agent, and a pass to go to the press event after the concert. It was just John, Paul and me – they were big fans of The Three Degrees, as were many people then. It was a big deal. I have a picture of the three of us with Valerie Holiday of The Three Degrees, and it brings back happy memories of the time.

A vox pop piece I was doing for *19* magazine was to seek out the best of London's disco scene. I once again engaged the services of John, Paul and Mandy to do the rounds of clubs with me. We had a great time, and most of the discos made us very welcome when they knew I was writing a feature. However, there was one that was not quite so welcoming.

The club was virtually empty when we walked in. We settled in and had a drink. I explained to one of the people who worked there that I was there to do a bit of research for a feature I was writing. Ten minutes later, a man of substantial size came and asked me to go with him to the owner's office. Off I confidently trotted. When I got in there, I felt distinctly uncomfortable. Another large guy, with an unsmiling face, sat behind a desk and started quizzing me about why I was there, what I was going to write about, why choose his club, etc.

Finally, I stood up, expressed my annoyance at having been dragged into his office for an inquisition, and we all departed toot sweet! Much later, when we were talking about how bizarre it was, we could only think it was connected to a drugs racket. I mean, please, you only had to look at my stature, all 4' 10" of me, to see I was not trying to take over his patch!

That wasn't half as scary, though, as the time I was in Morocco with my husband, testing out one of the holiday experiences that would then be written up as a feature review piece for the magazine. We decided to take a boat trip across to Gibraltar. Not long into the journey, I was approached by one of the crew and told that the captain wanted to have a word with me. I went with him to the captain's cabin, where a guy was sitting behind a desk, flanked by two others. On his desk was a gun and on the belts of the other two.

I was asked for my passport. I duly handed it over. He was quiet for a while and spoke in a language I didn't understand to his comrades. I was then asked to stay where I was, and he went off somewhere, returning minutes later asking me what kind of journalist I was. The penny dropped. I had handed over my passport to be stamped when I boarded, and my passport stated that my occupation was journalist.

Clearly, because of issues that had been going on for some years between Britain, Spain and Europe, the guy had put two and two together and made five. He assumed that I was a British newspaper journalist, out to cause problems between the three countries over the Straits of Gibraltar. It took me some time to assure him that I wrote for women's magazines, and I was not a newspaper reporter, war correspondent or any other type of journalist destined to cause trouble.

After what seemed a very long time, he violently stamped my passport and dismissed me with a wave of his hand. I have to say my imagination had run riot and I visualised myself not being allowed to get off on arrival at Gibraltar, nor when I returned to Morocco, in case I was responsible for some kind of coup! A life on the ocean waves was most unappealing at that point.

LIFE AFTER ALBERT!

In 1978, Albert left *19* magazine. He eventually moved to Spain and now lives a quiet life with his wife, children and grandchildren. Our days working together were special times indeed.

Albert's position as writer was taken over by the clever and talented Linda Newman (one of the co-writers of this book). I had worked with Linda in the early days when we were both 16-years-old, enjoying life at Tower House. Now, more than ten years later, here we were working together once again. Apart from gender, Linda was not far removed from Albert in personality, style and in being a gifted writer. We were a good match, and it softened the pain of losing Albert to Spain. Linda and I were both born under the star sign Aries in the same year. I was older by two weeks.

When Maggie recruited new people, she was very often a little swayed by the sign they were born under. I have since come to wonder if this explains why everyone who worked on *19* magazine got along so well together and, indeed, were a close knit 'community'.

Linda and I only worked together for about a year and a half because I became pregnant with my first son and went on maternity leave in 1980. I remember the time we worked together, though, as great fun. We had a similar sense of humour and, of course, a lot in common, having worked together previously. Suffice to say that we are still meeting for lunch today, over 50 plus years since we first met, and are still the best of friends. I have certainly been very lucky indeed to have worked with so many generous and talented people, who inspired me to take on challenges that I might otherwise not have had the confidence to do.

Sharing our office was beauty editor, Caroline Richards.

While I carried on with my research work in Features, I also assisted Caroline, which kept me on my toes and introduced me to the beauty side of the business. On first meeting, Caroline was a formidable character. She was tall, direct and didn't suffer fools gladly. Thank goodness then I was no fool! We made an odd couple when attending press events together, with me 4'10" and Caroline not far off 6ft. We made a good team, though, which held us in good stead on our next venture.

FIVE

1980

Hair & Good Looks was Born

Caroline Richards – as beauty editor – and I worked together producing several hair supplements for *19*. They turned out to be hugely popular with the readers. On the back of these pieces, the idea of the *1980 Hair Book* was born. This started as one issue a year, then the following year we did two issues, and by 1982/3, we were producing three a year. After having my son, I continued to work freelance for the *Hair Book*. Maggie was editor, with Caroline and I writing the editorial.

IPC Magazines, at that time, were looking for new titles to launch, so in 1984, *Hair & Good Looks* was conceived, as a stand-alone publication, cutting its sibling ties with *19*. The magazine specifically focused on hair and beauty. Caroline left the position of beauty editor at *19* to become editor of *Hair & Good Looks*. I was employed as features editor. Steve Poole, who I had worked with on *19*, and who I got on well with, was art director and Heather Warwicker worked alongside him. Anita Pai was production editor.

The magazine launched alongside two others, one a fashion title and the other a food title. Only *Hair & Good Looks* was the

*Left to right: Steve Poole, Editor Caroline Richards, myself, Anita Pai
and Heather Warwicker at the launch of Hair & Good Looks*

real success story though selling, at its height, 200,000 copies, which would be unheard-of today. Mind you, it nearly didn't launch at all. We were working on the first edition when the National Union of Journalists, of whom I was a member, came out on strike. We knew if the magazine didn't come out as scheduled, it wouldn't come out at all. We therefore took the decision to cross the picket line that stood menacingly outside King's Reach Tower. As you might imagine, it wasn't a popular thing to do, and I was extremely intimidated as I went into the building and when I came out again.

I was summoned to explain myself by the NUJ once the strike was over, along with Caroline. Both she and I were thrown out of the union. But we lived to tell the tale, and a highly successful magazine was saved.

Do Make Me Over!

Reader makeovers were extremely popular on *Hair & Good Looks*. We would enlist the help of top hairdressers and make-up artists to assess the person's look and give them an image transformation. I worked with many top beauty photographers and make-up artists of the time. If a reader puts their faith in you to give them a fabulous new look, you tend to build a small team of professionals that you trust implicitly to do the job.

Not all hairdressers were easy to work with though. It was the beginning of the era of so-called celebrity hair stylists, and one or two of them took the 'title' far too seriously. On one particular shoot, we enlisted the help of a top London salon, who subsequently sent one of their up-and-coming but rather arrogant stylists to do the shoot. This guy was eight years younger than me, and I soon found his ego far outweighed his talent and ability.

I recall that he was expecting the 'commander-in-chief' (Caroline Richards) to be running the session, not her 'petty officer' (me)! He complained to the photographer that he was not prepared to work with a mere assistant and instructed him to call Caroline. The photographer, a lovely guy I often worked with, was mortified on my behalf. However, Caroline wasn't free at the time to come over, so we called the salon to see if they had another stylist they wanted to send and explained why.

Thirty minutes later, the 'top man' appeared and took over the job of creating beautiful hair – with me in charge! He was a household name (married to a popular Scottish singer), and someone who was far more entitled to flaunt the 'celebrity hair stylist' tag, but he never did. He got to work on the hair, apologising to me for his assistant's behaviour. He was charming, good-looking and kind. He saved the day and I so appreciated him for doing that.

Hairdressers enjoyed working with us; it was good promotion for their business, plus *Hair & Good Looks* was a great magazine, well designed and well written.

As well as organising regular makeovers, I also wrote many of the beauty and lifestyle features. One that sticks out in my mind was a nine-page feature about eyes, aptly called 'Eye Society'. It covered everything to do with choosing glasses, face shapes, eye colour, eye make-up, and so on. I remember it well because it won an award for Best Eye feature from Dolland & Aitchison. It's the little things that make you happy!

Moving On...

In late 1985, I became pregnant with my second child, Amy. She was born in August 1986. I went back to work for a short while but then decided to go freelance. I wasn't confident that I would get any freelance work at all, if I'm honest – but I was wrong. Having been in the industry for a lot of years and having made many contacts and friends during that time, I was able to write to editors offering my services for hair features, beauty makeovers and general features.

I wrote a feature for *Practical Parenting* on the pros and cons of christenings and the different approach that is taken by each religion. After it was published, I was invited onto a TV programme to discuss the feature and chat about my findings. This was in 1988, soon after my third child, Michael, was born. I initially turned it down, citing the new baby (secretly, I didn't think I was TV material). However, that plan was foiled when they told me to bring the baby along. Embarrassingly, Michael cried throughout much of the programme and had to be taken off the set. Although it went okay, I was right. I was not TV material!

I know I was incredibly lucky to get the opportunities I did,

Kicking off my PR career with a profile feature in Hairdressers Journal. New beginnings!
Photo courtesy of: Hairdressers Journal Int. Reed Business Publishing.

none of which I really went looking for, but fate decided to take me by the hand and lead me from one fabulous encounter to another. I wouldn't change any of it.

I was sweet 16 when I joined George Newnes Publishing, and it was a year or more before I got to taste the real life behind magazine work – but what a joy it turned out to be, from the day I started to the day I finally left in 1987 to become a freelance journalist and take up my new career – as a Public Relations Consultant.

I would like to dedicate my story to my dear husband, who so sadly never got to see the finished result but, I know, would have been proud of what I (and the other Magazine Girls) have achieved. I would also like to thank my family and friends who have been so supportive and encouraging throughout this book-writing journey, and which really helped to spur me on.

JAN'S STORY

Stepping inside the star-dusted pages of Valentine *magazine, I come face to face with my pop idols whose posters decorate my bedroom walls. It's 1969, I'm 16 and thrust headlong into the creative colourful buzz of activity that makes up a magazine life.*

ONE

Ready, Steady, Go!

I come from a big-hearted family in an East London backwater beside the flowing currents of dockland life. Where girls like me left school at 15 to work in factories and shops, or, if they hit the job jackpot, in typing pools. I fantasised about being a writer or an actress although you couldn't get above yourself where I come from.

Girls like me didn't end up interviewing pop stars for a living.

Yet, here I am striding right out of those humble beginnings, stepping inside a swanky rock 'n' roll limo purring past downtown avenues all neon-lit and star-bursting. It's 1970, New

Music scribes posing for my camera before being chauffeured to a rock concert New York City. Circa 1970

York City, where rock is louder, jeans tighter and rules looser. I am being chauffeured to an Alice Cooper gig with a bunch of young journalists, while the scribe seated beside me with the big bouncy 'Afro' jiggles to a Byrds jangly guitar riff blaring from the radio.

Arriving at the theatre, we spill out into the night in our glam-rock glad rags, our feathers and fedoras when someone mistakes us for a coterie of rock 'n' rollers, steps forward and takes our photograph. No time to pose or offer our best profiles, it's *showtime...*

Welcome to the demonic, hot-as-hell domain of Alice Cooper's 'Nightmare' show featuring a giant Cyclops, decapitated dolls, outré explosions and special effects. The macabre figure of the Shock Rocker in his signature ghoulish face paint, sprayed-on leather leotard and top hat appears centre stage in the spotlight, cracking his whip like some demented ringmaster. Alice's '70s rock circus is over the (big) top, and the fans love it.

After the gig I am driven to meet Alice Cooper at the hotel where he's staying, half-expecting to find Alice's alter ego swinging from the opulent hotel's chandelier with a rotating reptile and a gaggle of groupies. No such luck.

Flopped in front of the telly, wearing a baseball cap, shapeless t-shirt and jeans, and surfing the TV channels, Alice is drowsy and looks ready for a cup of Horlicks and an early night. Being 'Normal Norman' seems weird on Alice Cooper. But then, in the decades working as a pop and showbusiness journalist, normal had nothing to do with any of it.

So how did a girl like me end up interviewing pop and rock stars in the first place? To crash a job on a top-selling national teenage magazine with only a handful of O levels when today the equivalent entry-level assistant/general dogsbody would need letters behind her name.

I left school in 1968 and got a job in a secretarial pool at a City of London bank. A few months later, I saw an ad in the *Evening Standard* for an office junior to work on a teen magazine, went for the interview and was offered the job on the spot. I was lucky to arrive just as they were throwing away the rule book. Within six months, I got promoted to junior features writer. It was as easy as that.

The '60s was an epic moment in time to be a teenager. There was a transformative cultural and fashion movement taking place, known as the Youth Quake, whose poster child was Twiggy. My childhood London of the '50s went from a post-war city scattered with bombsites – my rubble-splattered playground growing up – to a sassy style icon known as Swinging London. It teemed with musicians, models, fashion designers, artists and rock stars, all beautiful, all impossibly young and impossibly thin. Suddenly smart working-class kids like me were making good, and for a fleeting moment it felt as though the young ruled the world.

Bands could make a record in a fortnight. They could be stacking shelves at Tesco one minute and rocketing up the hit parade and appearing on 'Top of the Pops' the next. It was possible to discover the next big thing, and get excited about new forms of music.

A week into my job I came face to face with The Hollies in the corridor, and I almost fainted with the shock. One of the first pop stars I interviewed as a 'rookie' was Marc Bolan, who very sweetly insisted he walk me to the bus stop from his parents' home in Hackney when our interview ran late.

It didn't seem like work. At least, nothing like my dad's back-bending toil unloading ships' cargo down at the docks, with all the attendant strikes and militant action to improve poor wages and working conditions for himself and the men in his charge. Wasn't I the lucky one, then, being paid decent money just to swan around with pretty pop stars?

A mishmash of memory snapshots of celebrity encounters

such as... a game of darts with The Who...Waiting for the gasman in Phil Lynott's kitchen over mugs of tea, with the Thin Lizzy frontman high as a kite at 10am... An impromptu chat on the phone with David Bowie talking about cockney accents and his new album, 'Hunky Dory', that dog-eared copy he gave me I still have today and love just as much ...

I remember having the cheek to discuss body odour issues with Status Quo on a sweltering hot day, with Rick Parfitt inviting me to sniff his armpit as I took notes.

I even kidded myself that I might be in with a chance with Harrison Ford when he and I shared a beer on his day off from filming 'Star Wars' at Elstree Studios, while he pulled my leg about fancying skinny girls. It was all a bit mad, really.

I've Got The Music In Me

For as long as I can remember, there was always music in our house. As I kid, I would lay awake on a Saturday night in a trippy half-awake state to listen to the grown-ups singing their hearts out in the streets after they had been turfed out of the pubs.

My best friend, Patty, lived a few doors along the landing from us. We'd dress up in her mum's high-heel shoes, look at the pin-ups in her film magazines or play Cliff and Elvis singles. Patty liked Cliff, and I was a fan of Elvis. Years later as a journalist I met Cliff Richard, although sadly, I never met Elvis. Cliff had converted to Christianity and he showed up looking like a bank manager in a suit and horn-rimmed spectacles, bearing little resemblance to the rock 'n' roll heart-throb Patty had fallen for. I found Cliff charming, but I never liked his music.

I guess I was influenced to a degree by my teenage Teddy Boy uncles and the music at parties held at our house, when I would sneak out of bed and listen in the shadows to skiffle and rock 'n' roll. At such gatherings, I was captivated by the hyper-femme wiles of my aunties, Barbara, Kathy and the two Junes, with their petticoats peeping out from under full-circle skirts, and the scratchy 'shick-shick' sound of their nylon stockings as they danced in their stiletto slingbacks. Kathy came from a big East End family, genetically blessed with beauty and talent. She and her cousins, the actor Terence Stamp and his late brother, Chris, the manager of The Who and Jimi Hendrix's record producer grew up together and were very close as kids. "He's not the film star Terence Stamp to me, he's just 'Terry.'"

The day my dad bought a radiogram on the never-never, we celebrated with a massive dance-a-thon. If I close my eyes, I can still picture my parents jiving in the front room, with Dad turning Mum like a spinning top to Dion and the Belmonts rockabilly doo-wop. Dad was skint most of the time so he had to work overtime to pay off the weekly Hire Purchase payments.

The Second World War gobbled up my parents' youth. Dad joined the Royal Navy at the start of the war in 1939 when he turned 17, and fought until it ended in 1945. He was on the Arctic conveys to Russia, and participated in major campaigns in the Mediterranean, Africa, and the D-Day landings in France. He cavalierly kept his many medals in a shoe box, and he let me and my brother play with them.

Mum was 14-years-old at the onset of the London Blitz; living close to the docks, the area was a target for the Luftwaffe. When the bombs dropped, she would hide under the kitchen table or make a dash for the air-raid shelter with her mother and three younger brothers. To help with the war effort, she worked on her uncle's farm in Kent. From there, she would commute by train to and from London in the blackout to work in a factory making soldiers' uniforms.

Dad was demobbed when the war ended, having fought all the way through it. Post-traumatic stress syndrome wasn't acknowledged then, and there was no welfare state to fall back

My twin brother Jeff and I at The Tropicana Coffee bar 1966

on. Ex-servicemen like Dad had to somehow muddle through, find work and start their lives afresh.

My twin brother Jeff and I were born in the early '50s in the aftermath of the war when they still had rationing, but the deprivations of post-war Britain were somewhat diffused by living in a family of comedians, who resolutely looked on the funny side of life even if there was little to laugh about. All in all, I had a happy childhood although memory is selective, we filter out the bad and exaggerate the good. My parents were non-conventional for the times, as my dad was a hands-on parent. I adored them both. Mum lived to be 95, and in her twilight years had Marie the hairdresser come to the house once a week to style her still-lustrous silver-blonde mane, until the end.

Growing up, Jeff and I were close. As fashion-forward 14-year-old Mods in 1966, we dressed in mohair suits, made-to-measure from a stall in Poplar Market; we listened to Tamla, soul and bluebeat records and went to dances at the Ilford Palais. There was a pool of my brother's good-looking friends I could date. The lost East London pubs full of drag queens, live music, West Ham football stars and local villains were the entertainment palaces of our misspent youth. Always packed, you had to fight your way through the crowd to reach the bar. As soon as you opened the door, you were hit by the heat of the crowd, the whiff of beer mixed with ciggie smoke and Estée Lauder Youth Dew, and the roaring boom of sweet soul music.

As underage 14-year-olds, my friends and I hid beneath layers of pan stick, heavy eye make-up and strobe lighting, so we could order our gin and limes with impunity. One minute we would be dancing around our handbags to a live band or a DJ spinning some great sounds, or we'd be trying to emulate the groovy moves of the go-go dancers on the stage, the next there'd be a fight break out, and half a dozen blokes would pile on top of each other in a bundle of bodies; punching, kicking and thrashing the daylights out of each other. We got so used to pub brawls that at the sign of the first punch, we'd pick up our handbags, our drinks and ciggies and flee to the toilets.

Jeff wasn't a fighter, unlike our cousin Paul. When he and Jeff went out drinking it usually ended in a punch up. Paul was a lovable rogue with a temper that got him into trouble, resulting in a spell in Her Majesty's prison. Tragically, boys I knew got very badly hurt, and then it would affect you. My best friend's boyfriend had just turned 16 when he was fatally stabbed in a street brawl. I went with her to the undertaker's – so we could see his handsome young face for the last time and say goodbye. The tragedy haunted us for weeks.

After my Mod phase I turned into a Flower Child and bought my peacock-strutting hippy gear, my Ossie Clark knock-offs and Top Shop 'seconds' at Roman Road market stalls at knocked-down prices. And let's not forget all the clobber that 'fell off the back of a lorry', that endearing euphemism we used for stolen goods.

Mum took us to Watney Street Market where Alma Cogan's uncle had a children's shop, lined with racks of princess pink chiffon-layered party frocks, fluffy mohair boleros, boys' velvet suits and bow ties. On the walls were signed photographs of his superstar niece in a dazzling array of '50s décolleté evening gowns. My six-year-old self was magnetised by those glamour shots; I wanted to be like the voluptuous Alma Cogan when I grew up. Unfortunately, at 13, I was a beanpole Twiggy who stuffed her 32-inch bra with tissues. I hated my figure, yet, ironically, I had the perfect body shape for the skinny-obsessed '60s.

THE TEENAGE YEARS

A girl I knew lived next door to Kenny Jones, drummer with The Small Faces, and she got me in to see The Small Faces concert at Queen Mary College in the Mile End Road on 19th March 1966. I remember the date because it was my first pop concert and it took place two days before my 13th birthday and three months before The World Cup. That summer my family of dyed-in-the-wool West Ham United supporters went berserk with football fever: Not only was Bobby Moore England's skipper, the winning goals were scored by West Ham players Martin Peters and legendary hat-trick hero Geoff Hurst. It was The Hammers' finest hour.

Small Faces' 'Itchycoo Park', with its poetic references to ducks and 'dreaming spires', was supposedly written about Shadwell Park, where I played as a child. It's in an area steeped in maritime history, overlooking the Thames at Wapping, where Captain Cook had his lodgings following his marriage to a local girl.

Wapping today is an expensive waterside neighbourhood of *tony* condos and converted lofts; it was once a fully operational docks where my dad unloaded ships' cargo into the tall gothic-style warehouses that flanked the narrow cobbled streets, and where the old mariner-style pubs were located. After a hard day's graft, Dad might walk down the quayside stairs towards the Town of Ramsgate pub for a swift pint before alighting on his bike to wobble home. Captain Bligh lived in Wapping from 1785 and, like my dad, he supposedly enjoyed a pitcher of ale in the Town of Ramsgate before setting sail on his epic voyage on the 'Bounty'. He met Fletcher Christian in Wapping, the man who cast him adrift in the famous mutiny.

It was in this slither of Old London where me and my boyfriend did much of our early courting over a pint of Guinness and a packet of cheese and onion crisps in the historic Prospect of Whitby pub. To impress me, Andy, then an apprentice engineer, blew a week's wages on a slap-up meal in the pub's upstairs oak-panelled restaurant overlooking the Thames.

In the nearby Georgian square, we fantasised about someday owning one of the handsome houses that faced each other across a central garden that covered the former entrance to London Docks. But it was celebrities, lawyers and Harley Street doctors who bought up the old warehouses and properties, worth millions today, and the locals didn't get a look-in.

Back in 1966, there was a youth club in the basement of one of those splendid Georgian houses, where local kids could go, that kept them off the streets and out of trouble.

Descending the stone steps to the basement one night, I heard the perky staccato beat of Shirley Ellis' clapping song. Me and a friend rushed onto the dance floor to clap alongside two other girls, then afterwards we struck up a conversation. One of the girls was a tawny beauty named Olivia who lived in Wapping with her mother and brother and was studying Drama. Evidently too modest to tell us herself, I discovered from her friend that Olivia had won the coveted role of Juliet in Franco Zeffirelli's 'Romeo and Juliet', and was about to fly to Rome to start shooting the movie. My early claim to fame was doing the hand-jive with the 15-year-old Olivia Hussey.

Another not-yet-famous person, Paul Simon, had left his native New York to seek fame in London and was living in Wapping in 1966, with his girlfriend, Kathy, immortalised in 'Kathy's Song' and 'America'. Simon was staying at Dellow House, a faded Victorian tenement belonging to Judith Piepe, a German refugee involved in the London folk scene who was helping to promote Simon's work. Judith befriended struggling artistes and musicians who went on to become famous; Al Stewart, Cat Stevens and Sandy Denny would crash at the flat if they had nowhere else to stay.

My brother Jeff started a band in the early 1970s, so he and his bandmate John would visit Judith's flat with their guitars, to play and hang out. Jeff took me to meet Judith and her son, who handcrafted guitars, lutes and lyres, and he had dropped off a guitar he'd custom made for Jeff. Judith talked about Paul Simon's days as a struggling young folkie around the London folk circuit playing in smoky cellar clubs, launderettes and working-class pubs, or anywhere he could get up and perform before an audience who would listen. According to Judith, Simon wasn't motivated by money or fame but by sheer love of the music. He wanted as many people as possible to hear his songs.

When I wasn't listening to music, I had my head stuck in a book. I had a brilliant English teacher at school named Mr Casey, who won over his philistine pupils making language seem real and alive, magical yet accessible. Shakespeare, poetry and the Classics were as much fun to read as the magazines I read at home.

In my Girl Guide days, I devoured all the action-packed picture-strip comics with public-school tough-girl heroines from the pages of *Bunty* and *Judy*, then, as a fashion-freak teen, I progressed to *Petticoat* where I first spotted Twiggy modelling on its front page and I fell instantly in love with her 'gawky' style. I got to meet Twiggy some years later, when I interviewed her about transitioning from modelling to acting and singing, expecting her to be 'up herself', as she had gained a reputation for being a bit of a madam. *Au contraire*, I found her warm and funny, with a big honking laugh. Minutes into our interview, my tape recorder conked out and I couldn't get it to work for the life of me. Twiggy, like a heroine from *Bunty*, stepped in, fixed my tape machine and saved the day.

A MAGAZINE GIRL IS BORN

The 'white-collar' career prospects in the '60s – for working-class girls like me –were found in the typing pools of insurance companies, building societies, banks and the civil service. Many working-class kids stayed at home until they married and were expected to pay for their board and lodging once they started work. I handed over two pounds a week to my mum until I left home.

In my first job after leaving school, I spent a miserable few months miscast in a bank, doing clerical work, but I didn't hang about. In 1968, when work was plentiful, you could cherry-pick jobs. There were no unpaid internships then; you learnt on the job and you got your wage packet – paid in cash in those days – and sometimes with luncheon vouchers thrown in.

At the interview for the job on *Mirabelle,* it didn't start off very well. I got lost trying to find the editor's office, when a nice old lady I thought was the cleaner came to my rescue. I arrived flustered and late, so it was just as well the young bouffant-haired male editor Paul, with the vibe of a pop star, was laid-back. As I tried to explain the reason for my tardiness, the lady herself popped her head around the door and beamed at me. "Meet my mother," said the editor.

So began magazine life as a 'foot-in-mouth', tea-making office junior, earning the princely sum of seven quid a week, which in a careful and considered way I straightaway blew on a new Biba frock.

First, I was given the task of replying to the readers' letters, and I was directly under the watchful gaze of Bill, our dapper editor-in-chief, a spruce Scotsman with a penchant for sharp tailored suits, shiny shoes and pongy aftershave, who complimented me one day on my economical writing style. I assumed it was complimentary. I dashed over to the Features department to ask what 'economical style' actually meant.

A few months later, I flipped over to *Valentine* magazine, just around the corner from the *Mirabelle* office, as it offered better prospects for a writing job; they only had a Features editor, who wrote most of the magazine's editorial content and pop articles. I had a mentor-protégé relationship with its editor, Trudie, a clever 23-year-old rising star of magazine journalism and a dead ringer for Vivienne Leigh in 'Gone with the Wind'. The aforementioned Features editor Jackie and I hit it off right away and I quickly became her sidekick. Both women took the 16-year-old me under their wing and appreciated my energy and enthusiasm while just about tolerating my alarming frankness (which, in my defence, is an inherited trait). They showed great generosity in helping me and the other young staffers to develop and become part of the team. Despite this, the constant stream of amazing creative types I was thrown together with still left this Stepney kid feeling out of her depth, until I figured a way to feel less intimidated.

A new girl named Debbie (the Deb) joined the editorial team. She was the first upper-class 'toff' I'd met, although I doubt if there were any cockneys who lived in a council house among her social circle. In that regard, our respective backgrounds were a weird source of fascination to the both of us. She was all right, if you liked that sort of thing, and could be quite charming when she wasn't name-dropping about her 'friend' Lord-haw-haw-haw or bragging about being an 'Old Girl' of Benenden, the elite public school she attended with 'fellow classmate' Princess Anne. Then she was a proper twat. Debbie finally galloped off to work in advertising, and so, by default, I took on some of her writing tasks.

I was given a weekly column to write about the adventures of Tone, *Valentine*'s resident 'heart-throb'. The readers didn't have a clue that he was made up, or that we used the headshot of a gay male model. I didn't make a very convincing bloke, either, and sometimes Tone's ramblings came across as unintentionally funny.

Jackie and I got lots of invites to work-related events and parties. We went to singer-songwriter Labi Siffre's debut album release, 'It Must Be Love', the classic pop song Madness later recorded and had a massive hit with. We sat on the grass in Regent's Park to interview Mungo Jerry when 'In the Summertime' got to Number One and was being played everywhere in that summer of 1970.

We attended the screening of Paul Newman's latest film and afterwards his PR lady deposited him at the bar to have a drink with us. It was impossible to pay attention to anything other than Newman's classical Greek-god beauty, so I hadn't a clue what we talked about, but Jackie kept it together and asked all the right questions. Newman wasn't very tall, and he seemed to visibly shrink when we two Amazonians stood beside him. Newman's famous blue eyes really popped.

As he was one of the last great 20th-century movie stars, with classic roles in 'The Sting' and 'Butch Cassidy' with Robert Redford, just grabbing Newman for a 20-minute interview was considered a scoop. Back at the office, we padded out the interview to make a one-pager, added some eye-candy photos and trumped it up with a saucy cover line: 'Our Night with Paul Newman!' Ta-da!

Valentine, launched in 1957 – coincidentally the same year Newman became a star – emerged from the post-war austerity that lasted well into the 1970s. The readership was younger than *Boyfriend*, *Rave* and *Petticoat* and, like *Mirabelle* it featured illustrated picture strips and interviews and double-page spreads of pop stars. Leafing through some of my vintage copies, with their vast offering of '*Groovy brilliance*', is to witness the capriciousness of cultural trends and fashions: from rock and roll and the swinging sixties to the punk revolution and beyond.

When I arrived in late 1969, they still ran the picture-strip romances and the 1,000-word fiction stories I would later turn my hand to writing. As with most modern romance magazines, and the '50s pulp fiction before them, the illustrations for the strips were stylistically executed; the 1970 version when I worked at the magazine had a psychedelic vibe that mimicked the 'look' of the time.

Initially, readers picked up the teenage mags at the newsagents for those tempting headlines ('Boys! Boys! Boys!'), and then they were drawn in by the busy fun covers and the content within. At the height of their popularity, teen magazines practically flew off the shelves, owing to the access they offered their teenage readers to their favourite 'heart-throbs'. For young women longing for a personal connection with stars they might never meet in person, stacks of treasured teen magazines were the next best thing.

Writing for *Valentine* as a 17-year-old, I shared the dreams and aspirations of my peers. Most of the staff were young, and the few that were over the age of 30 we arrogantly dismissed as boring old farts. That makes me laugh today, because now I am one.

Valentine was located on the top floor of Fleetway House, just off Fleet Street in the small warren-like offices we shared with *Rave*, *Mirabelle* and *Loving*. Then we moved in 1971 to the Weldon building near Covent Garden fruit market. Fortunately, my bombastic teenage personality was no hindrance to forming friendships with colleagues who worked on those magazines, and have lasted to this day.

I was the youngest in our circle of Magazine Girls. A few of them had already eased themselves into editorships by the time I arrived: Janice Collier and Ann Carpenter, beauty and fashion editors of *Loving* respectively, seemed enviably sophisticated and slightly aloof uber-professionals. They inhabited a rainbow

Outside the Mirabelle offices. Left to right: Magazine Girl Sandie Robbie, Santa AKA Mirabelle artist Richard Brookes, Magazine Girl Linda Newman and me. Circa 1970

world of vivid make-up palettes and racks of fashion-forward clothes, where a revolving door of skinny models paraded with their huge portfolios. *Loving*'s fashion assistant, Penny Saunders, was usually joined at the hip with her hipster photographer boyfriend, Ian. Sandie Robbie was the young gunslinger at *Mirabelle*. Her colleague the pop-star-mad Linda Newman was all swishing long blonde hair and chutzpah – whose adoration for Scott Walker was part of the office folklore.

Once I found my feet, it was *very heaven* to work on teenage magazines with so many talented young creatives. Girls like us, secure in our beliefs and opinions, were able in no small measure, to shape the trends of pop culture.

Out of the blue, Jackie announced she was leaving the

magazine; she wasn't a mad crazy pop fan like I was, and besides, she had outgrown *Valentine* and the teen genre in general and had decided to accept an offer to work on the launch of a new woman's magazine called *Eve*. The question was, who was going to fill Jackie's big shoes and cover all major pop interviews?

Oh, go on then, I'll do it.

TWO

I REMEMBER WHEN
ROCK WAS YOUNG

For the purpose of researching this book, I spend an evening dancing and hanging out by myself, getting lost in the rhythms and the beats of the '60s and '70s: Led Zeppelin, Aretha, The Stones and Prince Buster on the turntable, up full pelt.

Absorbed in a glitter-tinged recollection, I sift through dog-eared photographs and a portfolio of yellowed press cuttings scattered across the floor – the ones I hadn't thrown away or lost in the move to Montreal in 1992.

I jot down some names of celebrities I'd met over the years, snippets of a broad church of artists.

Patti Smith holding court in a punk club in New York City, waxing philosophical about the Romantic poets, leather jackets and Bob Dylan's shades.

The gamine Jane Birkin, speed-knitting and chain-smoking Gitanes in the garden of her mother's home in Chelsea.

Steamy novelist Jackie Collins playing *hausfrau* at her palatial St John's Wood home, as she served home-baked fairy cakes and pots of Earl Grey tea along with ribald stories about some of the real-life characters in her best-selling books.

On walkabout with The Kinks' Ray Davies in Muswell

Hill when we were neighbours in Fortis Green in the '80s. Ray pointed to a Victorian cottage on the next street to where I lived and said: "I wrote my biggest hits there." 'Dead End Street', 'Sunny Afternoon' and 'Waterloo Sunset'. There was a tornado happening in Muswell Hill then and nobody knew about it…"

Time-travelling backwards in my mind, I remember being young when rock was young. Funnier still, I remember when Elton John was young… before his vanity hair transplants, Donald Duck stage suits, fake marriage, stimulant excesses and legendary tantrums.

Elton was my first big interview. Only months before, he and Bernie were flat broke and sleeping in bunk beds in Elton's mum's spare room, working as session musicians. Now Elton was on a high from his breakout success with 'Your Song' in the UK and the USA.

I didn't really rate him back then, being your diehard Tamla, Otis and Blue-beat girl, with a burgeoning admiration for Cream's psychedelic version of the classic blues form. I wondered why he sang with a phoney American accent when he came from Pinner.

I knew little about Elton and his music, so I contacted my friend Lyn, an Elton fan, who worked in the Fashion department of *Petticoat,* who convinced me she should come along to the interview. The three of us knocked back champagne at the hotel. Elton let me try on his 'Dame Edna' spectacles, but I couldn't see diddly-squat through the pebble-glass lenses. Lyn looked longingly at Elton, blissfully unaware she didn't have a hope in hell as he hadn't yet come out.

That interlude with Elton was an episode that marked a joyous, ego-free time in pop music, a time when ordinary people were making extraordinary music. I was a scatty 17-year-old interviewing rock gods and I just got on with it, although I was initially a little anxious about meeting anyone famous, until

I cottoned on that we were all trying to be cool, but everyone inside was probably as insecure and geekish as I was.

My friends thought I had the best job in the world and wanted to know if I'd 'got it on' with anyone famous. I never subscribed to 'kiss and tell', and I had a boyfriend I was crazy about. We didn't live in a world of oversharing like today, with so many confessionals on social media. Writer and satirist Nora Ephron's famous line, 'Everything's copy', didn't square with me. If someone told me something juicy, 'off the record', I would never tell, cross my heart and hope to die. I guess I was discreet to the point of stupidity given my career choice, although it would be a no-brainer to keep schtum if you saw a rock star you liked nod off in a plate of spaghetti. You wouldn't necessarily want to write about it.

FANDOM

There was a regular clique of *Valentine* readers who hung outside the offices, and whose leader was a sweet-looking blonde named Cheri Honey. I'd invite them into the office while ignoring the pissed-off looks from some of my grumpier colleagues. They'd rhapsodise about their pop star crushes and which stars they'd like to see featured in the magazine, then they'd leave armed with free pop posters and copies of *Valentine*.

One time, I took a couple of 14-year-old readers to meet Jack Wild and Mark Lester, the young stars of the hit movie musical 'Oliver!' The girls, from the provinces, had won a competition to come to London and have dinner with Jack and Mark, and then stay overnight in a fancy West End hotel, so the editor sent me along to be their 'chaperone' despite only being a few years older than they were. Fat chance of any hanky panky; the girls were too shy and awestruck to even speak to their famous dates. Mark Lester sat there looking cherubic, while Jack Wild was a bit of a

Go Karting with Jack Wild and the Valentine gang. Centre top photo: Jack gives me a push-start. Main photo: I try to catch him up as he cruises to the finish line. Valentine © Copyright Rebellion Publishing IP Ltd. All rights reserved.

sourpuss. I think he was fed up with his cheeky chappie Artful Dodger screen persona everyone expected him to be.

I met Wild again a few months later when I took him go-karting for a *Valentine* photo-feature shoot, after a tip-off that he liked to drive fast cars. He was in his element as he morphed into a rocket, pocket-sized Steve McQueen behind the wheel. Jack had to give me a push-start because I was hopeless. Even the nippy Art and Production guys, who had come along for the ride, were left in the dust.

SCREAMY-BOPPERS

I scored two premium tickets and a backstage pass to take my hot boyfriend's Bay City Roller-obsessed kid sister to see the tartan terrors perform at the Hammersmith Odeon. I stood in the front row with a swooning 13-year-old, singing and holding aloft our tartan scarves in unison with a swaying sea of Roller fans. The things we do for love.

That was a smidge less uncomfortable than being stuck in the middle of a maelstrom of screaming Osmond fans while trying to review their show with a thumping hangover. I watched with mounting nausea a sea of fans watching The Osmonds watching them. They were teenagers, mostly girls, many of them crying. When Donny waved or shook his bum, they openly sobbed and pulled at their hair. All I could think of was, who the hell designed their poncy-looking white cat suits with the stand-up collars, à la Elvis in Las Vegas during his fat period? On a subliminal level, this may have propelled me to spill a Bloody Mary all down the front of Donny's white onesie post-show, as we stood chatting at The Osmonds first-ever London press reception. He actually took it really well, but I was mortified.

The Osmonds were very nice, polite boys. I'd interviewed them several times along with their sister, Marie, but they weren't cool like their nemesis, The Jackson Five, who blew me away when I saw them perform at London's Talk of the Town at a champagne party for the British press on their first appearance and tour of the UK. What was special about the Jacksons was Michael. Michael could dance like James Brown. It's 12-year-old Michael who was the precocious talent onstage with his brothers.

When I met Michael later in his hotel suite, I saw how controlling his father was. As we talked, Joe kept walking in and out of the room. He seemed afraid to leave us alone for more than five minutes. Michael was gracious but shy, showing none of the sassy swagger of that stage performance with The Jackson Five. I was touched by his sweetness.

Jackson's later inappropriate relationships with young boys may have been in some warped way a desperate attempt to recover a childhood his controlling and abusive father had denied him. But that's still open to debate.

I first met David Cassidy in the grip of superstardom. The

second time, I had to bring my 9-month-old baby daughter Lara with me as my babysitter had let me down at the last minute. There was no way I was going to cancel on David Cassidy even though by now he had lost his lustre. I packed her bottle, dummy, cuddly toy and a supply of nappies, then called a cab, and off we went to meet David. He was surprised when I turned up at his hotel suite pushing a baby buggy but was charming and very sweet to Lara, pulling funny faces and making her laugh. He was less humble at the height of his fame, when I watched in amazement how he was fawned over like a little emperor.

The Stars Seeing Me

Marc Bolan was the only guy I knew who could carry off a pink feather boa. He mixed fantasy and folklore in his music and his life, and with him I experienced one of the silliest afternoons ever in the company of a pop star. For whatever reason, Marc had chosen to communicate through his guardian angel, who, according to Marc, was standing by his right shoulder, answering

my questions. Inexplicably, the funny thing was, we both got carried away and kept it up for the entire interview, until I almost started to believe our crazy charade.

The last time I saw Marc in 1975, a few years before his death at 29 in a car crash, he was bloated and blousy and trying to make a comeback. *Bon vivant* that he was, Marc insisted on opening one more bottle of champagne before

Interview with very fabulous Marc Bolan, Record Mirror, 1975.

wrapping up our talk, and as he did so, there was an almighty pop sending the cork flying through the air, narrowly missing my frontal lobe by a nano inch. The irreverent tongue-in-cheek piece I wrote, entitled, 'Whatever Happened to the Teenage Dream?' must have amused Bolan, for the following day 13 red roses were delivered to me at the office, signed, 'Luv, Marc'.

I really liked Bob Geldof, despite him loving the sound of his own voice and never shutting up. He could just as easily discuss sensitive topics such as the death of his mother, and then turn round and tell you he likes your shoes. I was invited to join Bob and The Boomtown Rats in their 'Rat mobile' on tour in France. Bob couldn't sing for toffee, but he had bags of charisma on stage. The fans went wild in Paris; he knew how to work the audience.

After his performance, Bob was buzzing, so we piled into a taxi to a smokey Parisian speakeasy in Pigalle where nightbirds hang out.

Interviewing Bob Geldof in Paris (Note the humongous size of my tape-recorder.)

If I was captivated by Bob's shape-shifting cleverness, I was dazzled by Paula Yates, and her overstated blonde ambition. We worked together on an ill-fated new rock music paper a mutual friend of ours edited. Paula was translucently pretty, funny and smart; all the guys in the office fell in love with her. Bob would joke, "we're just an old-fashioned couple who, "ate Mr Kipling cakes at teatime in our love nest in Clapham." Bob later married Paula, bought a medieval priory in Kent, got knighted for Band Aid, only for his world to crash and burn when 'Lady Geldof' ran off with the sexy Australian rocker, Michael Hutchence. The relationship had all the elements of a Greek tragedy ending in their untimely deaths.

Not all rock stars were as fascinating as Geldof, and some wanted only to discuss their new album and upcoming tour. With perseverance you might get them to open up as they would to their mates or girlfriends and then it would make an interesting read. The Who's Roger Daltrey and Pete Townsend, my rock heroes, always gave great copy.

Daltrey, a self-confessed hard nut in his youth, told me in one of our many interviews that if he hadn't become the singer of The Who, one of the most famous bands on the planet, "I would probably have been a villain and ended up in jail. I was always in trouble. I mean, even today me and Pete fight. I've knocked him out a couple of times. But I gotta say, music saved me from a life of crime..."

At The Who's studios in Battersea in the mid-seventies, I had been waiting ages to interview Pete Townsend and when he finally emerged, he mistook me for Roger's '*bit of crumpet*' (Townsend's words, not mine) when he saw Roger and me horsing around in a friendly but slyly competitive game of darts. (Reader, I 'thrashed' Daltrey at darts by the way.)

Townsend never censored himself with the press; on the subject of his sexuality, he said it was "fluid, some of the early

Roger Daltrey talking about his days as a young 'hard-nut'. 1980. 19/Future Publishing Ltd.

Who managers were bisexual or gay." Talking about his private life when I interviewed him for a women's magazine in the '70s was no big deal to him. Mick Jagger, in the early days of The Stones, was "the most beautiful boy I had ever seen," according to Townsend. "I've had a few affairs with men in my time, only one of which I've not actually resisted."

Unfortunately, these revelations didn't go down well at home. His wife apparently hit the roof.

I met Bob Marley through a haze of ganja smoke. Drugs at this time were everywhere in the media and music, but drugs weren't my danger zone. I sometimes smoked joints on the road with other journalists, but I didn't get heavily into them. I arrived late for the interview, nervy and frazzled having been stuck in a taxi in heavy London traffic. Furthermore, the sight of Marley's chiselled beauty, his cheekbones of a god and those iconic dreadlocks cascading to his waist rendered me speechless, and so I hoovered up his ganja for courage.

Marley parroted these strange undecipherable Rastafarian mantras, and the joints he chain-smoked weren't helping. I must have looked a total dumbass sat there with my mouth open, although I doubt if he ever even noticed. What do you say to a Rasta legend to calm your nerves? *"Hello, Bob, gis' a puff"*? Well, I didn't actually say that, but I did somehow manoeuvre the joint from his hand, took deep inhalations and sort of ended up sharing Bob Marley's spliff and almost melted into a puddle on his Persian rug. He played me some of his new record, but to this day I haven't a clue what we talked about.

Back at the office, the sub-editor attempted to help me piece together that Marley interview, but all he did was laugh and shake his head and mouth, "What the f...?" The next day, I played it back once more on the tape recorder, then made the whole thing up.

GIRL POWER

It was an interesting time to be a young female in '70s Britain, when women were pioneers of equality; fighting against misogyny and double standards in the workplace and beyond.

Female colleagues a decade older than myself, on the other hand told me stories of how terrifying life without contraception could be, while there I was, popping a daily little pill that gave me complete control over my reproduction. I took the pill for granted, if I'm honest. It's only as I look back that I consider myself lucky to be among that first wave of females who didn't have to worry about unwanted pregnancies.

The generation of women artists I grew up listening to – Dusty, Sandie, Cilla, Lulu and the American Tamla and soul sisters – were the adored songbirds of my youth.

I enjoyed interviewing female pop stars because you could relate to them and the challenges they might face as women trying to make it in the misogynist world of pop music, or simply to have a laugh with, as if chatting to a girlfriend.

On the other hand, Marianne Faithfull's cleverness and beauty intimidated me. I had been sceptical of Marianne's clichéd image of the convent schoolgirl turned Mick Jagger's consort and drug addict, but then she wasn't the sort to reveal who she truly was. Marianne got a lot of criticism for being the rock muse of her day, but she and other female performers were pioneers in their own way, intent on getting their voices heard independently of men. Women artists back then couldn't sing about their affairs or one-night stands in songs. Marianne saw through the hypocrisy inherent in the music business. "Women have to listen to men mock and belittle us, 'Under my Thumb', and the rest of it…'" her posh voice amplified by the acoustics in the half-empty bar where we sat talking. "So, then I thought, right, I'm going to start writing my own songs and tell it as I see it."

She wasn't using heroin when we met, but she had been struggling to stay clean. "People say to me, 'That's one thing about you, Marianne, you're a survivor.' That's balls!" Her parting shot was one of defiance: "Christ, it's been so interesting, I'd do it all again…" She looked back at me with a wan smile and wandered off somewhere into the Soho night.

Veteran Suzi Quatro was the ultimate truculent, mullet-haired rock chick in leather zip-up suits, and a low-slung bass guitar at her hips. Having left home when she was 14 years old to go on the road, she's still on it today.

I was invited to her home in the early '80's: a modest bungalow in Stapleford Abbotts in Romford she shared with her first husband and bandmate, Len Tuckey, and their two young children. There were framed gold and platinum discs on the wall and a vintage 1957 Fender Precision bass her dad gave to her in 1964.

The first thing she said was, "Please take off your shoes." She didn't want muddy footprints on her immaculately hoovered beige carpet. She served tea and cakes and insisted I help myself. Her American accent blended with Estuary Essex as she recalled stories of her crazy life as an underage rock 'n' roller. Fifty million plus record sales later, she can afford to live in an Elizabethan mansion in Essex replete with moat. Three chords and an attitude can take you far.

The avant-garde punk singer Siouxsie Sioux (of the Banshees) and Suzi Quatro have little in common except for their Christian name and a deep and genuine concern to keep their music unpretentious. In 1977 in a noisy, sweaty London dive, Siouxsie had just finished her set with the Banshees. After ten minutes struggling to get her to string a sentence together, I gave up and put the disastrous interview down to a personality disconnect, although I had niggling suspicion after some weeks interviewing various punk bands that this whole punk lark had become a bit of a racket.

What I loved and admired most about these and many other famous women of the time was their individual style. In my teens I adored Twiggy's pouty innocence and Jane Birkin's bohemian Anglo-French charm. When I later interviewed Jane B, my puppy-like adulation must have been embarrassing. In an attempt to emulate the Twig's short bob with the side parted fringe and sleek bangs, I lopped off all my hair, but I looked more dorkish than gamine, so I grew it back long, à la *Jane*.

On the one hand, I wanted to be like my female pop idols, but my impressionable young self slowly came to realise you can't imitate perfection, and this realisation inspired me to find my own groove. Image seems such a vacuous preoccupation, but it means everything when you're young. Moreover, it was important a rock journalist should look the part. Pop music and fashion were symbiotic, inextricably linked because music became a way of showing individuality rather than just homogenised entertainment. In the '60s and '70s, the music scene was the voice of the young generation and influenced the iconic fashions that were created during those decades.

Models, actors and pop stars and their consorts were the new aristocracy, and Biba their boutique of choice: Mick and Marianne, David and Angie. Being an early fan of Biba, I purchased my first pieces from Barbara Hulanicki's mail order catalogue before discovering the Biba boutique on Kensington Church Street. I was over the moon when Helen, my best friend, got a job at Biba's even cooler new store on Kensington High Street and she would squirrel things away for me before they got snapped up; the mulberry soft suede knee-high boots I particularly cherished. I was gutted when Helen suddenly went off to work in a building society.

Then I went from a Biba girl in bell-bottomed pyjama suits and pretty smock minis at affordable price points to a brief flirtation with American hippy princess, inspired by Joni Mitchell and her folk-rock music.

At work, fashion editors would sometimes ask female staffers to model a dress for a random fashion shoot up on the office roof against a backdrop of Victorian chimney pots. I loved posing like some kind of cut-price Twiggy, and I got paid a little stipend

Dressed head to toe in Biba. Boyfriend Leslie in Mr Freedom 'star' t-shirt. 1970. Photo: Mike Gilchrist.

so I could splash out on a new lippy or a pair of snazzy-patterned tights.

Magazine Girl fashion editor Ann Carpenter asked me to participate in a fashion makeover with the stunning Maggie, a designer from the Art department at *Rave* magazine. Maggie said I reminded her of Talitha Getty, whom I'd never even heard of; an actress/ model and heroin addict married to the oil tycoon and philanthropist Paul Getty Jnr, who partied with The Rolling Stones before dying of a drug overdose. Despite her sticky end, I loved the idea of looking like an edgy style icon.

Normally, I blew my modest wages on clothes I picked up for a song at markets and jumble sales, so when my *Valentine* colleague Jackie asked me to help on fashion, I was stoked. We'd spend afternoons with PRs selecting clothes and accessories for the shoots. Top Shop, Biba, Dorothy Perkins, Peter Robinson, Granny Takes a Trip, Kensington Market and Mr Freedom were our go-to boutiques.

Rave artist Maggie and myself posing up a storm for the 'Take Two Girls' fashion feature by Magazine Girl Ann Carpenter circa 1972. Loving/Future Publishing Ltd.

Jackie and I heaved piles of garments into a taxi to Marble Arch in central London, where Mike, *Valentine*'s fashion photographer, had his studio. Half-naked models then quick-changed into successive outfits in front of us, but they were so girlish and thin as to be non-erotic. "Lean more towards me... flick back your hair so we can see the collar…" Mike instructed the models as rock music blared into the rhythm of the shoot.

What, you may wonder, happened to the clothes afterwards? You could sometimes score a discount on a piece you fell in love with on a model or be given the occasional freebie. Helping yourself to the borrowed garments was a no-no, as every single item was painstakingly returned. Don't tell anyone, but I still have – and wear – that beige chunky cable-knit cardigan that I walked out with when nobody was looking.

Mary Quant was the designer who got me obsessed with fashion in the first place with her iconic mini skirt most girls of my generation wore whether they had the legs for it or not. "You're not going out dressed like that," my dad with his Victorian morals would shout when he saw how short my skirt was. My mum would usually spring to the rescue at such moments with, "It's the fashion, Jimmy."

Love Is In the Air

I met Andy, my future husband, in1971. Andy was a little bit rock and roll with his tall rangy frame enveloped in a military coat from the Army and Navy Stores, electric-blue velvet pants and Cuban-heeled boots. What the magazines termed 'dishy', but with edge.

From the start, we talked about everything under the sun, from what made us laugh and cry to our individual pasts and our imagined futures. He loved music, travel and books, as did I, and he didn't even object to wearing some of the unisex clothes I bought at a discount from the magazine fashion shoots. One of the first things we did as a couple was to go to Petticoat Lane's Sunday market in Aldgate and buy matching Afghan suede coats, which looked great on the both of us but reeked of old goat; so much so, Andy's mum refused to let him in the house.

Andy worked in north London, and by coincidence my new job on *Popswop* was based in nearby Holloway. *Popswop's* managing director was Jack Hutton, a legendary figure in the music industry. It was Jack's teenage daughter, Mandy, who had suggested its concept – a kind of pop version of *Exchange and Mart*, where fans could swap albums and singles from the listings at the back of the magazine. Lyrics to the latest pop songs, printed weekly, became a favourite with readers. Launched in 1972, *Popswop* rapidly achieved a massive circulation of 650,000. Wendy, my assistant on *Valentine*, defected with me and between us we were responsible for writing and overseeing most of the magazine's editorial and fashion contents.

Hutton had edited *Melody Maker* from the '50s jazz age to the pop invasion, and had met all the greats of pop, rock and jazz. When on a visit to London, Jack took the legendary jazz singer Billie Holiday shopping in Marks and Spencer. When it came to paying for her purchases, Billie shocked the cashier and shoppers when she lifted her skirt to retrieve a wad of banknotes tucked into her knickers. You really had to hear Jack Hutton tell it in his stoic Scottish slur to really relish the anecdote.

The editor, Sue, was the first lesbian and feminist I'd ever worked with. I had been raised in a feminist household – although it wouldn't have been labelled as such in the '50s – where both my parents worked and shared domestic chores and childcare, which became the blueprint for my adult relationships. Sue and her strident support for the women's rights movement intrigued me. She'd bring her copies of *MS* and *Spare Rib* magazines into the office to read and then pass them on to me, their clarion call for social, sexual and reproductive freedom for women was something I'd never encountered in mainstream magazines before, and was inspirational.

By 1973, *Popswop* had merged with the relaunched *Record Mirror*. For all its liberalism and radicalism, there was a woeful under-representation of females in the music press at that time.

After the merger, one 'dinosaur' scribe from *Record Mirror* refused to associate himself with 'girl writers from a teenybopper comic', and strode off into the sunset in search of hitching his wagon to a 'proper' rock music journal. I thought he was just being a dick. Funny, but after his petulant exit, I don't recall ever seeing his by-line anywhere. (Today with pop memorabilia in demand, I couldn't resist a smug smile when I came across a 1973 issue of Popswap on eBay selling for a whopping £100.)

In the early '70s, the nation went into an economic downturn with Heath's three-day week, and hemlines fell as quickly as the pound. I went through my Edwardian schoolmarm phase, in Laura Ashley leg o mutton sleeved blouses and long sweeping skirts. But then the economy picked up and disco-glitter had made its sparkling entrance by the midpoint of the decade. A pot-pourri of pot-bellied rockers lurex-ed their way onto 'Top of the Pops' in a poor imitation of the skinny glam-rock maestro Bowie. He led the pack in his persona of the androgynous Ziggy Stardust and challenged the concepts of gender.

Popular music was in a state of flux. The elements of spontaneity and fun that marked the '60s seemed lost forever as nihilistic punk music echoed the 'no future' mantra of mid-seventies social mayhem.

THREE

PUNK MANTRAS

In the summer of 1984, I was freelancing for *19* magazine, when I found myself suffused in scented joss sticks at the Radha Krishna Temple in Soho. I had come to meet punk icons turned Krishna devotees Poly Styrene and Lora Logic of X-Ray-Spex, to find out why they had strayed so far from the fame and fury of the punk scene.

I knew from personal experience that the spiritual life can be deeply seductive. Following the Summer of Love in 1967 and the hippy-dippy movement, many young people, like me, were connecting with themselves through eastern philosophy, and from the jump-off point of 1970 I began to meditate on a regular basis at Buddhist centres in London.

A decade later, pregnant with my first baby, I enrolled in yoga classes for expectant mums in a quest to relax our collective pelvic floor muscles for an easier and uncomplicated birth. It didn't go to plan for me, but I like to think yoga and meditation helped me survive an emergency labour induction when I suddenly developed pre-eclampsia in my last month of pregnancy – soaring high blood pressure which came from nowhere – which can be a potentially fatal condition to mother and baby.

In a different way, the spiritual life gave Poly and Lora some kind of solace after they fled the 'misogynistic punk scene' when they felt it had become 'toxic towards women musicians'. Aligning with the movement, they went the full nine yards: initiation from a guru, the study of the ancient Hindu text of 'The Bhagavad Gita and adopting spiritual names in the Sanskrit, while Lora entered into an arranged marriage with a fellow Krishna.

Music, though, was never very far away, and Polly's spiritual identity infused her chugging punk grooves with Indian music influences, while Lora Logic spliced it with her anarchic saxophone. They used ex-Beatle George Harrison's studio, a Krishna befriender, to write and record their songs.

Before I left the temple, I observed the punk ladies in their long white devotional robes bowing in loving devotion before a life-sized statue of a Hindu deity, and they looked as cheery as the happy monks bouncing down Oxford Street, I had passed on my way there. Seeing them glow with light, love and mindfulness, it made me wish there was some magical way I could bottle the transcendental alchemy that floated around the temple and take it home with me.

SPIT AND POLISH

Looking back, X-Ray Spex's super-charged sonic riffs with added rocket boosters, had made my heart go BOOM. For me, the punk girls such as Poly Styrene and Lora Logic always took it to the edge.

By 1977, the punk revolutionaries had stormed the ramparts of the music, art and fashion industries, and taken the genre beyond the burn-it-down-and-spit-on-it mantra.

As a superannuated flower child, I couldn't relate to punk's white-hot rage, although I got what the punks were rebelling against: all those self-indulgent reactionary old hippies selling millions of records and making tons of money, this happening before punk itself sold out and went mainstream.

When Johnny Rotten was singing about 'no future', I was preoccupied with nest-building, and feeling quietly optimistic about what tomorrow would bring, although 1977 ended on a bum note for me when the rock paper I was working on suddenly folded. I used the redundancy pay-out for a deposit on a modest flat in Highgate, which got me on the property ladder. I bought it with my boyfriend for the princely sum of £8,000 then we sold it three years later for £26,000.

I was in the middle of unpacking boxes at our new flat when I landed an interview with The Jam, and was stoked to be one of the first journalists to meet the new boy wonder – singer, guitarist and songwriter Paul Weller – on the cusp of the band's debut album release, 'In the City'.

Weller, in his mohair suits and two-tone weave loafers from Toppers of Carnaby Street, smashed the London Look. He emulated and personified the cool Mod boys I hung out with when I was a 15-year-old in the late 1960s, madly into soul, blues and Tamla Motown and whose backdrop was espresso bars, jazz clubs and Vespa scooters.

Paul, a teenager in 1978, was still living at home with his mum and dad and I met them when Paul and I swung by their council house in Woking, Surrey, before his dad, John, who was the band's manager, took us to the studio where The Jam were recording their first album.

Over the years, I followed Paul Weller's trajectory to success, pinballing from hit album to hit album – and never selling out on his musical integrity or his style.

And he still wears incredible shoes…

Revolution!

A call to action in the '70s era of civil unrest, mass unemployment, violence and political extremism marked many bands, such as

The Clash, as punk activists, whose political views were the cornerstone of their lyrics.

True to the times, many of my interviews with punks were typically conducted in local dives and 'caffs' with their heavy doses of Formica and Lino. Maybe the punk subculture was merely a form of inverted snobbery, a pose, to show what right-on proletariats they were, even if, like Joe Strummer, you were really an educated middle-class boy.

I spent a five-hour roundtrip train ride from London to Manchester to meet The Buzzcocks, Manchester's preeminent punks only to be taken to a seedy all-day breakfast bar and grill which you could find in any English city. At least the arresting presence of singer Pete Shelley, who had renamed himself after the Romantic poet, somewhat helped to blur the unloveliness of the place.

Ian Drury of 'Hit Me with Your Rhythm Stick' fame shared his irreverent humour with me in a south London Wimpy Bar. He spoke in cockney rhyming slang ("So I got on the dog and bone to me agent…"), and he winced with the pain from his piles: "They dun 'arf give me a sore bottles and glass…"

A diamond geezer who knew how to make a girl laugh.

Appropriately for The Clash, a band who scorned 'privilege', they liked to entertain journalists in their breakfast hang-out, at Mick's Cafe, on Ladbroke Grove. They didn't feel like discussing their recently completed American tour, except to say how great it was playing with Bo Diddly, who they personally invited to be their support. If the stories were true, most of the 30 grand or whatever they made from the tour, the band generously donated to Diddly, who was on his uppers at the time.

I love The Clash and their music, but interviewing the band was difficult; I felt like a supply teacher who couldn't connect with her class and I wanted to hit their knuckles with a ruler and scream: "*Sit up straight and pay attention!*" Instead, I took the coward's option, made my excuses and left, when really I should have told them to *eff off*. Anyway, I never did find out if The Clash were one more punk band who lip-synced to sloganising political clichés or were the real-deal humanitarians trying to change the world.

It's Only Rock 'n' Roll

When I switched from teen magazines to music papers, I thought gender wasn't supposed to matter, but it did and it shaped everything. Female journalists were sometimes given a hard time at interviews; my 'clash' with The Clash was by no means unusual. Girl writers were generally thought not to be so serious about rock and roll and more interested in the boys who played it. That was partly true in my case as I wasn't exactly a raving music purist. My premise was gossip-driven: *"Are you in a relationship?" "Is it true you are bi-sexual?" "How did your stint in rehab go?"* Those were extreme examples, perhaps, but I wanted to know what made some of these rock stars tick and less so about their virtuoso guitar playing.

I didn't think for one minute that being a girl writing about pop music was in any way disadvantageous. I think it helped because I didn't mind blowing what little credibility I had, and so I got away with asking cheeky questions that perhaps my male counterparts wouldn't ask.

Fortunately, there were pop stars like Bryan Ferry, smart, interesting and funny, who played along with me: "No, I'm not gay, perhaps I will be by the end of the decade," Ferry had responded when I asked if he'd ever had male lovers. Call me shallow, fun was my *raison d'être*. Although it wouldn't have been fair to deny all those dyed-in-the-wool rock bands their prerogative to be taken seriously.

I would coerce my music-savvy boyfriend to gigs and then

afterwards use some of his comments and observations of the show. We'd go in search of a public phone box to dictate the concert review to the copytakers if there was a pressing deadline to meet.

Andy was a whizz at theory and technical details; he would evaluate the acoustic quality of the music and the skill of the musicians, whereas I never strayed from the transformative nature of music because music to me was visceral: you danced and made love to it, laughed, cried, got high on it. I popped out baby number two while playing Simon and Garfunkel's 'Bridge Over Troubled Water' on a loop, and delivered him in record time.

In the mid-seventies, I worked at *Record Mirror*, which covered a broad church of musical tastes. Launched in 1954 as a weekly music paper for 'pop fans and record collectors', it stayed true to that formula. It was the first national publication to publish a feature on The Beatles and promote black American R&B artists. It folded in 1991, because it was reputed that the editor who had been running it as an online music paper had gone to prison.

Every issue required new content, and sometimes it felt like you were on a hamster wheel. Silly diversions and horse play in the office – water pistol fights with the subs and layout artists, and a liquid lunch at the pub – diffused the stress of looming deadlines.

My good friend David Hancock was the paper's off-the-wall

My colleague David 'I'm a rock star' Hancock and me. Record Mirror, 1976.

personality; we shared many a boy crush. One of the true hedonists of 1970s pop journalism, after a bender David would reappear as fresh as a daisy, and no one was bothered if he had to go for a quick refresher at the Lord Nelson across the road, as long as he produced his sparkling copy.

You'd struggle to beat assistant editor Rosalind's impressive list of top-drawer interviewees, and she counted Rod Stewart as a friend. One half of a rock 'n' roll love story, Ros met punk rocker Kym Bradshaw from the seminal Australian band The Saints on their first visit to the UK during the punk explosion of 1977. Kym never returned to Australia but took up residence in Ros' Camden flat, and they eventually got married and had many dogs.

Record Mirror shared an office with *Sounds*, a music paper brought out to rival *Melody Maker* and *NME*. All the so-called serious and influential rock 'inkies' were largely populated with music-mad, hairy denim-clad scribes, and some even played in bands on the side. To the delight of their legions of male readers, these word-magicians wrote hip and knowledgeable 6,000-word essays on rock criticism, which evolved into a new type of journalism, epitomised by *Rolling Stone* and *Creem* in which writing on rock was transformed into an art form '…Jimmy's solo tended to fly past transcendence and land squarely in the realm of self-indulgence', wrote one wordster. A lot of it was hogwash, but some of it was original, inventive journalism.

There were few women writers on rock papers in my time. Chrissie Hynde occasionally wrote for *NME* before she formed her seminal band, The Pretenders, and she was badass enough to get away with being 'one of the lads' in what was essentially a boys' club.

The late great Penny Valentine wrote for *Sounds*. She was a pioneer, a female writing eloquently about pop music in a man's world as it emerged from the days of Tin Pan Alley. Penny, along with Maureen O'Grady, started on *Boyfriend* and they later worked on *Rave* with Dawn James, sister of '60s pop singer Twinkle.

Those women were the first wave of female pop writers to emerge, fortunate to begin their careers when the likes of The Beatles and The Rolling Stones were beginning theirs. They had a major influence on the '60s music scene as well as on the female pop writers who followed.

Another major influence was DJ John Peel, a regular presence in the Spotlight Publications office. He blended his enthusiasm for many strands of music with a deadpan humour in his column *for Sounds,* and when he came into the office to write it up, he would invite me to his iconic radio show at the BBC. John and a group of us would sometimes walk over to the old geezers' pub on the Holloway Road for a pint, where he'd entertain us with his laugh-out-loud stories about his posh family background or what went on at the BBC 'Peel Sessions', all served up in his stylised scouseness.

Working and socialising with Peel and other rock scribes, I learnt (and intuitively recognised) that the main qualification for music journalism was you had to be passionate about the music. In Peel's case, his absolute dedication to music was enough to keep the art form alive.

My daughter's friend, Mitz, a 30-something furniture maker from Tokyo, is just one of today's ardent young John Peel fans, not even born when Peel was at his zenith as a DJ. Yet Mitz streams Peel's old radio shows and raves about his musical choices and his influence. He practically kissed my feet when he heard I knew the late legendary DJ back in the day.

Rock is a story about growing up. Loving something your parents or old people hate. You don't get that today because young people such as my daughter's friend actually like all the bands I liked when I was young. No wonder we baby boomers like to kid ourselves that we're still pretty groovy; that we like rap (but not really) and going to concerts. Realistically, how can you be cool when you are practically ready for the Chrysanthemums?

I wasn't even that cool when I was young. Just a little bit cocky and a little bit lost all at once. Like most shy people, I was a mash-up of extrovert and introvert. I wasn't cool enough for some of the jobs I did, but I could kid myself that I was, although I never felt you had to lead the kind of life you wrote about.

For the most part, I got on well with the people I interviewed. I had a naive way of just coming out and asking impertinent questions, which to my surprise (and maybe theirs), they answered.

I had nothing against David Essex, who I got on with in interviews because we were both from the East End. I wasn't a huge fan of his music; I liked his acting better. I was invited to his opening show in Manchester on one of his nationwide tours of the mid-seventies. I gave his performance an honest review and for some reason his overprotective manager took exception to what I had written and banned me from doing any interviews with Essex. This made me wonder what became of the critic who said Essex's singing sounded like 'a constipated stoat'.

ON THE ROAD

I enjoyed the peripatetic lifestyle of hopping on and off tour buses with bands, watching them play in TV studios, at rehearsals, clubs, gigs and festivals, and catching planes to Europe, America and beyond to cover gigs.

I was a huge fan of the exquisitely witty weirdo brothers, Ron and Russell Mael, of Sparks, whose music was an acquired taste. I covered all their London shows, whenever they were in town, and then their London PR arranged for me to see them play at the famed L'Olympia in Paris.

At their hotel on the Rive Gauche, Sparks were nowhere to be found. Still a no-show two hours later, I invaded the mini bar, unaware as I glugged another miniature bottle of brandy that the band were on stage. No one had thought to tell me that Sparks were doing a matinee show.

To make up for missing the gig, Ron and Russell took me to dinner at the expensive L'hotel in Saint Germain-des-Prés. Oscar Wilde lived (and died) there, Frank Sinatra, Johnny Depp, Princess Grace of Monaco and other famous faces have passed through its doors. We were seated around a large oval table while Jean-Claude, Phonogram's man in Paris, taught me how to eat *foie gras au torchon et escargots*. Unfortunately, I threw up in the hotel room later when it crossed my mind, I might have eaten one of *Les Canards* from the decorative water feature.

Drinking champagne in the back of a Rolls with Slade was the one time I got to experience their rare display of rock ostentation. Not given to showbiz histrionics, the nearest I'd seen Slade come to throwing a strop was when the band were about to go onstage and Jimmy Lea took one look at Dave Hill's truly preposterous lurex space-age cat suit and screamed: *"I'm not going on with him dressed like that!"*

Slade were the most down-to-earth blokes in pop: I wrote about them so often I should have been on their payroll. They were woefully underrated in my opinion; there was more to Slade than their terrace anthems and weird wardrobe choices. Don's mental drumming, for starters, and Noddy and Jim's masterful tunes. Noel Gallagher of Oasis thought they wrote genius pop songs.

It was Jim Lea's mother-in-law who suggested to the band: "Why don't you write a nice Christmas song?" Good job they listened to her. Today, 'Merry Xmas Everybody' is Slade's biggest-selling single. It's still played regularly on TV and radio stations, and you can't avoid it in supermarkets at Christmastime. Now in retirement, Slade need only sit in their garden acres and count the royalties.

My first encounter with Abba happened a short while after their Eurovision win with 'Waterloo'. I became the designated Abba correspondent for *Record Mirror* by default; oddly, nobody else on the paper shared my passion for the uplifting joy and the chirpy piano trills of Abba's music. Strange to think that at the height of their fame, they were considered a bit naff by the rock music establishment, until the likes of John Lennon, Kurt Cobain, Pete Townsend, even Sid Vicious, came out as Abba fans, and then it was cool to dig Abba.

Being Swedes, they had a Nordic distaste for grandstanding, and they didn't get over-chummy with journalists, so getting them to open up was like pulling teeth. I'd been *Record Mirror's* Abba correspondent for many years and the only time I saw raw emotion from an Abba person was Agnetha tearing up when I raised the thorny issue of her and Bjorn's break-up.

One of the most rock-steady marriages that endured until death did them part was Paul and Linda McCartney's. Even their

Getting to the heart of Abba. 1978. Woman's Own/Future Publishing Ltd.

dodgy musical collaboration survived the critics' slings and arrows.

During the Wings period, I was introduced to Paul at a party, and my first thought was how small he was. I had idolised The Beatles since I was 11 years old. Even after meeting so many rock stars in my job, I was still massively star-struck meeting Paul McCartney. Earlier, when Paul was dating Jane Asher, I wanted them to marry, simply for the silly reason that my neighbour and best friend banged on about how my 'teenage self' looked like Jane. (I wasn't quite as thrilled when someone else remarked my 'older self' resembled Paul's second wife, Heather Mills.)

I'd never been struck on Linda until I saw her with Paul that night and I thought how original and artless she looked with her choppy long hair and vintage vibe. Furthermore, I liked that Linda was not your subservient rock star wife waiting for her man to come home from months of touring; she was right there on stage with him.

Rock music was, after all, androcentric, and it operated in an environment where women were objectified or used as sex objects. Women were the focal point, the muses, but excluded.

A generation before the moral high ground of the #MeToo generation, groupies were key players in rock's inner sanctum, and that role could come with fringe benefits. Women like Barbie Buell, Cherry Vanilla, Lori Maddox, Sable Starr and the infamous Cynthia Plaster Caster (who made plaster casts of rock stars penises) had an innate understanding of how to make their sexuality powerful, and they wielded influence over the musicians they slept with. Some groupies progressed from courtesan to girlfriend – or in Courtney Love's case to wife, when she married Kurt Cobain.

I met the ultimate rock groupie, Pamela Des Barres, when she was promoting her racy memoir, 'I'm With the Band'. She was funny and unsentimental about her former life and had absolutely no regrets. Pamela was supposedly the inspiration behind Kate Hudson's character in the movie, 'Almost Famous'. She had a love affair with Led Zeppelin's Jimmy Page and made it with such rock icons as Mick Jagger, Robert Plant, Frank Zappa and Keith Moon.

Today she is a star on Instagram, where she peddles her stories and photos of groupie superstardom. Good luck to her.

Celebrated muses – Pattie Boyd, Anita Pallenberg, Marianne Faithfull and the unlikely Yoko Ono – were transmogrified into iconic rock figures. Unfortunately (for me), unlike those prototypical rock consorts and lovers, female pop writers rarely ever had rock gods write songs about them. Being complimented on a fetching belly button, unfortunately, didn't count. Really though, I wasn't bothered about winning any popularity contests. You might say, 'Chance would be a fine thing', but I wasn't interested in sleeping with someone just because they were in the Top 20 hit parade.

Anywhere there were underage kids there would be predatory old roués like Jimmy Savile waiting to pounce. At the 'Top of the Pops' studios where I'd sometimes go to meet the bands performing on the show, Savile would be all jokey-blokey as he pawed the underage teenyboppers in the audience. It was obvious he liked little girls.

But who'd have thought dear ol' Rolf Harris was anything other than a benign TV personality, who could speed-paint and play didgeridoo? He was all raised eyebrows and comical quips as we sat *face à face* in his dressing room at London's Talk of the Town as if butter wouldn't melt. Afterwards, he sent me flowers and a thank-you note for the nice write-up I'd done on him.

I spent a marathon interview session in a hotel room with Gary Glitter, littered with beer bottles, half-eaten pizzas and Gary hangers-on, for a two-part 'confessional': 'The Night We All Cried'. (Glitter was nothing if not a sensationalist.) I asked him if it was true that he wore a wig and lied about his age. He deflected questions he didn't like with a glib response — "What am I this week, 55 or 15?" It was impossible to get him to part with the truth.

When the article came out, Gary's personal assistant called and invited myself and the *National Rock Star* staff to Gary's Christmas show at Baileys nightclub. It was the silly season, so we wore something sparkly and barrelled down the M1 in a hired minibus to less-than-glittery Watford.

Gary was waiting backstage to say hello, and then we were shown to our front-row table. We ordered drinks and filled our faces with scampi in a basket as Glitter clunked on stage in his 4-inch platform-soled boots like a shimmering Frankenstein, and perversely acted out the lyrics to the coyly suggestive 'Do You Wanna Touch Me?' to an audience of over-30s.

Today, for their sins, the likes of Savile, Rolf and Glitter are the most loathed and detested names in the entertainment industry.

Whisky on the Go-Go

I learnt to drink at an early age. My mum and dad – who I thought were the best parents you could wish for – never appeared unduly worried about the implications that my underage drinking might have on my behaviour, or my health, because everybody drank where I came from. In today's world, where parents can be overprotective, that would probably translate as benign neglect.

'Boozers', as my grandfather called them, were woven into the fabric of our East End life. He knew most of the pubs in Stepney, and they served as his Google Maps of the day: "*Turn right at the Rose and Punchbowl, swing a left at the Ship, cross at the lights at the Hayfield…*" He loved those centuries-old watering holes with their many historical secrets: Lord Nelson and Lady Hamilton engaging in romantic trysts in the upstairs rooms at the Gun at Millwall's Coldharbour (where my son held his wedding party). Isambard Kingdom Brunel, a regular at the Ship on the Isle of Dogs while building one of the great Victorian steamships of the industrial age at nearby Burrells Wharf. The Queen Mum pulling a pint at the Queen's Head in Stepney (where we held my own mum's 90th birthday party). The Lord Morpeth in Bow, where according to family folklore, my Great-great-aunt Doll would repair with the suffragettes after 'all that marching'. If only walls could talk.

Like Grandad, Andy was a ligger and as such he was the perfect companion at rock concerts. We saw Bowie play his last Ziggy Stardust show at the Hammersmith Odeon on 3rd July 1973. We witnessed poor Frank Zappa get pushed off the stage by a jealous boyfriend, spread-eagled in the orchestra pit with a broken leg and a tour in shatters. Hanging out at The Stones' open-air headliner at Knebworth in 1976, and mingling backstage in the press enclosure with louche rock stars and other liggers and journalists, we were just another couple of music-loving long-haired freaks.

We once drove up to Yorkshire in our battered old Volkswagen Beetle, enveloped in fog on the M1, to John Vanbrugh's baroque masterpiece, Castle Howard, the stately home that was chosen to represent the great domed palace of the doomed Flyte family in the TV series 'Brideshead Revisited'. I was writing a freelance article about Evelyn Waugh's '20s saga for the travel and lifestyle magazine *In Britain*, and Andy had come along for the ride. Owner George Howard gave us a tour of its galleries aglow with paintings by Rubens, Gainsborough and Tintoretto, and rooms elegantly furnished with Sheraton and Chippendale. We passed Sir Laurence Olivier's dressing room where I saw him getting into make-up for his role as the paterfamilias Lord Marchmain.

We had tea in the drawing room with star of the future Jeremy Irons, whose hair was brillianteened into shiny patent perfection à la Fred Astaire as he discussed the afternoon's cocktail scenes with actress Diana Quick. Irons was having a marvellous time staying at Castle Howard: "You could say I'm living over the shop…" To observe these *mise en scènes* was like being in a film within a film.

SNAP, CRACKLE, POP

As I wanted to do more 'gigs' with Andy, I proposed to my editor that he should be the de facto snapper at the George McCrae concert I was going to cover on McCrae's upcoming UK tour following his number one hit record 'Rock Your Baby'. Surprisingly, Sue agreed.

Andy was into photography. I'd bought him a Pentax camera for his recent 21st birthday, and he took copious photos on our trip to Poland to visit his father's surviving relatives in Oświęcim, a small town 30 miles west of Kraków, which had the dubious

Young lovers, Andy and I, in our courting days. 1975.

distinction of being situated on the doorstep of Auschwitz concentration camp.

My father-in-law had told me some years previously stories about how as a teenage boy he had watched the distant glow of the crematorium fires from a window of the family farmhouse, seeing the smoke rising from the chimneys where they burnt the bodies. Now we were actually there in the camp itself and Andy captured some startlingly powerful images.

Surely, after this, you would think taking pictures at a pop concert would be a doddle, except not one of the photographs of McCrae onstage came out. Andy put it down to nerves and a cavalier approach to his research. Either way, bang went my dreams of working a double act with the boyfriend.

In 1977, *National Rock Star* folded, so I found myself out of a job. Several journalist friends of mine went over to the 'dark side' to work as PRs. I toyed with the idea of doing the same after a record company approached me to work as their press officer. While it had been good fun to be a ligger on various press trips abroad, to be a responsible PR trying to keep a bunch of scallywag rock scribes in line, I imagined, actually, I *knew*, would be a nightmare. Furthermore, schmoozing the metropolitan media to promote artists and bands whose music I might have hated wasn't on my list of dream jobs.

Pop music writers came with a lifespan; it was a young person's game when, after all, at 24, I was pushing it. I wanted to do something a bit more grown up. Shedding my scruff-pot jeans and t-shirts for my granny's twinset-and-pearls sensibility, I swapped the rock and roll circus for the more sedate world of the women's weeklies when I landed the coveted job of showbusiness writer for *Woman's Own*, Britain's leading women's magazine with a not-too-shabby readership of millions.

That's how I came to be eating fish and chips with a Hollywood screen legend...

FOUR

SEEING STARS

I walked into the office of *Woman's Own* on my first day as the new showbusiness writer, and passed a matronly journalist wearing more hairspray than a glam-rock star. She gave me a withering look from behind her typewriter, as if to say, *Look what the cat's brought in.*

It wasn't the welcome I was expecting. Being a bit cocky, I had assumed the staff would be a pushover, a walking-talking version of *Woman's Own* itself: kind, nurturing, even mumsy. Well, I was wrong.

Everything had gone so well at the interview. Iris Burton, the features editor, wanted me for the job, but I was the first person she'd interviewed, so I had to sweat it out for weeks while she waded through the rest of the applicants.

Of all the magazine's female hierarchy, I never had a problem with Iris. She was an

Editor Jane Reed introducing me in her editorial column as the new showbusiness writer. 1977. Woman's Own/Future Publishing Ltd.

249

exceptional editor, demanding but fair, and with empathy and charm coaxed the best out of her writers. Given the narcissistic women's magazine orbit she operated in, I admired her complete lack of vanity and being over 6 feet tall she radiated a strong aura of self-confidence that I found strangely reassuring.

Growing up, *Woman's Own* had been my mum's favourite mag and, as such, a benign presence on our front-room coffee table. I'd casually thumb through it, spot a fabulous new hairstyle, such as the Farrah Flick, tear out the page and tell the hairdresser: "That's the haircut I want." Even if you didn't read it, *Woman's Own* found a way to you in most doctor's, dentist's and hospital waiting rooms.

By the time I joined the staff in 1977, its editor, Jane Reed, had made it the most influential women's magazine in Britain, with a weekly readership nudging 2 million.

Reed's jolly head girl demeanour gave no clue as to the formidably tough cookie she was. Her reputation as an Olympian editor in the arena of magazine publishing was certainly justified, and her supreme authority employed as she saw fit.

Reed wasn't limited to steering her staff or influencing how her readers looked, what they ate for breakfast or how to do up their living rooms. She led ground breaking campaigns, like changing the tax laws to benefit women. She opened up discussions of once taboo subjects such as same-sex relationships, single motherhood, seniors sexuality and equality in the workplace, while also reassuring her readers that it was OK to be a home maker or a stay-at-home mum if that was their choice.

My job as showbiz correspondent was solely to entertain the troops, which in the wider world of strikes, riots, black outs and uncollected rubbish that was the latter part of Britain in the '70s, at least offered a form of escapism.

The queen bee of the Features department was the

supercilious deputy editor whose command I was under. She made a point of telling me she'd interviewed Brigitte Bardot in French, then translated and written it in English in her head, as if to say, *Beat that.* The main issue here was that senior female editors saw young female writers as a competitive threat, and so they would undermine their rivals pre-emptively. Summoning me to her office on my first day, with my new-girl need for approval on full beam, she came right out and said I wasn't her choice for the job. When she'd finished wiping the floor with me, I was dismissed with a curt, "That's all."

I love you too!

Despite all the playground BS, I loved the job. I mean, who wouldn't love flying all over the show interviewing stars for a living? But I had to grow a pair of balls and the skin of a rhino to deal with female rivalry and sabotage.

Behind The Cover

As I was used to working in the male-dominated rock press, it seemed strange at first that 85 per cent of the magazine's by lines were women, and women occupied key roles. The testosterone deficiency around the office was made up by the male-dominated Art department. Its silver-fox art director turned trouble shooter was one of the nicest people on the staff. *Thank God* for Dennis Whelan and his joyful explosions of laughter that echoed around the office, which told us life was a comedy. Dennis would pop into the writers' zone and throw Wimbledon tickets, theatre premieres and party invites onto my desk, as a magician might pull rabbits from his top hat. With his connections in the industry the length of King Kong's arm, he got me exclusive interviews with celebrities at their homes. I am forever indebted to his kindness and generosity.

For every gentle Paddy and charming, giddy Shelagh, two

commissioning editors who were a joy to work with, there were long-standing editors, wary of newcomers, who would put you down with a look or a snide remark at a meeting that rubbed at your confidence, who thought the right school and what 'Daddy' did for a living counted most. It was risible how many regional accents hid behind elocution-speak. All fur coat and no knickers, as my mum would say.

To be fair, a lot of people reinvented themselves just to fit in. One editor, real name Ethel, became the more magazine-friendly Janice. If you didn't act the part, you were as irrelevant as yesterday's news. I often wondered how the hard-nosed Fleet Street reporters got on if they were teetotal, because working in the media was one long piss-up. Newspaper and magazine editors installed drinks cabinets in their offices; a bottle stashed in a desk drawer for those little emergencies. An artist friend who freelanced at *Woman's Own* was tasked with collecting a crate of Guinness on his way to work of a morning for the hungover blokes in the art room.

Meanwhile, back in the editorial department I was reconnected with Magazine Girls Linda Newman and Janice Collier who was working down the hall as the Beauty editor. My writing colleagues Linda, Louette and Ruth bashed out immaculate copy on their typewriters without breaking sweat. I, on the other hand, grappled with the magazine's stylistic dictates. I was annoyed when a heavy-handed sub slashed an interview of mine to bits. I checked the proofs, and when no one was looking, I slipped the edits back in before it went to print. No one seemed any the wiser. Louette, was the only person I confided in, as she and I had struck up an instant friendship. Anyone with the bottle to drive their convertible MG sports car faster than the speed of sound was in my book a worthy partner in crime.

Woman's Own's massive reach and splashy entertainment coverage attracted PRs and agents on the prowl for publicity for their clients. We could tell their handlers what we wanted and we chose the photographer and photos. They needed us, because magazines were essentially all there was.

Nowadays, Twitter, Facebook and blogs have reduced the role magazines play. Now, the publicists rule. A young journalist friend of mine tells me today they book you like a doctor's appointment. "You can have Monday at three for an hour." And most topics are a no-no, especially the affairs, the domestic fall-outs, the drugs. Now, the celebs mostly get copy approval, and if their demands aren't met, they walk. Unless of course they are promoting their autobiography.

ONCE UPON A TIME IN HOLLYWOOD

The best part of the job, hands down, was interviewing the stars. Looking back at some of those interviews from the 1970s, they have a cinematic quality that plays out in my mind's eye like an old Super 8 home movie.

In 1978, I interviewed the indomitable Bette Davis over lunch at Pinewood Studios on her day off from filming

Lunch with Hollywood star Bette Davies at Pinewood Studio. 1978.
Woman's Own/Future Publishing Ltd.

'Death on the Nile'. Being a no-holds-barred interview, I could ask her whatever I liked. Except I couldn't because she was cantankerous and scary and refused to speak until she had lit the first of many Marlboros. Beneath her black leather Bob Dylan cap, Bette threw me a look that said: *Your cue. C'mon, deliver your line.* Before I could say anything, she steamed in with her put-downs on modern-day films and how 'utterly disagreeable' it was to shoot in the heat of the Egyptian desert. "In the old days, they'd have built the Nile for you."

Fellow actors smiled and waved from nearby tables. Maggie Smith, her co-star, floated by. Christopher Reeve on a break from his 'Superman' movie stopped to chat. I like to think we bonded over our battered fish and chip lunch, as we puffed away like trains and talked about her divorces. But Bette Davies wasn't really best girlfriend material.

I was warned by Cary Grant's publicist: "Be punctual, he doesn't like lateness." So, I arrived on the dot at the Hollywood actor's personal suite at the Hilton, only to find him on a transatlantic call. At 73, with cropped silver hair and black-rimmed spectacles, he was timelessly elegant.

He told me he was due to fly to Monte Carlo in his role as ambassador for the cosmetics company Fabergé, involving Henry Kissinger and the first-ever meeting of Prince Charles and Princess Caroline. He apologised for all the name-dropping: "I am not trying to impress you... and anyway, you may know the Queen for all I know."

He didn't want to discuss his films or Hollywood; he would much rather talk about his only child, 7-year-old Jennifer. "She's my greatest production." When his daughter was born, he quit films to be with her. "I wanted her to be raised with love."

Cary Grant asked if I had children. When I answered no, I was only in my early twenties and there was plenty of time to have kids, he said he wished he'd started earlier and not waited until he was in his sixties. 'My advice to you, young lady, is to stop wasting your time with me, go home to your boyfriend and make babies."

It was so weird to get baby-making advice from the likes of Cary Grant. I headed straight to the lobby bar for a large glass of *vino collapso*.

Postscript: A few months later, I went to see Dyan Cannon, Grant's ex-wife and mother of Jennifer, who was in town to shoot a movie. Dyan put into perspective much of what Grant and I had previously discussed. When Grant – real name Archibald Leech – was 11-years-old, he believed his mother had abandoned him, only to be told when he was 30 that his father had in fact committed his mother to an institution. He experimented with LSD and other drugs, with psychoanalysis and primal scream therapy to rid his demons, but it was fatherhood most of all that provoked a sea change in the actor. According to Dyan, "Jennifer's birth was life-changing for Cary. He was instantly besotted with his daughter. He had so much love for her, it was beautiful."

Omar Sharif was sprawled on a chaise longue, chain-smoking pungent Gauloises and flirting with me outrageously. Those famous eyes of melted chocolate marshmallow made me feel quite giddy, or had I inhaled his French cigarettes too deeply?

The interview spilled into overtime and it was growing late. My boyfriend

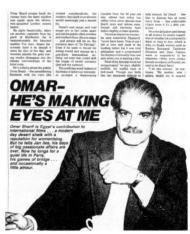

Omar was making eyes at me. 1978. Woman's Own/Future Publishing Ltd.

arrived and was waiting outside in the car to pick me up and take me to the country for the weekend.

I asked Omar one last question about 'Doctor Zhivago', which I'd seen a dozen times, and I told him that if I ever had a daughter, I would name her Lara, because the romantic in me loved Julie Christie's performance in that role. "Do you know, that beautiful creature ate bacon butties every morning for breakfast? I adore Julie, but it wasn't pleasant filming our love scenes."

Omar asked me to have dinner with him, and I heard this discombobulated voice in the room say she had already made plans. Had I really just turned Omar Sharif down?

I got up to leave, trying to elegantly extricate myself from the chaise longue without showing my knickers, then I thanked him and fled.

Downstairs, another surreal scene was unfolding – a comical contretemps between my boyfriend and a roly-poly gentleman in pinstripes who had somehow squeezed himself into the passenger seat of our little VW Beetle. It turned out to be the portly actor Robert Morley, who'd mistaken my boyfriend for his mini cab ride. We managed to heave him from the car and safely deposited Mr Morley onto the forecourt, before we sped off.

I never got another chance to have dinner with Omar Sharif. But I did name my daughter Lara.

THE ROYAL BEAT

Woman's Own excelled at its royal coverage. Back then, Buckingham Palace successfully imposed restrictions on the reporting of royal matters, as you weren't allowed to 'let daylight in upon its magic'. If reporters overstepped their mark, 'The Firm' would complain about intrusions and would accuse the press of being 'bloody vultures' and 'pests'. Can you imagine them getting away with that today?

At the whisper of her romance with Prince Charles, I managed to get hold of Lady Diana Spencer's phone number. Diana, a plummy 19-year-old Sloane Ranger working as a nursery assistant in a posh kindergarten, was sharing a flat in Kensington with her friends and I could hear shrieks of laughter when I called. She was far too polite to slam the phone down on me and said she was sorry but she couldn't talk, although I imagine the 19-year-old Diana, in love with her prince, wanted to shout from the rooftops that she had won the heart of the heir to the throne, but protocol wouldn't allow her to discuss any of it. I called her back a few days later, but Diana had been shunted off to the Palace and the phone disconnected.

Occasionally, I would be assigned to write a royal puff piece. I was dispatched to Gloucestershire to talk to the locals about their new royal neighbours, the newlyweds Princess Anne and her husband, Captain Mark Phillips, who'd purchased Gatcombe Park from the Conservative politician Rab Butler. A few months earlier, my Magazine Girl colleague Linda Newman had received a tip-off from a 'reliable source' and was sent to a completely different part of the West Country on what turned out to be a wild goose chase trying to track down the couple's first home, later revealed to be in the village of Minchinhampton. I spent a freezing January weekend there on a walkabout doorstepping homes and businesses, before heading over to the Crown Inn to pick up some royal gossip over a pint of Guinness. There was a herd of cows laying down outside the pub's door, looking like they were waiting for opening time, blocking my way, and I was scared to disturb them because they were bigger than me. I was ready to flee back to the safety of the Big Smoke when Princess Anne rode by on horseback, flanked by her lady grooms, and I could have sworn she told the pesky beasts to 'naff orf'.

Prince Charles had a tenuous connection with my *Woman's Own* predecessor Clive Harold, a brilliant journalist and *bon vivant*. Clive would swing by the office, and I was warned not to talk to him because he might steal our ideas. So, we'd adjourn to the local across the road where the 6' 2" bouffant-haired Clive would sweep in trailing his floor-length fur coat. The looks on the locals' faces said, *What a prat*, though it never bothered Clive. In his mind, he was a star.

We lost touch in the intervening years. In the early '90s, out of the blue, I received a call from a friend telling me Clive had fallen on hard times and was living on the streets.

The story made national headline news. "One morning, I woke up and found myself in a shop doorway in the Strand," he told the *Daily Mirror*.

Clive was selling copies of the *Big Issue*, a widely circulated street newspaper in the UK, which offers homeless people the opportunity to earn a wage. It was in the magazine's London offices that he encountered Prince Charles. "I don't suppose you remember me," he asked Charles, "but we used to go to school together." Clive and Charles were in the same class at Hill House prep school in Chelsea when they were children. "I remembered you," he told Charles, "because we both had big ears."

I googled his name, checked on social media and talked to his former colleagues, but no clue of Clive's whereabouts materialised. I was left with the uneasy feeling this was a story without a happy ending.

OUT OF PRINT

In the late '70s, I freelanced for John Blake's Ad-Lib column at the *Evening Standard*. Working on Fleet Street was an education in itself, observing all the scallywags, the geniuses and larger than life characters of the print media. Blakey was the Street's breezy young pop music maverick in a sea of besuited hacks, and great fun to work with. As soon as we finished our copy around noon, he would march us over to the pub.

Home of British national newspapers for centuries, Fleet Street was like a time capsule, with historical buildings, law courts, inns and a labyrinth of alleyways, where the lorries carrying huge rolls of paper struggled to negotiate the narrow side streets to the printing presses. Two of my uncles started working 'in the print' at the *Daily Express* after discharge from National Service in the mid-fifties. Johnny and Georgie sported the square-jawed good looks of Rank matinee idols. You could always find them propping up the bar with fellow printers and hacks in one of the street's smoky pubs, hijacking the crowd with Max Bygraves impressions ("I wanna tell you a *story*") and other people's terrible jokes. I lived in fear that the two would sneak up on me while I chatted at the bar with some Harrovian gossip columnist and take the piss.

Today, the printers have become obsolete, the newspapers have moved on, and Fleet Street is a drab monochrome of law firms and sandwich bars. The exodus started in 1986 when Rupert Murdoch took the *Sun*, the *News of the World*, *The Times* and *The Sunday Times* off to a purpose-built complex at Wapping in East London. It marked the dawning of computerised printing technology when the screeching of hot metal print was replaced with the feathery tap of a keyboard. The music papers have folded, the UK music press as I knew it is no more. It had its flash-bulb moment, and then, *kechung*, disappeared. Whoever dreamed rock 'n' roll would end so quickly?

The Old Becomes the New

Here I am today, in an age of fake news and fluid policies, noticing a slide away from the authentic celebrity interviews

My daughter Lara and I, photographed in Yours, for Magazine Girl Janice Collier's Vintage fashion feature. Courtesy of Yours magazine.

to the celeb-on-celeb puff pieces we get in magazines now. It's the stars, photoshopped on social media, airbrushed in music videos, who call the shots.

Old rockers never die. Why would they get off the stage and let someone else have a turn when they can pack arenas with inflated ticket prices and make more money than ever? When I go to their shows, the only difference between me and every young person around me yelling and bopping is that I'm the one checking out where the 'Exits' for the toilets are.

Like the pop stars I once idolised, I have too many candles on my cake. I'm the 'mum' in the mother and daughter fashion spread that my Magazine Girl colleague Janice Collier produced for a vintage fashion spread in *Yours*. I'm fine with my daughter raiding my collection of '60s miniskirts, because I can't get away with wearing them anymore, except in my dreams.

While I have no desire to regain my lost '*yoof*', amazing as it was, I feel I still have a way to go before my pop-ups online will be for hip baths.

Then again, time has a sneaky way of catching up with all of us.

On a recent visit to a senior's residence in Montreal with my Polish author friend, Roma, I was introduced to her acquaintance who turned out to be William Shatner's sister. With her still delicate bone structure and China-blue eyes you could tell she had once been a beauty.

While we sat chatting, I mentioned I'd met her brother more than 50 years ago at the height of his fame as Captain Kirk in 'Star Trek'. Shatner had arrived for the interview looking a little shaky because just as he was leaving his hotel he got mobbed by a group of over-zealous 'Trekkies', and he thought they were going to tear his clothes off.

"Well, fancy that!" she said with a chuckle as she sipped her tea. "I guess that's fame for you…"

ANN'S STORY

Mᵐᵉ *Ann Carpenter*
Nationalité
Adresse

Nᵉ Carte professionnelle
est accrédité auprès de la Fédération Française de la Couture,
du Prêt à Porter des Couturiers et des Créateurs de Mode,
en qualité de :
Assistante
par : *Evening Standard*
(GB)

My 'official' passport to the Paris fashion collections.
Photograph: Roger Charity.

It was official; bespoke haute couture no longer solely dictated what women should wear. The inspiring, innovative ready-to-wear of the Pret would steer fashion into a huge classless arena, dominating the fashion market for decades to come as cheaper brands interpreted the looks to permeate every city and town throughout Europe, America, Asia and beyond. And I was there to see it happen.

ONE

YOUR WILDEST DREAMS

It was 1970, I was 21 and covering my first-ever Paris fashion show. The designer was Issey Miyake who, along with Kenzo Takada and Kansai Yamamoto, represented the new wave of Japanese ready-to-wear fashion designers at the Paris *Pret-a-Porter* collections. I will never forget the exhilaration of being present at such a thrilling event. The venue was packed to the rafters with international press, fashion buyers and photographers. The whole atmosphere was fired up and the female fashion silhouette was changed forever.

Gradually, the lights dimmed and voices faded to silence. Then came the models; Asian, black, oriental, multi-national; a trickle to begin with, then scores of them forming a continuous gliding performance along the catwalk. Each model walked in the same way – eyes to the front, arms to the side, with erect fluidity; the emphasis was on the designs, rather than the body within.

And the clothes were awesome, like nothing I'd seen before. Glorious, clashing colours in waves of fabric billowed behind the girls. This unstructured, loose and flowing silhouette, which employed Japanese clothing tradition, was in electrifying contrast to the skimpy, body-shaped mini that had dominated the 1960s. The mini skirt was aligned with the sexual liberation that began at the start of that decade, and some claimed it was a symbol of feminism. The voluminous cut of Miyake's cloth, a look being delivered by other emerging young designers, exemplified a new and contrasting kind of liberated feminism. This was one that critically challenged the conventional, thigh-revealing, voluptuous female shape of previous generations.

Throughout that memorable week, I witnessed creative alchemy in collections from names such as Sonia Rykiel, Jean Paul Gaultier, Thierry Mugler, Yves Saint Laurent, Jean Charles de Castelbajac, Claude Montana and the genius Kenzo Takada, designers who overturned every rule in traditional dress code for shake-up-inspiring yet practical ready-to-wear.

The sheer audacity of their risky imagination and the way they demolished the restrictions of convention were thrilling as decades of received good taste in dress were not only confronted but shredded. The modest-breasted slenderness of those self-assured, clearly bra-less models boldly celebrated the rule-

My striking invite to Thierry Mugler's 1980 summer collection.
Credit: Mugler Archives.

breaking atmosphere of the day. Many sported ultra-short boy-cuts, projecting an androgynous look that heralded things to come. The whole theatre lasted well over an hour – breathtaking fashion designs, one sensational theme after another. And then the bride. *Pret-a-Porter* brides were like no other – think black, Day-Glo and 'your wildest dreams'– traditionally signalling the end of the show and the appearance of the designer to the cheers of the audience.

It was official; bespoke *haute couture* no longer solely dictated what women should wear. The inspiring, innovative ready-to-wear of the *Pret* would steer fashion into a huge classless arena, celebrating women of all colours and cultures and dominating the fashion market for decades to come as cheaper brands interpreted the looks to permeate every city and town throughout Europe, America, Asia and beyond. And I was there to see it happen. Pure *zeitgeist*, of course, since rules were being toppled all over, politically and socially, and this was reflected throughout popular culture and the arts and, most strikingly, fashion.

But I'm getting ahead of myself. Looking back over these years, I can freely admit that the early signs were not auspicious; on the face of it, my prospects did not look great.

TWO

ALL EQUAL AND ALL STUPID?

When I turned five, my family overlooked sending me to school, rectified only by a visit from the school inspector. Mum was divorced – still frowned upon in the late '50s – was suffering from severe depression, possibly postnatal, and we lived with my grandparents. My father had left, taking my two-year-old sister, Janet, with him. She was never returned. Mum and my grandparents were also a little casual when it came to the 11+, which didn't seem to be on their radar.

At primary school, I was one of three kids in my class to pass the exam. No one was more surprised than me – except my family, that is. After learning I had passed, I rushed home in anticipation of interest, which didn't happen. Eventually, I asked why no one had enquired about the results. "Well, we didn't like to ask," was the anxious reply. Soon after, it became clear that passing the 11+ was an achievement held in pleasing esteem. Kids in my 1950s social circle received presents only at Christmas and birthdays. So, it came as a great surprise when not only did Dad post me a watch but Mum bought me a Kodak Brownie 44A. All were thrilled.

On the brink of my teens, I was a mix of low self-worth and far-reaching, hugely unrealistic ambitions. Passing the 11+

certainly helped the latter, and I was already showing signs of challenging established ideas and pathways. In the summer of 1960, instead of choosing to attend the prestigious Eltham Hill Grammar School for Girls, I opted instead for Kidbrooke Comprehensive.

Completed in 1954, Kidbrooke was one of England's first comprehensive schools, employing ideas way ahead of its time – ones that are finally being meaningfully implemented today. It was officially opened on 15 June 1955 by Countess Mountbatten of Burma, encompassed just under 2,000 girls and served a huge south east London catchment area. The diverse multicultural student population presented a ground-breaking vision of social inclusion.

Back then, I didn't fully understand what social inclusion meant, but the concept permeated my thinking, influencing me for the rest of my life. The dad of one girl in our class became the first black mayor of Lewisham. Another was from the first communist family I had come across, which I found seductively exotic. In my class were girls from posh, left-wing, middle-class Blackheath and feisty females from the sprawling south east London housing estates, who used colourful language and got into fights. Whatever their backgrounds and capabilities, all girls were expected to leave that school with the skills to earn their living.

Fashion was already playing a part in our lives. And it was the Mods (known then as 'modernists') who stood out. They were self-confidence personified in their mid-calf skirts, boys' haircuts and Hush Puppies, while the rest of us were still rolling up our waistbands to shorten our skirts and swaggering around with curious thick wodges of material betwixt shirts and hems – one retro idea that never found its way onto the catwalks.

This comprehensive school 'social experiment' proved an invaluable experience for many of us, though, naturally, there were doom-mongers who predicted it would sound the death knell for educational opportunities for the girls of south east London. The right-wing publication *Time and Tide* suggested the school's motto should be: 'All Equal and All Stupid', and questions were asked in Parliament by MPs worried about its likely impact. Alas, it seems today the visionary capabilities of MPs have not managed to develop.

Maybe the doom-mongers were concerned that us girls would want to work, rather than go straight into the role of 'housewife', thus threatening the very stability of our society. After all, the comprehensive plan was being drawn up at the end of WW2, when men were returning from conscription and many women who had carried on the 'men's work' had to give up their jobs.

Then everything changed again. My mother had remarried and gone to Nigeria with her new and very much younger husband, who I had previously met for half an hour. I was left with grandparents ill-equipped to look after a challenging 11-year-old who yearned to do things they didn't approve of, like go to dances in dark halls. After a year, Mum returned to England with her husband and we began a sequence of house-moving to fit in with my stepfather's job relocations.

First stop: Bushey, Herts, where I found myself in a backward and boring all-white middle-class grammar school. It was mixed education, so boys did Woodwork and girls had Cookery classes. I remember the humiliation at the sorry state of my pastry case, and then in the gym with my non-standard shorts, home-made by Mum. At Kidbrooke, we had 'Housecraft' instead of Cookery, and our Physical Education tutor directed us in expressive movement: "Pretend to fight your way out of a balloon…" which led to some super-inventive, contorted body language and a good amount of hilarity. Back at Bushey Grammar, why would anyone attempt to pointlessly jump over a horse? As for hockey, I soon discovered that if you convincingly messed about in the changing room, the punishment was to be barred from hockey. Job done.

A PASSION FOR FASHION

Soon, things perked up through making new friends and our introduction to the wonderful world of fashion through the growing movement of street culture. This was 1963 and on Saturday evenings, us 14 year-olds hung out at the Watford Trade Unionist and Labour Club where bands such as The Who, The Yardbirds and Georgie Fame and the Blue Flames performed live.

A bonus was that the Trade acted as a hub for the Mods. These guys were the real deal, older than us and part of the working-class movement that was rapidly spreading out from London. Mods adopted the coolest style in music and fashion: rhythm and blues, ska, Prince Buster, The Specials, The Who, Small Faces. Mods lit a fire under the whole street style culture that was to influence fashion and sounds for decades to come.

The cool, unmacho look of the original clean-shaven male Mods who coasted, sunshaded, on Lambretta and Vespa scooters, belied their taste for purple hearts and 'a bundle' with the rockers, who had greasy hair down to the collars of their skull-printed, studded leather jackets and rode ear-blasting motorbikes. Mods adopted loose 'GI' t-shirts, chinos, desert boots and the iconic parka, all to become classics in fashion 60 years on. The girls looked like boys with their cropped hair; long, coloured leather coats – from canary yellow to deep green to aubergine – Hush Puppies; ankle-skimming pants; mid-calf, slim skirts; pierced ears; Max Factor Pan Stik foundation and pencil-thin eyebrows. This female look was truly revolutionary. They may have been in 'kitten' heels and twinsets and pearls for evening wear, but these girls had claws and could weigh into a bundle with intent. The Mod movement made the big screen when 'Quadrophenia' was released 16 years later in 1979. And us kids were part of that.

My increasing passion for fashion nearly did for me when I became an enthusiastic member of a small group of schoolgirls who developed an interest in Saturday visits to Welwyn Garden City department stores to nick clothes, notably the expensive classic tweed suits so favoured by girl Mods. We sought no pleasure out of conning the stores; it's just that we lusted after clothes we couldn't afford. How we got away with it, I do not know, not least as our haul was so bulky. Try slipping a tweed suit under your coat. We even tried them on in the changing rooms beforehand. Inevitably, my partners in crime got caught. I was extraordinarily lucky not to be with them as, yes, we had just moved house again, so I missed that particular shopping trip. My schoolfriends' names and their headshots were published in the local paper. I felt so ashamed to have been part of that and, although mighty relieved, a bit guilty at getting off scot-free. Mercifully, my brief excursion into shoplifting came to an abrupt end.

On to a new town and the prospect of the next school. There was no hope of catching up academically and, aged 15, I disengaged from the education system and got a job working part time in a supermarket while attending typing classes in the afternoons. Yet another move one year later, this time back to the London suburbs. Since art had figured strongly at home, art school was an attractive proposition. But then, my clever mother spotted an ad in the *Evening Standard* for an office junior in *Woman's Own* Beauty department, general office duties for £6 a week.

THREE

RIGHT PLACE, RIGHT TIME

The interview was brief and I was hired on the spot. My interviewer, who was exquisitely dressed, was probably well past middle age at the time, but she was still a stunning beauty with a warm smile that shone favourably upon me. Only later did I come to learn and appreciate that Phyllis Digby Morton, beauty director of *Woman's Own*, was a publishing legend in her own lifetime.

Since they already had one Anne in the department, she briskly altered my name and, employing my middle name, I became Ann-Louise for the next four years. Next, she put me on a diet to lose a stone for a *Woman's Own* feature. My hair was cut into a fashionable bob and, having lost said stone, I was despatched to have my photograph taken by Murray Irving at the John French Studios in Bleeding Heart Yard where Terence Donovan and David Bailey began their careers and with whom I worked in later years.

It was like that in the 1960s, when jobs were freely advertised

Age 17 and a soft new hair look for a long-forgotten magazine.

and East End working-class lads and a comprehensive schoolgirl with no formal qualifications could be interviewed, get hired and start work a week later in a job with prospects. If you were reliable and showed initiative, you could work your way up. But back in those days, you could also be fired with equal rapidity. I remember a secretary, a rather catty French girl, speaking to me very rudely, but even I was surprised at the speed with which she was dismissed. No first or second warnings in those days.

I loved PDM as she was known, primarily because she took a special interest in me. It was a turning point in my dull, suburban, few-prospects life, and I owed the rest all to her, not forgetting Mum, of course, for spotting the ad.

PDM was known in publishing as 'The Grande Dame of the Glossies'. Her editorship of *Woman and Beauty* magazine, published by Fleetway in the early 1930s, was noted for breaking new ground in the women's magazine market. Previously dominated by subjects such as needlework and cookery, PDM introduced sexual issues such as virginity, frigidity, fertility and infidelity. She later recalled, "We tackled all the 'ity' subjects, and what a fuss they caused with all those gentlemen on the Fleetway board."

I remember Phyllis telling me how, when she worked as a young newspaper reporter, she was sent to cover a divorce case and was barred from court by the judge because of her gender. The explanation: the case was no fit subject for a woman. She lived in a grand Mayfair mansion apartment with her husband, Henry Digby Morton, universally known as Digby, who was a couturier.

I recall the time members of the Beauty department were invited to a drinks party where waiters circulated with champagne and mini pizza canapes. Having a look around the flat when I arrived, I had been hugely impressed by the spacious and elegant bathrooms; one for the boys, another for the girls. I had never before come across two bathrooms in one household. Overdoing the booze and pizza, I am still mortified to remember staggering to the 'girls" bathroom and throwing up on the marble floor.

There are certain characters who go down in journalism folklore. PDM was one, Dennis Whelan another. An unforgettable character, for the best of reasons, Dennis was a respected graphic designer and artist whose career was mainly freelance, largely for the International Publishing Corporation (IPC), Carlton Publishing and Bauer Publishing. He also worked on *Vogue* in the 1960s. Dennis gained a reputation as a trouble-shooter. If a magazine was falling in readership, he would be brought in for several months to work alongside the editor and reshape the title, responsible for a complete redesign and overhaul. Dennis always encouraged young talent and went on to teach Art and Design at the London College of Printing and PMA Media Training.

At *Woman's Own*, Dennis and PDM enjoyed collaborating with exaggerated secrecy on special projects. Both loved the conspiratorial aspect of keeping their assignments well under wraps and would theatrically cover up layouts if other staff members walked in. Dennis was funny, wonderfully irreverent, sometimes acerbic and prickly but essentially respectful of people and was much admired and loved in the business. He certainly made me feel I was valued as part of the team.

Dennis cropped up regularly in my life over the years, as we were both living in Putney at the time and had mutual friends. Not that he was always an easy character. At one stage, my pal Caroline Richards got together with him, moved in and invited me over to supper. Dennis was out and Caroline showed me the kitchen cupboard where he had written DW in thick, indelible felt pen over all his condiment jars. Dennis arrived home a little later and the pair of them fell out over something. I remember feeling rather awkward but also highly entertained as they stood at opposite ends of the room shouting "Bollocks!" and "Well, bollocks to you too!" at each other. That relationship foundered and Dennis went on to marry his girlfriend Ronnie. They were together for 20 years and married for ten, up to his untimely death far too young. We need people like Dennis, and not only in the media; people who through their generosity of spirit, skills and encouragement give real hope to youngsters, including ones like me from troubled backgrounds.

I still have a beautiful first edition of 'English Fairy Tales' exquisitely illustrated by Edmund Dulac that he gave me after a birthday supper party at my flat. The message inside – in bold felt tip pen – reads, 'Thanks for supper – what a hangover!'

In those days, both *Woman* and *Woman's Own* were selling in the millions and magazines had vast staff counts and fat budgets. The Beauty department was showered with freebies from beauty product companies – everything from cellulite-busting treatments to perfume, cosmetics and what were then called anti-ageing creams. For the beauty editor, there were boozy, schmoozy lunches courtesy of big brand PRs and even all-expenses-paid trips abroad for the launch of new ranges. Rich product companies, particularly the ones who could afford to advertise, reaped generous editorial mentions. Products were taken very seriously and office staff chat involved intense discussions around eyeliner and face packs.

Once, the staff team were despatched to different beauty salons to test innovating fat-busting techniques. My thighs were subjected to an intensely painful suction treatment by a grim-faced beautician in a white overall. The next day, they were covered in huge blue-purple bruises and, naturally, there was no sign of weight loss. Madness.

Working at *Woman's Own* was intensely competitive for staff, and tears were frequently shed after altercations. Some of my 'Magazine Girls' friends passed through WO (pronounced 'woe') at different times, surviving to share their experiences in this book. As for me, an unsophisticated south London teenager, life was pretty limited in the fun department. I felt disconnected from the others in the Beauty department who were older and posh. One had been brought up on a royal estate, and another had a boyfriend who was a sheriff. The 'wild west' and Robin Hood's nemesis aside, what on earth was a sheriff in the 1960s?

Looking back, I can appreciate that I was rather a dour teen and no doubt sometimes a pain to have around. They were always asking for cups of tea which I got fed up with making and it showed. I adored PDM but she occupied a separate, spacious office upstairs, with a huge desk and drinks cabinet in the famous 'tower' of Tower House in Southampton Street. I was one floor down amid the 'debby' types as I called them, with their posh voices and perfect pronunciation of French cosmetic brands – accents so very different to my own south London enunciation. I didn't realise it at the time, but I was periodically suffering from serious depression which continued throughout my working life. Fortunately, medication today is far less invasive and that, mixed with a complete change of lifestyle, has helped enormously.

There wasn't a great deal of respect for the readers in the Beauty department – I remember the beauty editor of the time saying disparagingly, "Our readers don't read books." Those who wrote in with beauty problems were dealt with by a separate department altogether where the staff were virtually ignored by the editorial team. The beauty editor, who appeared to be the object of schoolgirl-type crushes from the other members of the department, had run-ins with some management person or another, returning tearful and shaken, describing them as "absolute shits" and demanding one of my precious fags.

A particular disappointment for me was being excluded

from the occasional long-lunch staff shopping expeditions to the most exciting and original fashion shop in London – Biba in Kensington. I had to remain behind to mind the office and feel hard done by. That beauty editor eventually left to go to a better-paid job with a cosmetics company. She had frequently lamented being hard up and eventually became a best-selling author of blockbusters and presumably extremely rich. She was succeeded by Caroline Richards, a former *protégée* of PDM's who'd been working on *Petticoat*. It was Caroline who encouraged me to move on from being an office junior and, very soon after, an astonishing opportunity arose.

James Wedge shot the photographs for Biba's 1978 brochure promoting the new store at 22 Conduit St, W1. Cosmetics' shades mirrored the clothes colours.

FOUR

RAMPED UP AND RECKLESS

The 1960s was a decade of counterculture, an anti-establishment sensation marking the growth of the civil rights movement, women's rights, gay rights, alternative lifestyles and challenges to traditional forms of authority. People around the world joined the protest against the continuing war in Vietnam. It was also the beginning of the mass environmental movement. Bob Dylan prophesied a wave that could engulf the whole world and messaged it in his brilliant 'A Hard Rain's A-Gonna Fall'.

Into the early 1970s, the youth market was being ramped up in the media to capitalise on growing interest in pop music and fashion and the increasing spending power of teens. Glossy magazines such as *Vogue* and *Harpers & Queen* had dominated the fashion scene, but the new magazines – *Honey*, *Petticoat* and *19,* launched in the 1960s – targeted a younger market. As office junior in the Beauty department of *Woman's Own,* I'd been given increasing editorial responsibility and was writing short pieces of copy. Then, when an editorial job came up in a new 'love story weekly' aimed at adolescent girls, I quickly applied, got an interview with Bill Willamson, managing editor of several teen publications, and, aged 21, was hired. And that was how I

In the Loving office. Photograph by Jeremy Fletcher.

became fashion editor of *Loving* magazine and got to attend my first-ever Paris fashion show...

Bill's titles were based at Fleetway Publications in Farringdon Street at the end of Fleet Street. Fleetway was one of the companies that, in 1963, merged into the International Publishing Corporation (IPC) until 1968 when all IPC's publications were consolidated into IPC Magazines. Who'd have thought I would be working for the publisher of comics that had transfixed me in my formative years – *Playhour*, then *Girls' Crystal* and *School Friend*?

Fleetway House comprised a warren of rooms housing publications such as *Mirabelle, Valentine, Fab 208, Rave, Hers, Loving* and later *Love Affair*. How wonderful it was to be working with a whole group of people of my age and with similar backgrounds and interests. My new workmates were such a colourful bunch. There was one guy who called himself Che, after Che Guevara, another called Xy (pronounced Zye) and my new friends from *Mirabelle* – Linda Newman and Sandie Robbie – who were always going off to interview pop stars. Then there was glamorous Dodders in the Art department, who mystified us by running two long-term boyfriends at the same time, one a famous sportsman.

I shared an office with *Loving's* beauty editor, the impressively elegant Janice Collier, always immaculately turned out and who entertained us with her spontaneous and startlingly convincing comic impressions of Cilla Black. The third member of our department was 17-year-old Penny Saunders, tiny of stature, dressed in long skirts, Biba crochet skull cap and looking like a mini Pre-Raphaelite heroine, yet strong enough to carry around the armfuls of clothes that constantly passed through the office. Penny later edited the *Pennywise* column for fashion on a budget. Later, we moved next door to Magazine Girl Shirley Dunmall, working in an administrative role at the time but who was later to become one of the foremost beauty PRs in the business.

In the Features department were youngsters Jane Butterworth (whose husband Brian Wright made up the crosswords) and Ruth Pitt. Jane later made a name for herself in another booming market, that of self-help books, while dispensing advice as the agony aunt for the *News of the World*. Ruth, already mega career-focused, moved into TV. Others who journeyed on their careers through our offices included journalism trainee Penny Junor, later carving a role as a royal biographer. What a gift my new job was, not least since many of my colleagues, including Jane and my fellow Magazine Girls authors, were to remain lifelong friends. It was Jane who, 15 years on, was to introduce me to Geoff, my second husband and best friend.

Despite our youth and lack of experience, we were allowed a remarkable – some would say reckless – amount of freedom and responsibility. Feature writers each had a designated number of

Double-page fashion spread for Loving. Photographs by Frank Murphy.

pages in the magazine – a weekly two-page fashion spread in my case – and were basically left to get on with it. That said, failing a deadline was never tolerated by the management, who had eyes everywhere and didn't miss a trick. The work was intensive but together we also went clubbing, partied, holidayed and engaged in juvenile horseplay around the offices, involving ambushes with water-filled squeezy bottles and more imaginative larks such as being Sellotaped into cupboards.

Yes, we drank too much – not least at press junkets. I still cringe at our adolescent lack of manners as I recall accompanying my mates from the *Mirabelle* team to some launch or other where the young Elton John played live just a few feet from our table. Having drunk and eaten our freebie fill, we rose *en masse* to depart, while Elton was still in full voice.

I had no personal experience of drugs in our corner of the media, certainly not in the office, although my then boyfriend, Frank, rolled joints which we passed around in the flat I shared with a fashion assistant on *Flair* fashion magazine. And I once scoffed some cannabis cakes unaware of the special ingredient. Those substances were far weaker than they are now and, if imbibed, just made everything seem hilarious. But having now read Nick Kent's brilliant book of essays, 'The Dark Stuff: Selected Writings on Rock Music 1972–1993', I appreciate things were getting seriously 'developed' in the rock media.

Two of my special friends at Fleetway were Sara Kotch, who edited *Mirabelle's* fashion pages, and Janet Impey, who became fashion editor of *Loving's* sister magazine *Love Affair*, both multitalented and highly accomplished, creative craftswomen who had studied Fashion at college.

Sara came from a media family and was a hybrid between posh (she was educated at the French *Lycée* in South Kensington) and totally down-to-earth 'everywoman'. She was very striking – quite small with hair heavily layered, long at the back and standing up on top, adding several more inches to her height. She dressed in paintbox-bright clothes such as satin shorts over coloured tights, t-shirts appliquéd with ice cream cones and multicoloured platform shoes. One of her favourite shops was the renowned Mr Freedom in the King's Road which sold eye-socking pop-art fashion. Sara also created her own distinctive knitted designs for both adults and children. She regarded knitting as fabric, hand-working it into myriad surfaces and textures. Her works were included in 'The Sweater Book, 50 Original Handknits by Top Designers', published in 1984. As with most arts, the best in fashion design, however outrageous at the time, became classics, and the knits in that book are fine examples.

Each spring and autumn, Janet Impey and I travelled together to the Paris *Pret-a-Porter* to cover the spring and autumn collections. We stayed in a little hotel on the Left Bank and I remember our favourite restaurant at the end of the road where, after an inspiring if turbulent day being pushed and shoved at the fashion shows and sketching endless outfits for all we were worth, we enjoyed supper of *cassoulet* followed by unforgettable strawberries and *crème Anglaise* tarts.

FIVE

GLITTERATI AND CATWALK CABARET

On arrival at the Gare du Nord, we would hurry along to the hotel hoping our tickets to the fashion shows had arrived. Despite the required marathon of form filling for the powerful ruling Chambre Syndicale, we always had trouble getting tickets, which was hardly surprising, as teenage love story weeklies just didn't carry the cachet of *Vogue*, *Elle* and *Marie Claire*.

If we didn't have tickets we would turn up early then hang around for an hour or so hoping to be allowed in on our press cards. There were bouncers on the doors, and even with tickets, gaining entrance to the shows was physically challenging. People would queue in a terrific crush as hundreds of journalists, photographers and general *glitterati* from around the world jostled to gain entry while actresses, style gurus and fashion editors from the most influential media were waved straight through to their front-row seats.

Once inside, Janet and I would usually spot the legendary Bill Cunningham, master of ground-breaking street style fashion photography for the *New York Times*. Clad in his signature French 'workman's' jacket and with a beaming smile, the wiry Bill moved like liquid mercury as he snapped movie stars, royals and key fashionistas clad in their designer outfits.

The incomparable Bill Cunningham.

But he also had the creative imagination to snap the 'unknowns'– those dressed in the most individual and inventively put-together outfits. Bill was at all the shows, travelling from one to another by bicycle.

Crushed in our seats, pencils and pads at the ready, we set about drawing the hundreds of garments paraded before us. Yes – we *drew*. Speed being crucial, we perfected a visual shorthand skill that, in a few convincing lines, would clearly show what a garment looked like. As the models paraded past, the key design themes became clear. Out of all this, we crafted our copy, paring down all we had seen into snappy text that flagged up the strongest fashion looks and the ones most likely to be influential.

Back then, a mere handful of the garments actually reached production as cautious retail store buyers dictated which of the more 'wearable' outfits would go into their shops and stores, thus editing out the more thrilling designs. The electrifying, one-off boutiques run by fashion designers were yet to claim ownership of our high streets, thus editing out the store buyers. Many fashion show garments were pure theatre, created simply for impact on the catwalks (today termed runways). When later working on the *Evening Standard* and *Evening News,* I would write up my fashion collections copy then phone it over to the speedy copy takers back at the London office to meet the deadline for the following day. Back then, we had no World

Wide Web, so my photographer would drive the photo film to the airport.

DARKER SHADE OF PALE

Previously at *Woman's Own,* all the major international womens' magazines were regularly circulated in the Beauty department. Even back then it was conspicuous how the 'black' models featured in American magazines such as *Glamour* and *Seventeen* had light coffee-coloured complexions and hair straightened into the soft waves of American housewives. In other words, they were required to become slightly darker versions of white models. Not a Marsha Hunt afro to be seen. At least they were featured in the US glossies; during my time at *Woman's Own,* I don't remember ever seeing a black model featured in the fashion or beauty pages.

But at the Paris *Pret,* conventions around race and gender were being overturned along with everything else. This was in the days before Botox, breast 'adjustment' and enhanced bums. In the fashion modelling world of the 1970s, the top girls were not only striking to look at, but individuality – sometimes startling – was celebrated. These catwalk models were the cream of their profession, and two who were in special demand were Pat Cleveland and Donna Jordan. Not as famous as their contemporaries Jerry Hall and Somalia-born Iman, later to marry David Bowie, but today recognised as two of the most influential models of all time for their explosive fashion show performances. The sheer sassy revelry with which they chose to rhythmically parade the clothes, in what can only be described as a catwalk cabaret, has become the stuff of fashion folklore.

Pat Cleveland was to become one of the world's first 'supermodels'. But, at the age of 16, she was told by a leading American model agency that she would never make it as a model

Firecracker supermodel Donna Jordan aka 'Disco Marilyn'.

because of her colour. Disillusioned with the general racism of American modelling, Pat relocated to Paris and became a house model for the legendary Karl Lagerfeld. Today, Pat can be seen on YouTube performing her celebrated 'runway dances'.

In total contrast appearance-wise, Donna Jordan was commonly known as 'Disco Marilyn' and was one of the most influential models of all time. She had striking white-blonde hair and bleached her eyebrows. Pat later said of her friend and frequent catwalk partner: "Donna was like a firecracker. She'd come into the room and wake everybody up and be lively and make the room come to life." Donna, who was also an actress and singer, spent time with the Andy Warhol Factory. She said in an interview: "We came from Andy Warhol. We were superstars."

Jamaican-born singer, songwriter and actress Grace Jones was another stand-out presence at the Pret. Having moved to New York at 18, she had successfully gained work as a model before moving to Paris in 1970. The Parisian fashion scene immediately took to her arresting, androgynous, dark-skinned appearance and bold stance. Top designers hired her for their shows, and she was photographed for the glossies by leading photographers of the time such as Hans Feurer, Guy Bourdin and Helmut Newton.

We met a few years later for a photo shoot on the *London Evening News* when she was developing her singing career and had just released 'La Vie En Rose', her first single for Island Records. Grace's appearance did not disappoint. She had shorn her hair to a minimalist scalp shine and drawn in the parting with yellow paint. At time of writing, she is 74 and, like so many performers from that era, she continues to rock.

This celebration of individualism and diversity was way ahead of its time. Today, I struggle to understand how we have reverted to such a dependence on an 'ideal' of beauty. Body contouring, Botox, line filling, etc… have collectively resulted in a homogenous ideal in looks, with everyone ending up pursuing a bland 'similar'. The ageing process is airbrushed from magazine covers. They may now project faces that include all ages and genders but that are, nonetheless, very obviously enhanced into a more acceptable blended image. So we have gone backwards. What a lamentable turn of events. That ridiculous thigh-bruising suction experience I underwent on *Woman's Own*, which belonged in the Dark Ages, was instead a portent of things to come…

SIX

WHEN AN IMAGE STARTS TO SING

A key experience for me at the Paris fashion shows was watching the hundreds of international photographers that lined either side of the catwalk, snapping the high-speed trail of models. Back at *Loving*'s London offices, I had the opportunity to work with some brilliant young names in fashion photography who were just starting out in their careers. The painter Wilhelmina Barns-Graham spoke of the struggle involved in making a painting – and then the breakthrough moment, describing it thus: "…when the painting starts to sing."

Some photographers are able to go far beyond technical skill; they have that fugitive ability to recognise the moment when an image 'starts to sing'. I was lucky enough to work with three who had that gift – Roger Charity, Frank Murphy and Tony McGee, who were just starting out in fashion photography. Each had that magic touch of alchemy that is hard to describe and can't be learnt but makes a photograph a classic. Like a wonderful painting or piece of music that thrills the heart and ignites an immediate connection with the viewer. Some years ago, a friend of mine cited the first time he heard 'Layla' by Eric Clapton, saying: "It felt as though the song had been written just for me." And that's as insightful a response to art as anything I've heard since.

It was thrilling to watch these photographers tease out the magnetism in an image – frequently to the sounds of the great rock bands of the time if we were working in a studio. When it happened, that magical atmosphere was highly conducive to seduction and I was susceptible as any of the models. I recall one famous photographer, in between shots, suggesting sex with me over a formica topped table while the model, hairdresser and make-up artist worked their alchemy in a separate room. Charismatic as the photographer was, the formica topped table just didn't resonate and anyway, married men were off limits.

Two established iconic photographers I worked with were Terence Donovan and James Wedge. Each with immense skill and substantial creative vision plus their distinctive brands of charisma – Donovan dressed in a smart suit and Wedge a gentle Heathcliff. Both men came from working-class backgrounds and, with their friend David Bailey, contributed to the transformation of the fashion photographic landscape of the 1960s.

One memorably special time, I was the subject of the photo shoot and experienced the genius for myself. I was in my mid-twenties, had just joined the *London Evening News* as fashion editor and was photographed for a promotion by the incomparable Barry Lategan, known significantly for discovering and producing iconic images of Lesley Hornby, better known as Twiggy. His photographs are now in the National Portrait Gallery collection.

Being photographed by

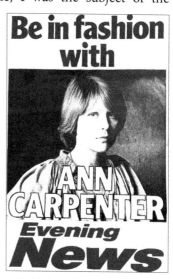

Suddenly I'm poster girl for London's Evening News.

291

Lategan is something you never forget; for a start, you have the setting: his Victorian Chelsea studio was said to be once occupied by Dante Gabriel Rossetti. He didn't want a hairdresser or make-up artist and liked the peasant blouse I arrived wearing, so we went for the shoot *au natural*. He made me feel oh-so-special, and I'll swear the spirit of Pre-Raphaelite romanticism still occupied that studio. I loved the resulting photo – although it didn't look particularly like me – which was blown up to poster size, proclaimed 'Be in Fashion with Ann Carpenter – *Evening News*' and was plastered on billboards all around central London as well as on the side of a bus.

RESTLESS

Looking back over my time as a fashion editor, on both magazines and newspapers, I wonder how I managed to produce a fashion spread every week, 50-odd weeks of the year. The job involved visiting the collections in wholesale showrooms, which were mostly in the West End at that time, and selecting garments for the shoot, booking photographer, models, hairdresser, make-up artist and finding locations. I have worked with the best-known names in the fashion photographic world – John Swannell, John Adriaan and Terry O'Neill as well as Wedge, Donovan and Bailey. These guys were spellbinding to watch when practising their art (apart from Bailey, who wouldn't allow me in his studio). However, my role at these photo shoots, which involved dressing the models and then standing around while the hairdressers and make-up artists got to work, was beginning to feel repetitive and I was becoming restless. I wanted to be the creator and not the facilitator.

Back in the world of teen magazines, the ground-breaking publication in the 1970s was *19*. Australian-born Norma Moriceau was the fashion editor and my hero. She innovatively and thrillingly styled the latest fashion looks in ways that had never been seen before. On returning to Australia, an inspired Moriceau forged a successful career in movie wardrobe design, notably creating the astonishing warrior-motorcyclist costumes for the 'Mad Max' films.

For the character of Aunty Entity in 'Thunderdome', played by Tina Turner, Norma created a chainmail gown from a collection of feral objects, soldering together coat hangers, butcher aprons, dog muzzles and chicken wire. Entity's earrings were industrial-sized springs. Reported figures for the weight of the dress vary between 70 pounds and 150 pounds

How I longed to work on *19*, instead of on *Loving* where my fashion pages were surrounded by romantic stories for adolescents. I also had constant battles with the Art department who insisted on being 'decorative' with their layouts and fancy fonts when all that was required was simplicity and space, with photographs used as large as possible. Then an unexpected opportunity arose. I'd written a strange short story which involved some kind of 'being' in a crisis situation who turned out to be a dot on the edge of a teacup. I can't actually remember it that well, other than it was called 'Microbe'. My mate Linda Newman, who worked on *Mirabelle* before moving to *19*, got wind of it and, being the supportive friend she was, encouraged me to submit it to *19*'s visionary editor, Maggie Koumi, who liked it enough to publish it. I was over the moon.

SEVEN

CREATOR NOT FACILITATOR

The genes were kicking in. All my family were creative in the arts. Mum – Doreen – had attended Woolwich Polytechnic aged 14 with standard lessons in the morning and Art for the afternoons. You could do that in the 1930s. Both Mum and Grandma Alma had been classically trained in singing and Grandpa Hugh attended art evening classes while working in his day job as a sales rep. He eventually became a cartographer in the Admiralty and, on retirement, painted exquisite watercolour greetings cards which he sold for a song to commercial card companies while also making for me little books with hand-painted lettering and illustrations. The three of them were keen actors in the local amateur dramatics company The Arcadians, acting and singing at Eltham Little Theatre which was formed in November 1943 to promote drama, music and allied arts in Eltham and the surrounding area. When the theatre hit hard times in the late 1970s, Bob Hope, who originally came from Eltham, stepped in with the necessary funds and in 1982 it became the Bob Hope Theatre.

Although my sister Jan Sheppard and I had been brought up separately, we kept in touch. This was despite our father, who had remarried and had four more children, never revealing to his second family that he'd been married before. Jan has inherited our family genes and is a multitalented creative specialising in photography. I find her work hugely inspirational and her photographs feature in my book 'Wild Margins, Drawings and Inspirations'.

Like so many others, Mum's artistic ambitions were cut short by WW2 when she had to work in the munitions factory at the Woolwich Royal Arsenal. The 'Munitionettes', as they were known, were drawn from all areas of society and Mum found herself working on the production line alongside a ballerina. It was a dangerous place to work, not least because of the toxic substances the women were handling and the ever-present threat of bombing raids. During WW2, 103 people were killed and nearly 770 injured during 25 raids. Mum would walk to work carrying an artist's drawing board to shield herself from shrapnel rather than having to throw herself to the pavement, in case it spoiled her peach-coloured coat.

When WW2 ended, people struggled to fit into grey post-war suburban life. Many women had enjoyed working before getting married and then again during the war. My grandmother never took to being a 'housewife', but she looked after me well while Mum was at work and always read me my *Playhour* comic directly it arrived through the letterbox. From a young age, I was encouraged to draw and paint, making and illustrating my own magazines.

Mum, Doreen McCoy, in her Arcadian days.

YOU NOW HAVE EIGHT MINUTES

While working on *Loving*, exposure to innovative fashion design, together with getting a story published in the great *19*, brought with it the realisation that I wanted to write more than just a title and brief introduction to the fashion pages followed by a list of captions. I was 23 when a job came up in the Fashion department of the *Evening Standard*, a job that would enable me to broaden my horizons, and I jumped at the opportunity. The vacancy arose because Janet Street-Porter, the current deputy fashion editor, was off to pursue a career in television. The fashion editor was Suzy Menkes, a force to be reckoned with in a range of ways and who, at time of writing, continues to brilliantly dominate the fashion industry via social media.

I learnt that relations between Suzy and Janet, two immensely capable and ambitious women, had been less than affable, and Suzy appeared relieved to hire me, inviting me to lunch at the Mermaid Theatre. Somewhat overawed by this super confident embryonic icon of the fashion industry, I was completely nonplussed when offered an aperitif and remember how she swiftly put me at my ease by suggesting a gin and lime. And what with the wine that followed, that's all I remember of the lunch.

Writing this, I am aware how I frequently recall events and trips by food and drink. New Delhi: fierce cocktails; Amsterdam: delicious hot cooked beetroot in a side-street café; Paris: canapés, champagne and life-sized ice swans in a tiny art deco museum; Monte Carlo: mega carbohydrate breakfasts in the Hotel de Paris, after late-night clubbing. Nearer home – Pembrokeshire coast: prosecco with cheese scones; Hay-on-Wye: bowls of steaming, curried vegetable soup on a bitter day; Dublin: the most expensive single fresh pear on the planet; train from Glasgow to Oban: large iced vodka and tonic while settling back to soak up the passing mountain scenery.

A world away from the young magazines, the *Standard* was a hub of high achievers and well-connected toffs. I was surrounded by the likes of the Eton-educated, the Oxbridge-graduated, the titled, the honoured, legends in their own lifetimes. Suzy had trained as a historian at Newham College, Cambridge where she became the first female editor of *Varsity*. Today, she has received numerous awards including membership of the French National Order of the Légion d'Honneur, and the Order of the British Empire for Services to Fashion Journalism. The features editor was Simon Jenkins (to become Sir Simon); Brian Sewell, dedicated adversary of conceptual art, was earning his reputation as Britain's most controversial and acerbic art critic; features writer Mary Kenny was a founder of the Irish Women's Liberation Movement; a granddaughter of Sir Winston Churchill worked on the Diary column. The place was heaving with 'names'.

Suzy had a reputation for being imperious but her qualities were ones I admired: hard-working, straight-speaking, professional and fair. However, she was rather remote, operating in a high-fashion parallel world to the rest of us in the open-plan Fashion department, and she was certainly in thrall of high-status designer labels. She led a grand lifestyle married to David Spanier, foreign and diplomatic correspondent of *The Times,* and, with two young sons and a magnificent St John's Wood house to run, juggled all this with her own career. She was also, unlike me, a very shrewd operator. Mindful of working in a Fleet Street culture staffed mostly by old-school male journos, she frequently and with creative subtlety often managed to inject sex into her columns. Remember, these were the days of Page 3 women, and Fleet Street was pretty macho then.

Well, I wanted to write and that's what I did, churning out words at breakneck speed to meet endless deadlines and learning to think on the hoof. That has stood me in good stead ever since, although I wish I'd been far less naïve and adopted some of Suzy's shrewder skills at the time. The news and picture desk staff were formidable. They worked all together on a huge open-plan floor, dispensing colourful language with impressive imagination. To this day, I remember the picture editor's withering comment on a batch of Paris fashion photographs I'd just delivered, saying of the photographer: "He needs his balls chewing off."

The news desk, which was three flights down, often rang up for a sparky fashion caption to go with a paparazzi photo, such as Mick and Bianca Jagger leaving a nightclub. The first time this happened I ran down the three flights to be handed the picture with the command, "We need 200 words in ten minutes." Then, brief explained and duly received, to be told, "Right, you now have eight minutes." By the time I'd run back upstairs it was more like five, and I still had to think what to say. Thinking with speed has proved a handy skill ever since.

The big-deal wedding of the time was when Princess Anne married Captain Mark Phillips on 14 November 1973. The evening before the royal nuptials, news editor Stuart Kuttner briefed me on how I would be responsible for the next day's front page. Soon after sunrise I was to collect a copy of Maureen Baker's design for the wedding dress from the West One showroom of ready-to-wear design label Susan Small then speed back to the *Standard* office to write the piece for the early edition.

I have never forgotten how, first thing on the big day, I woke up feeling sick with nerves at this burden of responsibility. The taxi picked me up from home and dropped me off in the West End... and I couldn't find the showroom. Panic meltdown. Not having the confidence of Churchill's granddaughter, I realised there was no point returning to the office empty- handed as I wouldn't have a job. However, suddenly I spotted a small sign in an upstairs window, grabbed a press copy of the dress, then dashed back to the *Standard* to complete the task. Stuart

A first (and last) front-page byline.

directed me to remain on the news desk should further fashion copy be needed for the next edition. Perched in the midst of 'proper' reporters, all racing around waving bits of paper, I was terrified of being asked to write something else at great speed and in front of the great and the good of Fleet Street, all bristling with uber-confidence.

My four years on that paper were full of vigour, excitement and terror, in equal quantities – and everything carried out on the double. I loved the clothes, creating the fashion pages and doing the interviews. And yet it was 208 weeks of unmitigated stress and self-doubt.

Fleet Street of the 1970s was in the days before corporate clones became the norm. Newspapers were staffed by highly individual, frequently eccentric characters. Liquid lunches were commonplace and, at the end of the day, ashtrays overflowed and empty wine bottles reclined bottoms up in waste paper bins. Political *in*correctness (the original term first appeared in Marxist-Leninist vocabulary following the Russian Revolution of 1917, but was virtually unknown in the early 1970s) was rife, romances flamed and occasional fist fights broke out on the news floor. Long-term grudges were nursed. It was common knowledge that two fashion editors who, for years, had shared an office on the *Daily Telegraph* were renowned for never speaking to each other. Long-suffering fashion PRs had to treat each of them exactly the same, and *always* separately.

My friend Beryl Downing, who doubled as both the 'Quick Cook' and the agony aunt on the *Evening News,* was embroiled in a lengthy, consuming feud with the women's editor, Anne de Courcy. Beryl once confided: "Anne de Courcy is the last thing I think about every night in the bath." This was not in a good way.

Beryl told me she had never wanted to be the agony aunt, complaining that *Evening News* editor Louis Kirby made her do it because there wasn't anyone else. She once lamented to me how sometimes she felt like replying to a reader's problem: 'You find the ledge and we can jump together'. She was eventually released from her misery when offered, in her words, 'the best job in Fleet Street', that of shopping editor on *The Times*. I still have a few of the exquisite contemporary Scandinavian wine glasses she gave me when I married my first husband. They became a design classic, as anything would on being selected by Beryl Downing.

These were the halcyon days before 'corporate clones' and team-building away days. Individuals bordering on eccentricity flourished and the system, ruled by strict deadlines, worked. Back at the *Evening Standard*, the Fashion department was one floor up from the newsroom, next door to 'Jak's Cabin', home to political cartoonists Jak, Frank Dickens (each a law unto themselves) and Rick Brookes, husband of Magazine Girl

Linda. Directly outside us were 'the greyhounds': rows of men who listed the dog races and betting odds. Next to them was the Stationery department – a sort of railway ticket office-type booth with a window over a counter. This was the territory of George Palmer, a man respected for his unyielding resolve not to hand out too many biros and notepads. You had to mind your manners with George, treat him with due respect, and it helped if you thanked him for all he did for the SOGAT Union. You then swiftly received your six notebooks and four black biros.

Further up the corridor was the office of features editor Marius Pope, described thus in his *Times* obituary (11 January 2010): 'If there had been a Colourful Journalist of the Year award Marius Pope would have won it many times'. Marius once suffered a coronary at work which, according to a paragraph in 'The Glossy Years' by Nicholas Coleridge, wasn't noticed for some time, as his colleagues thought he was slumped over his desk asleep after a pub lunch. 'Colourful' Marius, actually a rather serious, self-contained character, one day astonished me by suddenly exiting his chair and pursuing me round his desk, hands outstretched, saying, "You have such lovely breasts..." Out of the blue and certainly out of character and no threat to me because of the recent coronary, he was still overweight and I was faster. I swiftly exited his office and put this aberration down to another liquid lunch. Marius was not the type of man who needed to be avoided; besides, back in the day, women journos had no trouble giving unwanted behaviour extremely short shrift.

While on the subject, for me personally, unacceptable sexual conduct arose only once – with a most unpleasant man from the *Daily Mail*. He contacted me about freelancing, invited me to dinner (odd, but it was a good gig, so I went along) and spoke about his wife in a way that appalled me. Suffice to say, his designs on me were glaringly clear but I was having none of it. I actually got the freelance work anyway. This was a rare occurrence since the difference between my role and many of today's victims of sexual abuse at work is that I was usually in the position of giving out the jobs.

The Summer of Love social phenomenon happened during the summer of 1967, when an estimated 100,000 mostly young people sporting hippy fashion in dress and behaviour converged on Haight-Ashbury, San Francisco. In the same year, the National Health Service (Family Planning) Act of 1967 empowered local health authorities to give birth control advice, regardless of marital status. Nicholas Roeg's film 'Performance', made in 1968, took two years to go on public release due largely to the graphic exploration of gender and sexual identity. 'The Joy Of Sex' was published in 1972.

We were still living in an age of 'free love', and people – women as well as men – were far less cautious about trying their luck. In the office environment, one was propositioned from time to time and no damage done. You weren't always buying even if it was free. That said, it was pretty flirty on all sides and journalists often had affairs. Couples, newly enchanted and probably already married to another, would sidle out of the office at lunchtime for a romantic tryst. Not a hope of being unnoticed since most areas were open-plan and, once they were spotted, the general alert went up to general hilarity.

The 1970s may have been a decade of challenges and rule-breaking but solid traditions remained. It was largely immigrants who shaped the British fashion industry. The French Huguenot refugees arrived in the 1700s with a range of skills, particularly in silk weaving with which they became hugely influential in fashion. The Courtauld family were descended from Huguenots and the Courtauld textile business was founded in 1794. Around 100,000 Jewish people immigrated to Britain between 1881 and 1914. They were mostly from eastern European countries, and entrepreneurs such as Michael Marks from Poland established brands like Marks and Spencer.

I worked with many leading Jewish designers, brands and fashion PRs based in London and it was not unusual to visit their offices on a Friday afternoon in winter to find the occupants working in candlelight. When I lectured at the London College of Fashion, one young Jewish student asked me, with some anxiety, about starting work and observing Fridays. I was happy to say I thought there would be no problem, as I knew of leading Jewish PRs who observed the Jewish Sabbath – Shabbat in Hebrew – which began at sunset on Friday evenings.

Another time-honoured tradition was practised by the workforce in the newspaper composing room. At the time, it was all men in the Standard's 'engine room'.

THE HOT METAL MEN

One of my favourite colleagues was the *Standard's* features brilliant staff photographer Roy Jones. Roy was one of the angriest men I had ever met. We got along well but he seemed to intensely dislike an awful lot of people – particularly on the subs desk. The sub-editors held great power; all were highly intelligent and imaginative and they had little time for us features writers if they thought they could do a better job, which they often could. Roy worked closely with the *Standard's* arts editor, Michael Owen, photographing the most famous faces in the theatre world of the time. He was frequently sulky and uncommunicative and could issue expletives for England, but he had a gentle, sensitive and humane side, plus a fine sense of humour which emerged when not being crushed by his demons. Our fashion shoots took place in the *Standard's* basement studio, which was next to the composing room. The compositors set the pages and created the plates from which the paper was printed.

They were central to the existence of newspapers and were very much a community who shared customs such as initiation ceremonies and bang-outs (making a cacophony of sound to draw attention to unusual behaviour).

Setting the type by hand and laboriously casting the words in the stories and headlines out of molten lead required great skill and concentration. They had to be able to think back to front, putting all the letters and punctuation in the right place and to do this at speed to meet deadlines. A slab of stone or metal, on which the type was set into a layout, was used to align the text. Compositors had an iron-strong union and even more power than the sub-editors. It was an unwise journalist who didn't take time to get on the right side of their assigned hot metal man. As the *Evening Standard* was a daily paper with several editions and everything was carried out rapidly, if an article didn't fit the available space, it was simply cut from the bottom. Hence the wisdom among us writers never to put anything important in the last paragraph. The composing room was where editorial staff – mainly the 'stone sub' – met the compositors.

Sometimes other editorial staff were allowed in but never to touch the type. I had the privilege of being allowed 'on the stone' as Suzy Menkes had already judiciously made it her business to work well with compositors. Like Suzy, I respected their skills, and our collaboration on press day helped ensure the successful production of the fashion pages.

There were two ways out of the photographic studio – the most direct being turn left out of the door and up one flight of stairs to the main entrance. The other was out of the door and keep going straight ahead on a very long walkway through the centre of the composing room to a second flight of stairs and exit. Very occasionally, Roy took an aversion to a model who was rude or uncooperative and, fashion shoot concluded, he would smilingly direct her out through the latter route. The hapless girl would wander through this alien metal jungle, gradually finding herself accompanied by a sinister, raw drumming sound reaching a crescendo as dozens of compositors hammered hot metal rods on their tables in a rhythmic 'bang-out' timed to her steps. Just one more curious happening to add to the folklore of Fleet Street.

EIGHT

SUFFERING INTERVIEWEES

The short-lived relationship between the journalist and the subject of an interview was an interesting, often intense experience connecting two people never likely to meet again. For the fashion spreads, I organised many photo shoots and interviews with actors promoting new films or plays. Those who were interviewed came in all types: witty, sulky, charming, angry, super keen, sensationally boring, great fun. Some were uncomfortable about being interviewed and suspicious of journos, probably with good reason based on past experiences where untruths had been published. Others just didn't want to be there but had been pressed into it by their publicists. One actress, who is on TV today in a long-running hit series, failed to turn up for the photo shoot, leaving me, together with hairdresser, make-up artist and photographer, waiting for an hour or so. Twice. No reason given despite conversations with her agent.

I love the story told by my friend Jan Iles-Kaluza in this book of her encounter with Bob Marley. Jan had been despatched to interview this man who had already achieved near deity status, and who then, startlingly, replied to all her questions in Jamaican *patois*. Having barely understood a word, she cried all the way back to the office to be told, "Just make it up." So she did and apparently no one noticed – or cared.

Journalists can, of course, arrive very ill-prepared and I must confess to the occasional inexcusable gaff when I hadn't done my homework. Like asking actors after their famous husbands to whom they were no longer married, or completely overlooking significant recent movie appearances, or dressing them in clothes that looked awful on them. A usually competent colleague related to me how she had once conducted an entire interview with Robert Plant of the mighty, globally-famous band Led Zeppelin, assuming Plant's first name was Led. It appears her newspaper bosses were none the wiser (this was in New Zealand) since the title of the published article was: 'Led Said'. Again, no one seemed to notice, including Robert Plant, presumably.

Roger Charity became a great friend and we had a ball regularly working together on shoots which often involved the celebrated. It was Roger who photographed Helen Mirren for one of my favourite fashion spreads. Mirren had just opened at the Royal Court Theatre in the play 'Teeth 'N' Smiles' by David Hare. She was giving her all in a gutsy performance in the role of a rock singer, basing her character on Janis Joplin. The production was an important play of the time (1975), when London's theatres were filled with old-school socialist machismo, and where male writers dealt mostly with issues of politics and society, involving very little collaboration with women. Helen Mirren revelled in this key part. She was pure gold to work with – an exciting model, injecting masses of oomph and sex appeal into the clothes. I read this quote of hers somewhere: "I never really like 'middle' anything," which would account for her swathe of brave, risky and diverse portrayals from Shakespeare to 'Caligula' to 'Teeth 'N' Smiles'.

Another time, Roger and I drove in his trusty white van to

Helen Mirren in a jacket by Wonder Workshop, photographed by Roger Charity.

photograph the immensely likeable Susan George, who lived somewhere in the home counties. Such a game girl, hard-working, friendly, nothing too much trouble, and up for a good laugh. For several hours, we three made a great team and the pictures demonstrated that. Filled with good spirits, Roger and I sang aloud to Beach Boys tapes while seat-dancing (no seat belts then) all the way back to London.

I was welcomed at a Ritz hotel suite overlooking Green Park by an immensely attractive (yes, another one) Italian man exquisitely yet casually dressed in open-neck white shirt and rolled sleeves. As he departed to organise coffee, Sophia Loren entered the room. I was there to chat about her new book 'Women & Beauty'. That well-used term 'lighting the place up' must surely have been inspired by this woman's presence.

As well as beautiful and fabulously glamorous, she was polite, warm, interesting and interested. Every bit an original superstar.

Delightfully down-to-earth, Olympic champion Daley Thompson modelled designer pyjamas and no doubt would have been a thrill to work with if photographer David Bailey had allowed me into the photo session. I had arrived ten minutes late for the shoot. Bailey was seriously pissed off and made me wait outside the studio. Sheila Hancock seemed extremely wary of the whole fashion shoot scenario, and of journalists in particular, but relaxed into a thoughtful, original interviewee, and the pictures were terrific.

Zandra Rhodes remains one of my very favourite designers and was a refreshingly calm and direct person to talk with. We travelled together to Yorkshire TV where I was to interview her for 'A Touch of Fashion', a pilot programme that came to nothing. No surprise to me, as those producing it appeared to have little clue of fashion. That said, true professional Zandra dazzled on camera and gave a fruitful interview. She continues to express

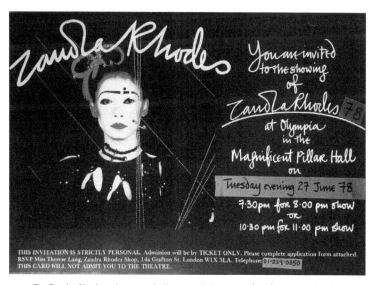

The Zandra Rhodes take on punk. Photograph Grant Mudford for Zandra Rhodes.

inspiring individuality and integrity in her work and her vision is unsurpassed, as demonstrated by her founding of the Fashion and Textile Museum in 2003 which is now run by Newham College. I believe it is the only museum in the UK dedicated to showcasing both retro and contemporary fashion and textile design through exciting, innovative exhibitions. The orange and pink (what else?) building nestles perfectly in Bermondsey, housed in a converted warehouse which was redesigned by the Mexican architect Ricardo Legorreta in collaboration with Dame Zandra.

Establishment Pond Life

Another part of the job was speaking at schools and colleges and taking part in public discussions and debates. A memorably uncomfortable experience took place at the Institute of Contemporary Arts in the Mall when I agreed to be interviewed on stage by someone whose name I have deleted from memory (today they would be called an influencer), followed by questions from the floor. The audience was composed largely of fringe players in the fashion world, some highly innovative and talented who would become household names.

Near the front was a young man with thick, tousled hair accompanied by a fragile-looking young woman. Producing innovative, exciting clothes that would become adopted as an international movement, this man had self-belief by the shedload and was, understandably, raring to challenge the fashion establishment. Thus, perceived as a member of the establishment and naively unprepared for a dousing of criticism, I was roundly cross-examined by Malcolm McLaren and came off the worst. His key grouse seemed to be that fashion journalists like myself only featured the big design names.

His companion, Vivienne Westwood, was more sympathetic,

trying to gently restrain him and pointing out that, as a fashion journalist, I was simply earning a living. I found Westwood's comments, although well meant, ill informed and patronising. In fact, the pair of them probably didn't read the *Evening Standard*, where I worked at the time, and didn't have a clue what I did.

As deputy fashion editor, I made a point of seeking out lesser-known fashion labels, covering culture at the borders that were about to make an impact. For example, the Swanky Modes shop in Camden Town. Formed in 1972, it was run by a group of young women designers which included the splendid Esme Young who, in her seventies, was to become judge of BBC Television's series 'The Great British Sewing Bee'. Young remains an iconic and original *fashionista*. Who else would have the *chutzpah* to appear on TV wearing a bold multicoloured necklace made from a row of discarded plastic sanitiser bottles, each filled with different-coloured liquids?

At that time, I was wearing second-hand clothes from charity shops and dresses made from recycled vintage fabrics from Van der Fransen, a small shop at the end of the King's Road, Chelsea. I visited places such as the three-storey indoor Kensington Market in Ken High Street. It opened in 1967, lasting until the end of the 1990s, offering music, body arts, crafts and fashion through three decades of subculture – hippies, punks, new romantics and goths.

Between 1971 and 1976, Westwood and McLaren ran their Chelsea fashion boutique under several different names: Let it Rock, Too Fast to Live Too Young to Die, Sex and Seditionaries, before reinventing it in 1979 as Worlds End. The latter was one of boundary- breaking fashion brands featured in the Alternative Clothes Show at Camden Palace. Vivienne Westwood was quoted in the culture monthly *The Face* as saying, "I'm using my shop as a crucible. The stuff that's in there is what will sell elsewhere… It's kind of market research…" Unlike today

Publicity poster for young designers show at Camden Palace, possibly early 1980s.

when brand name is everything, decided by layers of design and marketing professionals, the freethinking Westwood and McLaren made changes as their inventiveness took them. As the clothes ranges developed, the shop name was re-invented and decor altered accordingly. Under whatever name, all the shops specialised in clothing that helped define the punk movement.

At the ICA discussion, seeing me as representative of the media establishment pond life he so despised, McLaren ran rings round me as I struggled to summon a coherent voice. Nonetheless, among his glib judgements, he made some valid points – ones that I would subscribe to today. Well-known designer names, ones with degrees from fashion colleges and/or wealthy backers and slick PRs were getting the cream of publicity and indeed a proportion of the powerful fashion press were either too lazy or unimaginative or pressed against deadlines to seek talent below the radar, like McLaren and Westwood, who were producing fresh and exciting designs and ideas.

At the mercy of an individual allegedly described by Johnny Rotten as 'the most evil man on Earth' for his reputation for treating people like personal income-generating projects, I got a soft ride but, back then, I was easily cast out of my depth. Interestingly, like so many highly provocative culture changers, impresario McLaren gradually carved his position in the world of the revised mainstream and Westwood was made a dame for services to fashion. I regret now not giving him a run for his money in that interview, but that's the trouble with hindsight – never around when you want it.

Confidence was not one of my key qualities and despite, or perhaps as a result of, how easily I slipped into exciting journalism roles, I harboured an underlying, discomforting feeling that 'there must be some mistake'. Looking back, my lofty professional roles felt rather like teetering permanently on the edge of a very high cliff. Jobs were never long term or secure. People were sacked when a new editor arrived – which was frequent – and began culling. New bosses moved in and suddenly your face didn't fit. Malcolm McLaren unwittingly pressed that button.

NINE

New Directions
and Direct Action

After I moved to the role of fashion editor at the *London Evening News,* the gloss began to tarnish. I was increasingly finding the weekly routine very tedious. Alongside this was growing awareness of the shocking abuse of non-human animals in the world of fashion and beauty, largely through the new voices of protest against the wearing of real fur and the massive use of animals in cosmetics testing. I began to take every opportunity to write about issues such as this from my fashion journalism platform, seeking out those to the forefront of the protests and discovering more about the cruelties of the fur trade when interviewing campaigners like Mark Glover, co-founder of the anti-fur organisation Lynx. Lynx had collaborated with Greenpeace to successfully produce a shock-making poster campaign direct to the public, challenging people to stop thinking of fur as glamorous and instead regard it as grotesque and morally unacceptable.

David Bailey shot the campaign in 1984. The huge poster appeared on billboards featuring the lower body of a woman in short, tight black skirt and stiletto heels, dragging behind her a bloodied fur coat with a trail of bright red blood. She appeared like a model on a fashion runway, as the vogue for fur was still sadly promoted by designers at that time.

The Greenpeace campaign had a massive impact on public thinking, and Mark Glover put this success down to the fact it was one of the first to adopt a direct-to-consumer strategy. Lynx co-founder, Lynne Kentish, wanted to professionalise the animal rights movement and her vision was to become reality through the work of organisations like Animal Aid, People for the Ethical Treatment of Animals (PETA), Viva!, Compassion in World Farming and the British Union for the Abolition of Vivisection, which became Cruelty Free International. Today, Mark Glover heads up Respect for Animals which emerged in 1993 following the demise of Lynx. Lynne Kentish is the director of the Lynx Educational Trust for Animal Welfare.

Through my own involvement with animal rights, largely through the Religious Society of Friends (Quakers) of which I became a member in my thirties, I have seen the movement grow across the globe, impacting industries such as bullfighting, whaling, circuses, bear bile farming and the appalling dog meat trade. Many of these campaigning groups were started by women, and it's women who lead the crusade today.

The innovative poster for the Greenpeace/Lynx/Respect for Animals campaign against the fur trade shot by David Bailey. Image (c) Respect for Animals.

A watershed event in my discontent with mainstream fashion writing took place in a swish Mayfair cosmetics showroom. There I was, sitting in a facsimile of an Edwardian railway carriage with the PR of an upmarket cosmetics brand and leading exponent of animal testing. The PR enthusiastically 'unveiled' their new season's range of ludicrously expensive lipsticks, eyeshadows and blushers, and I wondered, *What has this charade cost and what on earth am I doing here?*

However, alongside fashion editing, I rejoiced in the new age of enlightenment, exploring the emerging alternatives to conservative medicine; complementary therapies such as shiatsu, meditation, yoga, Indian head massage, homeopathy, aromatherapy, acupuncture, and so on…

A Wedding, An Omen and the Same Mistake Twice

Some 'opportunities' are best given a wide berth. I met and married a graphic artist. Yet another 'colourful' character; handsome, charismatic and previously twice wed. One grown-up daughter by the first and two young boys by the second. The second probably foundered when said husband bought a Dutch sailing barge that sank when he took it to sea (they were designed for inland waterways) and the whole family had to be rescued. This was featured in the local press at the time alongside a photograph of the weary-looking family group, clad in blankets, departing the rescue vessel.

Our marriage lasted just 16 months, which was about 15 months too long. I was 28 and old enough to know better; the warning signs were there but I chose to ignore them. After the registry office ceremony, we had our marriage blessing at All Saints Church, Fulham. Our photographs were taken on the very spot where Father Brennen in 'The Omen', played by Patrick

On leaving the Evening News, the magnificent, imaginative copy takers presented me with this must-keep card.

Troughton, is impaled to the ground by a lightning conductor that falls from the church. It's a great scene – you can watch it on YouTube.

Disenchanted with fashion journalism and although mightily relieved to be exiting a bad marriage, I was emotionally shattered and struggling to cope. Reason in disarray, I left my well-paid full-time job and went freelance, losing a huge amount of redundancy pay when the paper folded six months later.

BEAUTY WITHOUT CRUELTY ON THE *COVER*!

Soon after, I embraced yet another doomed relationship when I was offered the role of health and beauty editor on *Good Housekeeping* magazine. Experiencing a further relationship of mutual incompatibility, I parted company with the publication after six months – to great relief on both sides. Almost from the start, it was clear that my idea of health and beauty was not that of the editor's. It must be said that '*GH*', as the staff called it, was at that time middle everything – class, England, of the road. Yet, naivety to the fore, I pressed on with my 'new- age' agenda.

GH was *really* not ready for this. I discovered that I didn't enjoy being 'pampered' on the posh health farms of the day, even if they were 'freebies', preferring to revel in events like the annual Mind Body Spirit Festival which first took place in London in 1977. This moral and cultural event, which defined the era, celebrated the unity of religion, spirituality, natural healing and personal growth. I embraced it full on.

Yoga was to become my lifelong fitness and mental practice of choice. Together with my inspirational first yoga teacher, Daya Ramjee, and fellow evening class students, I attended a memorable seminar given by the legendary BKS Iyengar: 'Live happily and die majestically'. It was a surprise to find one of the foremost yoga gurus in the world was pretty tough with students; I personally witnessed him thrusting a student's arm into place with a firm foot as she performed a headstand. As for beauty products, becoming further aware of the cruelty that went on in laboratories behind the luxury brand names drove me to seek out companies that didn't test on animals. I was very naïve in those days, failing to understand that what was obvious to me could be incomprehensible to others. At the time, since she was easily impressed by authenticated status and grounded in a solid lack of vision, it was no wonder that my snobbish editor must have viewed my approach to 'health and beauty' as beyond the pale.

My job included organising the cover shoots, which usually featured a close-up of a model with make-up credited to one of the big cosmetic companies which also advertised in the magazine. The highlight of my working experience on GH was when I managed to get Beauty Without Cruelty – one of the original cruelty-free make-up ranges – on the front cover. I left soon after and was later informed that this had practically caused a meltdown. Featuring a company that advocated non-animal testing in such a prominent position was deemed near catastrophic, as the advertisers would feel threatened and might even withdraw. At the time, the big names in beauty products were vigorously resisting giving up testing on animals.

In the event, it was too late to change the photograph and I got non-animal testing on the cover of a best-selling glossy monthly. Oh joy! Nevertheless, my confidence at losing the job had taken a hit and, with a mortgage to pay, it took a while to get back on my feet.

TEN

REFLECTION

In the 1960s and '70s, the Women's Liberation Movement was in full swing. In 1973, Virago Publishing was launched from a house in Chelsea, providing a resonant voice for women writers. Although back then I never saw myself as a feminist, I now value just how much we owe them. I was a high earner, particularly in Fleet Street, yet when I walked into a branch of the Abbey National seeking a mortgage, a man appeared from the back and dismissively told me over the counter, "We are not giving out any mortgages at the moment." End of conversation.

Gradually, women were moving more into business and securing key appointments. In later years, I worked in the less glamorous but nonetheless absorbing field of business publishing where advertising was the priority and journalism was almost seen as adjunct to sales. Despite working at breakneck speed with little time for research (although doing rather well financially), I learnt much about how business organisations, big and small, operated. Editing a variety of professional niche publications proved instructive in PR, marketing, working in teams and, perhaps most importantly, thinking creatively and laterally through two recessions. This has not only led to a far more rounded professional life but has also been immensely helpful to my work as a professional painter in both approach to subject matter and exhibiting. In subsequent freelance years, I have had books published on health and lifestyle, one of which I am particularly proud of – 'Why Am I Afraid to Grieve?' – written with my husband, Geoffrey Johnson, on grief and grieving after loss.

The passing years have seen ground-breaking and encouraging changes for the good. Nonhuman animals continue to be exploited and abused, but campaigning groups have expanded enormously and have achieved significant successes. It is not unusual now to see fashion and cosmetic brands adopting a vegan approach. I have engaged in my share of direct action, through protesting and writing about exploitation of nonhuman animals, making many new friends in the forefront of protest. But my commitment to art has continued throughout. One wonderful experience was an 18-month residency at the Raystede parrot sanctuary in East Sussex. Not only did it provide an informative and enriching time working with dedicated staff and their wonderful avian charges but the proverbial icing on the cake was to have a painting of Icecream, my favourite Raystede rescue parrot, accepted and hung at the Royal Academy Summer Exhibition. I have also published my first art book, 'Wild Margins'. Meanwhile, fashion continues to play a key role in my life, not least in providing inspiration for my art.

Journalism has been central to the whole of my adult life. It has offered me experiences that cause me to pinch myself as I recall them and to pose the question, *Was that really me?* or to ask myself, *Did you **really** do that?* Journalism has given me an opportunity to meet some wonderfully creative and inspiring people, but even more importantly it has opened the way to making lifelong friendships. During my career, there have been successes to celebrate as well as failures causing pain and triggering self-doubt. I have been both exhilarated and frustrated beyond measure, while often it has seemed that any excitement has been matched by sheer drudgery and grind. However, irrespective of the level of engagement and type of experience, journalism has enriched my whole life-journey.

I am not a fatalist but I do believe opportunities are there for us. The thing is, they frequently aren't what we expect and we need to recognise them lurking behind the everyday. Then there was my family, unconventional when it came to bringing up children and still actors, opera singers and artists at heart; dreamers, you could say, and dreams are well worth having. Ambition is a bit of a puzzle – where it stems from and how it develops. Where did mine come from? Mum held the belief that one would get through life just fine if you were bright, with a bit of talent and aspirations. In many ways, this provided a sound pathway. Thanks, Mum. You had your demons and struggled through life – but got it right for me.

Susan George and me after a photo shoot with Roger Charity (c) who took the photograph. Happy days.

PENNY'S STORY

I was THRILLED with my press card

My job working in fashion was to go out and select and collect the new season's accessories for magazine photo shoots —shoes, hats, belts, gloves, scarves, and so on. That's how it was until I joined Men Only magazine. From then on, instead of finding clothes to dress the models in, I was helping to take them off...

ONE

BREAKING BOUNDARIES
(1967)

I was born in Dulwich and grew up on a council estate in south London along with my two sisters, Cherry and Coral, and my brother, Barrie.

We all got on pretty well as far as families go, and there is approximately a two-year age gap between us all. At Christmas, we only got one present each, but it was always expensive and what we wanted. My pride and joy was that one Christmas I got a navy blue twin pram; it was gleaming with big shiny silver wheels – it was nearly as big as me.

We didn't have a lot, but Mum and Dad worked hard to give us what they could. Dad had a sweet stall in Brixton Market and his nickname was 'Sugar', and Mum had three cleaning jobs in grand houses in Victoria. I would sometimes help Dad out on a weekend, selling sweets, although I probably ate more than I sold.

I was a bit of a sickly child, in and out of hospital with bronchial pneumonia, tonsillitis and appendicitis, but then growing up as a teenager, I guess I was a bit of a wild child. When I was about fourteen, I stayed out all night, telling Mum and Dad I was staying with a friend, but the truth was I was mad

Sisters left to right: Coral, Cherry,
older sister Gloria and me.

Brother Barrie enjoying his
favourite pursuit, fishing.

about The Monkees and when they were over here, my friend
and I went to the Royal Garden Hotel in Kensington and waited
outside all night hoping to catch a glimpse of them.

On this occasion it paid off, as after we spent a long night
waiting with the other fans, they actually came out onto the
balcony and waved to us. As there was only a small group of
us, about a dozen girls, they sent their minder down to bring us
all up to their suite for coffee. We were so excited; we couldn't
believe our luck. They were really lovely and friendly and very
funny. I was mad about Davy Jones, so I was in my element
when he started talking to me. They were really interested in
their fans and what we all thought of their music. I remember
thinking that I couldn't wait to go to school and tell my friends.

After an hour or so, they asked us if we'd like to have some
pictures taken in the park with them, as a little thank-you for
waiting all night to see them. Of course, we didn't have mobile
phones to take pictures then as now, so we jumped at the chance
of a photo with them. I treasured those pictures and I was glad
I had them as proof that I'd met them, because I don't think my
school friends would have believed me. Shortly after, I sent one
of the pictures to my favourite magazine, *Mirabelle,* and to my

surprise they published it on the readers' letters page with this letter:

> *When the Monkees were here in July, we were actually invited by Davy up to his hotel suite and were laughing and joking with him and his friends. Later we walked in the park and had photos taken with Davy and kissed him goodbye. How about that then!*
> *Penny and Doreen, London SE5*

I showed it to all my family and friends and was quite proud that I'd actually had it printed in the magazine. Little did I know at the time that I would end up working there.

Of course, now I had to confess to my mum and dad and they weren't at all happy because they were worried about my safety, but at the same time they knew how mad I was about The

Me in mini skirt to the right of Davy Jones – I couldn't believe it if I tried!

Monkees and they accepted it. With the pocket money I saved, I bought their records and I still have a collection in the loft. Whenever I hear their music, it takes me back to that fabulous day when we met them.

I was never particularly interested in school, as I was eager to leave and earn my own money. I went to an all-girls school in London and the only subjects I liked were Typing, Art and Geography. My mum and dad didn't mind if I left school at 15 or wanted to stay on; there was no pressure either way.

What I do remember, though, is school friends staying on until 18 because their parents had said they would get a better job. As it turned out, I left at 15 with certificates in Typing and Art and got the best job ever!

I was passionate about fashion/make-up and always trying different looks. I was known as the girl who wore mini skirts and false eyelashes. I'd always dreamed of working in fashion, and my first job was in fashion of a kind – not exactly what I had in mind. It was working in a school outfitter's in Victoria!

I was an office junior and did the typing and filing, running errands and making the tea. I shared an office with two older ladies who weren't particularly nice to me and looking back, could have been a little bit jealous because I was young and pretty.

Every morning, one of the ladies used to sing, '*If I were a rich man*' and it used to drive me mad. She was always bossing me around and ordering me to make the tea before I'd even taken my coat off and so one morning I'd had enough of being bossed around and walked out of the job.

This was a bit of a trait I adopted many times, in many jobs! Another was when I was temping as a receptionist/telephonist for a large import company. On my first day, I kept getting the wires crossed on the huge dolls eye switchboard I was operating; it became manic, I panicked, went to lunch and never went back.

Mum and Dad were disappointed but not surprised, because I was a bit rebellious and never liked being told what to do. The very next week I got another job, because you could in those days. It was a temporary Christmas job working in Woolworths in Oxford Street on the Christmas decoration counter. I chose Oxford Street because I didn't want to work locally – I have always been a West End girl at heart.

I liked working there because I could decorate the counter using my art skills and own initiative. There were no calculators or tills that added up for you; it was all mental arithmetic and actually I was quite good at it and surprised myself sometimes.

Another temporary girl working there was actress and former model Lorraine Chase, although of course nobody knew her then. That was in the days before she shot to fame with her catchphrase 'Nah, Luton Airport' on the TV ads for Campari.

Lorraine and I used to flirt with some French guys in the stockroom, so we were always looking for an excuse to go in there. Sometimes, we used to take it in turns to go to lunch with them. I used to have to wear this hideous green overall that came down past my knees so was always hiking it up to mini length and was constantly in trouble for doing so.

After Christmas, I needed a full-time job and found one working for a pearl importer. My job was to take pearls to different jewellers for them to buy. I found the job boring and didn't stay there long. While I looked for a full-time work, I got myself a Saturday job with my sister Coral, working in Miss Selfridge in Oxford Street. I loved working there because it was in fashion, and my sister and I spent all our wages (before we'd even earned them) on the latest fashion!

I didn't have lots of boyfriends. I wasn't interested in boys of my age, as I found them to be childish and a bit annoying. I was more interested in going to the 'Top of the Pops' studios in

Shepherd's Bush and waiting around for the pop stars to come out and get their autographs. Boys could wait.

I liked going to concerts and used to go quite a lot to the Marquee in Wardour Street to see bands like Small Faces and Canned Heat to name but a few. My favourite band then was The Stones, but I'd never seen them play live, so I was very excited when they were going to play a free concert at Hyde Park. You can imagine my disappointment when I was let down by a friend on the day we were going; she never turned up and gave her reason later as being ill. I never forgave her.

A New Beginning

I always loved reading my magazines and my favourites were *Mirabelle* and *Jackie*. I couldn't believe it when my dear mum spotted an ad for an office junior on *Mirabelle*, so I decided to apply for the position and was so excited when I received a letter back for an interview. I was 15 and couldn't wait to start a proper job.

I was a happy-go-lucky teenager. Nothing really fazed me, so I wasn't particularly nervous about the interview, only very excited. I can remember walking down the Strand past the Savoy Hotel, which seemed extremely grand and thinking, *Little ol' me in this big, wide world!* I found my way to Tower House, a lovely old 1930s building, and made my way up to the second floor. I remember there was a clunky old lift that seemed to take ages to arrive!

The first person I met was a friendly blonde called Linda Newman, who made me feel very welcome. It must have been around Valentine's Day, as I can remember her giving me a handful of cards which had been sent to the magazine as samples for readers to see, and she told me to hide them under my coat – which could have got me the sack before I even started! Linda then took me to a lady called Miss Palfrey who was going to interview me. At the same time, I also met two lovely girls called Karen and Shirley. Karen was Miss Palfrey's secretary. Shirley was responsible for answering readers' letters. (Magazine Girl stories from Linda and Shirley appeared earlier in this book.)

Miss Palfrey explained what my role would be, which was running errands and typing letters. I felt quite confident, as I had come first in my typing exam at school, and I left the building on a high hoping that I'd get the job, although I didn't let it take over my life.

I received a letter about a week later saying I had been accepted and my wage would be £7 per week. I started shortly after that.

Karen, Shirley and Linda have been my friends for more than 50 years and have told me about what happened at my interview. Apparently, there were a lot of girls being interviewed for the job, some of them highly qualified. Miss Palfrey asked Karen and Shirley which of the girls they thought would be most suitable and who they would like to work with, as we would all be sharing an office. They both agreed they would like me to work there, as we had got on well, so that was that.

I spent the whole of my first week's wages on a pair of high-heeled brown suede shoes from the shoe shop Ravel. I felt bad for not giving Mum her housekeeping that week, which I think was about £2 at the time, but I justified it by telling myself that I had to be fashionable for the magazine, and Mum was fine.

I looked forward to going to work every day. The work I did was mainly for my favourite magazine, *Mirabelle*, running errands, typing and sometimes helping the Fashion department return clothes after shoots. One day, when I was asked to collect some clothes, I bumped into Sandie (one of the Magazine Girls) in the lift. Both of us were buried under a mountain of clothes.

We didn't really speak but just looked at each other and raised our eyes as if to say, *It isn't that glamorous*, but it was.

Karen, Shirley and I all got on really well and one day in particular, when it was one of our birthdays, we all got drunk in the office on apricot brandy that one of us brought in! We were so giggly that we had to hide under the desk when a client came in to see the art director, and later sobered up with strong coffee.

Invitations came into the office all the time from big fashion, music and beauty companies who were launching new products and artists. The press receptions were always held in grand hotels and always involved lots of champagne. I'd never really drunk champagne before, but I soon became accustomed to it, as I was often asked if I'd like to go along to many of the pop and beauty launches.

I actually didn't appreciate at the time just how lucky I was choosing which of the champagne receptions I'd like to go to! One that I definitely wanted to go to was the launch of Linda McCartney's new vegetarian cookbook. When that was on, Shirley was working on *19* magazine and I was on *Loving*, and we met for lunch that day. I'd been chatting to a photographer at work who mentioned that he was going to the Linda McCartney launch and I could go with him – he had a VIP ticket!

Shirley didn't have an official invite, so when she went back to the office, she asked Maggie Koumi, her editor, if she was going. Maggie said she had the invitation but wasn't planning on attending. She told Shirley to go in her place and to get a quote from Paul about his favourite fragrance. Unfortunately, Maggie couldn't find her 'official' ticket, but we didn't think that was going to be an issue. *19* was one of the leading magazines of the time after all.

We met the photographer a bit later and went along with him. He waved his ticket and got himself and me in. Shirley told the doorman that she was Maggie Koumi from *19* magazine but had left her invite in the office. He said no invitation, no entry! At which point I grabbed Shirley by the arm and yanked her past the doorman into the venue.

We grabbed a glass of champagne each on our way through and proceeded for the next 15 minutes to hide behind every column available, convinced security were on the look-out for us and we would be thrown out on our ear! (I also wanted to avoid the photographer, as he had become a bit too 'clingy'!)

We were both really excited that Paul McCartney was going to be there; also, Shirley had a bit of a crush on him. We drank so much champagne and spent the whole evening following the Beatle, glued to his side. Eventually, Shirley patted him on the shoulder, told him she was writing a fragrance feature for *19* magazine and asked him what his favourite perfume was! He said he liked '*Eau Naturelle*' and that he preferred a woman's own body fragrance to that of a bottled scent.

Paul chatted to us for a long time. His son, James, hadn't long been born and Shirley had also recently had a son she called James, so we talked about schools, and he confided that he wanted James to go to a local school and not a private school – which I believe is what happened. After a little while, one of his 'minders' tapped him on the shoulder to say there was someone they wanted him to talk to. Paul berated him by saying, "That can wait a moment. I am talking to these two lovely girls right now." He certainly went up in my estimation that day. We went home two very happy – and very drunk – Magazine Girls!

Loving Days

I was 17 at the time when the job as a fashion assistant came up on a new weekly magazine called *Loving*. I didn't hesitate to apply and when I was accepted I was over the moon. I was going to be sharing an office with Magazine Girls Ann Carpenter, who was the fashion editor, and Janice Collier, the beauty editor. The office was always buzzing with different people coming in and out. Mostly art editors, photographers and models. It was there that I met Ian Potter, who was a junior in the Art department and who later became my boyfriend.

Ann was lovely and so was Janice, who at first appeared to be a bit prim and proper, but would often have us in fits of laughter with her hilarious impressions. My job was to collect and deliver clothes that Ann had chosen for the latest fashion shoots.

It was while I was working on *Loving* that I met another Magazine Girl, Jan Iles-Kaluza. Ann had asked Jan to do some modelling for the fashion page and when she came into the office, I went with her to help her try on the clothes and afterwards I went on the session, which took place on the roof of Fleetway House. Jan and I were a similar age and hit it off straight away, and so now I had met all the Magazine Girls who were to be my friends for life.

My column 'Pennywise' in *Loving* made Mum so proud. *Loving*/Future Publishing Ltd.

I often used to go with Ann on the fashion shoots, which I found really interesting, and would sometimes go to fashion receptions. The most memorable fashion reception was when I flew to Paris with Ann for a bridal company called 'Pronuptia'. It was so exciting, as I'd never flown before, but I must admit a little bit nerve-racking, as it was quite a small aircraft.

On arrival at the venue we were greeted with champagne and canapés. We were shown to our seats for the fashion show – the dresses were fabulous and fairy-tale like. It was an all-day event and the champagne kept flowing, but after consuming large quantities, I really can't remember getting on the plane home.

After a little while I was asked by the editor-in-chief, Bill Williamson, if I would like to have my own column. We called it 'Pennywise', which featured some of the more affordable clothes for our readers. I would go round to the stores, choose the clothes, get them photographed and then write it up.

This was my first shot at writing something under my own name, so I was excited as well as a bit nervous about it, but everyone seemed pleased with what I did and as I became more confident I really enjoyed doing it. What's more, mum was so proud that I had my own page.

As well as my job in fashion, I was asked to do quite a lot of modelling for other features for different magazines. I always had to sign a model release form – I used to really enjoy it, and getting paid was a bonus.

One of the sessions I was asked to model for was with my friend Karen, who worked for Roger, the art director of *Rave* and *19*. The photo shoot was with the singers Paul and Barry Ryan, and after the shoot we should have gone straight back to work, but were asked by the singers if we'd like to go back to their flat for some drinks. We were very young and impressionable at the time so did not give going back to work a second thought.

Sweet 17.

When we arrived at their flat in Mayfair, they gave us some

Friends for life –in our twenties on the left and later in our fifties.

champagne and chatted to us for a while, but they then said they had to go somewhere and would be back. We didn't think much of it at the time, as we were getting a bit tipsy on the champagne. It was only when one of us noticed a tape recorder hidden behind the coffee table that we became nervous because we knew that our conversation was being recorded. Neither of us could remember what we said, but hopefully it wasn't anything embarrassing. We had no idea why they did that, but we just assumed it was kinky eavesdropping. That's what we thought at the time anyway.

Needless to say, we finished our drinks and left. When we did eventually get back to work that afternoon, we were in big trouble. Karen's boss never really forgave her, and not long after that Karen left the company.

As for me, I got off lightly and Ann never mentioned my late return.

TWO

FASHION FASHION FASHION (1970–1974)

From *Loving* I went on to work on *Petticoat* as a fashion assistant on accessories. The fashion editor would say, "Here is the spring collection, these are the clothes we are using." My job was to go out and select and collect all the accessories necessary for the latest season – shoes, hats, belts, gloves, scarves, and so on. I would then bring them back to the office and the fashion editor would lay the clothes out and match them accordingly.

Once everything came into the office, the fashion editor would book the models, photographer, make-up artist/hairdresser and a location van. On the day, we would load up the van with the clothes, food and drink for lunch, and then about six of us would pile in. We would then go off to a lovely country or seaside location and shoot the fashion pictures. Although it was hard work and long days ironing all the clothes and helping the models get dressed, it was fun.

I loved my job. It was like going on a constant shopping spree without spending any money. I would go around all the shops and fashion houses and select the items that I liked and thought would be suitable.

My favourite shop was Biba in Kensington. It was always so

Ed's letter introducing me to the readers. Petticoat/Future Publishing Ltd.

exciting and busy. You would often catch a glimpse of someone famous. If there was something that we really liked after it had been used in the shoot, we were sometimes able to keep it.

Lots of models and photographers popped in and out of the office, and one of the models was Jo Woods (who later married and divorced Rolling Stone Ronnie Wood). She was very pretty.

Although I loved the job on *Petticoat*, the girls I worked with were not as friendly as those I'd worked with before – they didn't want you to mix or talk to anyone outside the Fashion department. For instance, there was a time when I was talking to a girl on the switchboard, and when I went back to the office the fashion editor asked me why I had been talking to her. It was as if the switchboard girl wasn't good enough.

So when my friend Mary and I talked about travelling around America, I decided to hand in my notice. I was 21 and had been on *Petticoat* for a year by this time, so I thought if I didn't do it now, I never would.

Did I ever regret leaving? Not for the experience of travelling around the USA, but I do sometimes wonder where I would have been job-wise today if I'd stayed.

IN BETWEEN MAGAZINES

Mavy and I were away for about three months and had a great time travelling through the night on Greyhound buses. We would stop off at various launderettes where we stripped off apart from our coats, washed our clothes, dried them and put them back on. We travelled very light, just a gym bag each!

Mary, left, and me – the start of our new adventure.

We started off in New York and travelled to the West Coast, stayed in Los Angeles and then up to Vancouver, Canada. We used to stay in little motels, look at the map in the morning, decide where we wanted to go and then hop on a Greyhound.

We wanted to try and get ourselves a social security number so we could work, and someone – and I have no idea who or why – told us to use a different name. I remember calling myself Penny Thompson, a name I made up.

We did manage to get a few jobs. One was cleaning a large house, and once we put the hoover hose on back to front and it blew all the dirt out. We didn't keep that job. Then we were washing cars for a while, and when the money ran out, we reluctantly headed back home.

After being back home for a couple of months, I saw an ad in the paper and went for a job working for a small company called Dart, which was in Haymarket, Piccadilly. I did secretarial work for the two guys who ran the company, Clive Stanhope and Tim Satchell. They were both lovely, but Clive used to frighten me a bit sometimes with his loud, posh voice.

The three of us got on really well together; I would often stay behind late and tidy up the office for them and used to take the net curtains home to wash. Then one night I got locked in – the office was up in the attic and it felt really scary. I had visions of the fire brigade coming and hoisting me out of the window, but eventually I got hold of Clive, who had just arrived home. He came back to the office, let me out and I never stayed late again.

During that time, strangely enough, I was introduced to a girl whose name was Penny Thompson! I met her via a photographer friend of mine – and it was through Penny Thompson that I got my next job on magazines. But this time, instead of dressing the models, I was undressing them. It was, of course, a soft porn magazine called *Men Only*, owned by the strip king of Soho, Paul Raymond himself.

Clive and Tim were upset that I was leaving and used to ask me whether the girls who came for the interview were like me. I just laughed and promised them I would stay in touch and send them copies of the magazine, and I kept my promise.

THREE

SEX, DRUGS AND ROCK AND ROLL (1976–1986)

The *Men Only* offices were in Soho above the Windmill Theatre, and they were looking for someone young and vibrant to help with readers' letters and general office duties. I was a bit apprehensive at the time, but eager to see the set-up, so I went for the interview and remember thinking perhaps I should go bra-less, as it was a men's magazine. I did and I got the job.

I shared an open-plan office with two girls: Helena, secretary to the advertising manager, and Carole, who was secretary to Tony Power, the editor-in-chief of *Men Only* and *Club International*. (Tony was a friend of Penny Thompson, who introduced me.) Paul Raymond's office was just along the corridor so we used to see him quite a lot.

I would often find myself sharing the office lift with half-naked men and women who starred in the shows, on their way up to see Paul Raymond. It was a bit strange at first but I soon got used to it.

Very quickly, I went on to assist the art editors and photographers on photo shoots and I became a stylist. My role was to find pretty underwear, high-heeled shoes and anything else needed. I used to go to the big prop houses, who supplied items for film sets, to choose furniture and props for the photo shoots. It was fascinating and I would spend hours looking at all the different displays for lights, rugs and furniture, all from different eras and different parts of the world. I always made sure I went around lunchtime because they would offer you lunch and a glass of wine.

I remember the time I went into a fetish shop called 'She and Me', looking for some thigh-high boots in PVC, size 5. They only had sizes 10 and 11 there, so I approached the sales assistant who informed me that they were for men. At this stage, I was a little bit naïve, so I was shocked and hastily left the shop.

Even so, I soon became accustomed to going in and out of sex shops looking for all sorts of things – handcuffs, whips, rubber masks, etc., and thought nothing of reaching up to the top shelf of the newsagent's to flick through the latest copies of *Men Only* and *Club International* to see the results of my work. Quite often, I used to sit in with the editor and art editor going through transparencies of the girls to choose which ones would go into the magazine, and some were explicit soft porn. *Men Only* also featured general interest, men's fashion, cars and celebrities of interest to the readers.

I remember going on a photo shoot with Christine Keeler for a feature about the Profumo Affair. It was in the early 1980s and she must have been in her forties. Christine was concerned about having her photo taken and, of course, being ripped off again as she had been in the past. The photographer thought Christine might feel better if another woman came with her for moral support and so I went along. We met Christine in a pub in the King's Road beforehand, so that she could feel that she could trust us, because she had lost trust in everyone.

At first, she seemed a bit reserved and a bit paranoid about having her photograph taken – it was going to be a portrait shoot and she was being paid for it – but after a few drinks she seemed relaxed and a bit more confident. Even so, the photographer said that when he saw her, he thought this is going to be a difficult shoot, because in his view she had let herself go. She had put on some weight and didn't look so pretty.

We went back to her council flat in World's End to do the photo shoot; the place was small and a bit scruffy. She was drinking and smoking dope throughout the shoot and was glad when it was all over. At one point, she went into the kitchen to light a cigarette on the gas stove, when her hair caught fire. Luckily, we were able to put it out quickly.

I even did the occasional bit of modelling myself and appeared on the front cover of *Club International*. I only modelled for Ian, who was now also working for Paul Raymond and was the art editor and one of the photographers for *Club International*. We once went to Greece and took some pictures on one of the remote islands. It was a bit nerve-racking, as the tide was coming in so quickly and it was hard to get the little boat back out to sea.

When we managed it, it got quite choppy out at sea and then a bigger boat pulled up alongside us. We had to swap boats, and the only thing my boyfriend was worried about was his camera equipment. As for me, I was terrified.

I did pose for a few more pictures after that and was approached by Steve Lewis, one of the photographers from the *Sun* newspaper to put me forward to appear on Page 3, which was quite a big deal at the time. My one

A magazine cover girl! Photo: Ian Potter.

regret was that I didn't take Steve up on it, and that was only because Ian didn't want me to pose unless he took the pictures, and he couldn't, because the *Sun* used their own photographers.

I became good friends with Debbie Raymond, Paul's daughter, who used to come into the office regularly. We became like a family; me, Ian, Tony and Carole (who had got married), Debbie and Paul Raymond, or 'P.R.' as he liked to be called.

I got on quite well with P.R. If you worked hard, he liked you, especially if he thought you were a bit gutsy. If he came into work and I wasn't there (perhaps I was out looking for props, then again, perhaps not), he would say, "Where's Madam?" He was very camp-looking with his mink coat and long gold chain. He was a shrewd businessman, and he had a reputation for being ruthless and could be arrogant, but socially he could be quite generous.

Sometimes after work we would go to one of his clubs – Madame Jo Jo's or the famous Raymond Revuebar – and then go back to his penthouse suite in Portman Square for more drinks, where there was always cocaine available if you wanted it. Once or twice, I did indulge, as it gave me a buzz and the energy to go on to various other clubs. We'd go in his Phantom 6 Rolls-Royce to 'Wedges' in the King's Road, 'White Elephant' in Mayfair, 'The Embassy' in Piccadilly and however many more we could fit in. I'm told I was so drunk one evening in 'Tramp', Rod Stewart helped carry me out to the taxi. We would continue drinking until the early hours of the morning, and I have been known on a few occasions to go straight to work the next day.

We also used to go out on Paul Raymond's boat, which was moored at Cheyne Walk in Chelsea. Some weekends, P.R. used to take the yacht up to Oxford or just up and down the Thames locally. There were usually the six of us and it was always a real party atmosphere, with plenty of champagne and other substances available.

I began to get used to living the high life, mixing with the rich and famous. I once went on holiday to Miami with Page 3 girl Jilly Johnson and her boyfriend. We met Paul Raymond out there and joined him for oysters at one of the famous restaurants. A couple of months after we got back, Ian was asked to go as a photographer to the Cannes Film Festival, and there was no way he was going without me! Paul Raymond wanted him to cover the red carpet and snap celebrities going in and out of the Carlton Hotel.

I loved Cannes; it was so glamorous and everyone looked like a film star. When we went to the beach, there was no throwing on an old pair of flip-flops and a squashed sun hat; it was full make-up, skimpy bikini, designer sunglasses and high heels. Everyone wanted to be discovered!

After five years of working for Paul Raymond, I decided to leave and work for the company on a freelance basis. It was okay and I quite liked it for a year or so, but although the money was better, I missed the structure of going to work. Although I was getting work, I didn't like the uncertainty of not having a regular job and income. So when P.R. called to ask me if I would like to work as a receptionist for his new Burlesque show, 'La Vie en Rose', based on the Moulin Rouge, at the Windmill Theatre, I accepted.

A few days later, I was picked up from home in P.R.'s Rolls-Royce by his chauffeur Charles, and taken to a fashion designer in the King's Road, where I was kitted out in glamorous attire. I was dressed in this gorgeous pink wraparound designer dress, which tied up at the shoulders, plus a black bow tie, fishnet stockings and high heels. I worked on reception with another girl called Lisa and the head doorman, Dave, who I went on to marry five years later.

My job at the Windmill entailed me meeting and greeting the customers, answering the phone and taking table reservations.

Dave and I married in the Seychelles in 1991.

On arrival, I would take the customers' coats and take them upstairs to their tables. The whole place had a great atmosphere, it was buzzy and quite exciting, and when I had my break I used to sit at the bar and watch the show. P.R. once asked if I'd like to be in it, but I laughed and said I'd rather be on this side of the stage.

Funnily enough, I didn't miss being a stylist; I think it was just time for a change.

There was a funny incident one evening when the whole rail of fur coats collapsed on the floor in this tiny cloakroom. I'd gone to put one coat on the rack, which was already too heavy, and the whole lot came down on the floor. To try and sort them out I had to trample all over them and put them back, but in the tumble, a lot of tickets came off and so when the customers wanted to leave, it was a nightmare sorting out whose coat was whose. Luckily, Paul Raymond's mink coat wasn't one of them that night.

I enjoyed the reception work, as I loved meeting people, but when a position as a cashier became available, and it was nights rather than shifts, I decided to swap jobs, as I liked having the days to myself and also it was more money. I was a bit hesitant at the time, because it was very different and behind the scenes, but surprisingly I got to like it.

When the show closed three years later, I was offered a different job again, this time as a receptionist in the offices, but I'd got used to night work and preferred it, so I declined. P.R. wasn't prepared to pay me redundancy, so I took him to court. Believe it or not, we didn't fall out over it. Looking back, I don't know how I had the guts and just what possessed me to take this ruthless millionaire businessman to court. I wasn't worried about it – I just thought I owed it to myself to get what I deserved and so I applied for legal aid. On the day itself, when we went to the magistrates' court, we settled on a payout of £900, which was enough for me to take my dear mum on holiday to Tenerife. That was something I had always wanted to do. When my dad was alive, we would occasionally go on family holidays to Ramsgate. After my dad passed away, I promised myself I would take Mum on holiday abroad and when I got that payout, at last I was able to.

About six months later, Debbie Raymond called offering me a job back with Paul Raymond Publications working on another project. I reminded her that I had just taken her father to court. She laughed and said I should have got more money out of him and that he admired my cheek! I didn't accept, as I had already got another job at a restaurant called 'School Dinners', where all the girls were dressed in school uniform, but that's another story.

Mum and Dad on holiday in Ramsgate, Kent. 1960.

Looking back, when I was an innocent 15 year old and enjoying life on teenage magazines, I never imagined that one day I'd be working on a raunchy men's magazine, and loving every minute of it.

SANDIE'S STORY

On the journey at 15.

A wild child before the name was even coined, I was hell-bent on securing my journalistic ambition. The path was sometimes rough and rocky but never boring, as the next chapters will illustrate in full technicolour.

ONE

THE BACKDROP
1967–1968

'Rolling Stone Brian Jones found dead in swimming pool', screamed the headlines almost the first week I began my stint as junior features writer and pop reporter on *Mirabelle*, a magazine aimed at teenagers which offered advice to tweenies on life and love interspersed with pop and rock interviews, reports and features.

Brian Jones was found dead in his swimming pool one month after he had been asked to leave the group, partly due to his drug habit. Jones founded the group in 1962, was the original leader of the group and a widely recognised member of The Rolling Stones.

Police ruled that it was an accident due to the drugs in his system, but there are many who thought there was more to his death than was originally reported. There were a few who said that a contractor working in his home murdered him. Later on, a builder apparently confessed on his deathbed to murdering Jones, but police did not take his confession seriously. On a brighter note, the group has continued to remain ageless, with many band members from the original line-up still performing despite being at the ripe old age of 70 plus.

Unfortunately, this was not an unusual occurrence during the late '60s and early '70s, especially within the world of pop and rock. The swinging sixties were an emotive mix of hedonism and enlightening adventures tinged with a slightly innocent aura. But the innocence was a façade, with tragedy always lurking on the outskirts of the shadows and waiting to strike and rear its ugly head just when you least expected it.

Many pop stars avidly embraced the drug culture under the illusion that it would help them write better music, attain the impossible notes on their electric guitars or just generally feel better about themselves, but in many cases they just became addicted to Class A drugs, which would inevitably lead to an untimely death.

Working on a pop magazine and mixing with the music fraternity, I was constantly around people who dabbled quite heavily in the drug culture. However, it was a habit I never really understood. I took marijuana once at a party and, contrary to everyone else's feelings of euphoria, it made me feel irritable and so I never bothered to touch any drugs again. I also hated going to some supposedly cool parties where everyone was so stoned they never spoke to one another because they were incapable, and they certainly didn't dance, which I found extremely boring. After all, isn't that what parties are for?

The pocket-rocket ace guitarist, Jimmy McCulloch, originally of the Thunderclap Newman trio that released the iconic 'Something in the Air' number one hit in 1969 died of a suspected overdose at the age of 26.

I interviewed Jimmy when he was around 16, and I was 17 when I was working on *Mirabelle*. He and his older brother, Jack, were very photogenic, with their natural Peter Pan image, so we took plenty of opportunities to put them on the front cover. It's fair to say there were a few sparks flying between Jimmy and me – although never consummated – so, obviously, I felt very sad when I learnt of his demise a few years later.

I even ghostwrote a couple of features for him – one column based on ghouls and scary creatures, funnily, although I am pretty sure he had never seen one in his life. We white-lied a lot back in the day!

I also carried out the same task for child star Jack Wild, who played the Artful Dodger in the 1968 version of 'Oliver!' alongside Mark Lester, who played the lead role. I think Jack was quite attracted to me but, unfortunately, I didn't feel

Ghost writing for Jack Wild Mirabelle

the same way about him. Sadly, by 1973, when Jack was 21, he was already an alcoholic and diabetic. Due to his addiction, his career stalled and he never fulfilled his full potential as an actor and consequently died in 2006.

Back to Jimmy McCulloch's tale. He began his career at the tender age of 11 when he joined a Scottish band called The Jaygars along with his brother, Jack, a handy drummer to have around. He and Jimmy were part of a juvenile and elite group of musicians within the music industry and by the time he was 14, Jimmy had already made an impression on the music industry, with mentors backing his professional prowess, such as John Entwistle from The Who and John Mayall.

Once he left Thunderclap Newman, Jimmy became a member of Paul McCartney's Wings group, which at the time included, among others, Paul's wife, Linda, and Denny Laine, formerly of The Moody Blues. In fact, many people observed that Jimmy even looked like a smaller, younger version of Paul

McCartney himself. But he never seemed to settle into the Wings style of performing, preferring to be on tour rather than stuck in a recording studio.

Paul Kossoff, yet another eclectic blues rock guitarist who lost his life to drugs, was a shooting star who burned out too quickly. He and I went to the same school in north London and his father was the late actor David Kossoff.

Paul was a nice guy, a bit crazy but in a good way, and with bags of talent as a guitarist. He made his name with Free, a very successful group who produced a number of hits including 'Alright Now' – a tune once heard, never forgotten. Unfortunately, Paul, who was ranked 51st in *Rolling Stone* magazine's list of the 100 Greatest Guitarists of all time, died at the age of 25 in the toilet of a 'red-eye' flight from Los Angeles just as it landed at New York.

It may be a brutal introduction to my story about life on a young pop magazine, dear reader, but there is no apology. It was what it was, and I'm afraid it is still happening today, for example, Amy Winehouse, Whitney Houston and Avicii.

The only other person of note who was at my school was long-distance Olympian runner David Bedford. Indeed, I once ran around the track at the same time as David, but I think he beat me!

He went on to greatness in the Olympics, holding the 10,000 metres world record and improving it by 7.6 seconds with his time of 27 minutes 30.80 seconds in 1973. After he retired, he held the position of race director for the London Marathon until 2012. Apparently, he always ran in red socks, but I don't recall that quirk.

His prowess on the track also inadvertently caused me to have a marital spat with my hubby at the time, but when my dear mother found out, she said she hadn't a clue who David Bedford was and – in her words – 'didn't know him from the King of Siam'.

The positions of head girl or prefect were never honorary positions bestowed on me during my school days, nor could I have been ever described as a model pupil. There are occasions, however, when I wish I had paid more heed to the excellent Scottish education I received before I left Scotland at 12, but there is no use crying over spilt milk. And to be fair, I have done quite well for myself in spite of my lack of studious intentions.

English and History were the subjects I excelled in at school, and I was pretty good at PE because it gave me the freedom to run around and indulge in my favourite pastime at that time: mucking around and having a laugh. Due to circumstances in my family life, I had moved around a lot and been a newbie at more schools than I care to remember.

Without making excuses for my lack of enthusiasm for scholarly work, I found I fitted in quicker and more successfully if I played the class 'clown' and daredevil – traits that have not diminished with age!

Writing has always been in my blood; I have always had a very vivid imagination, sometimes too much for my own good. No pristine sheets of paper were safe, even my father's discarded cigarette packets. When I was 14 and attending Whitefield Bi-Lateral, my last school in London, I decided I would become a journalist, and nothing was going to change my mind.

Mind you, I may not have achieved any academic firsts but I certainly achieved a few at the University of Life. I was one of the first in my peer group to share a flat platonically with three heterosexual males and also to live 'in sin', as they used to call it, with an intimate partner. This is not a boast but it shows how times have changed. In the 2020s, there is nothing unusual or shocking about sharing a flat with other genders, and most couples carry out a 'dry run' before walking down the aisle.

My family were open-minded about a mixed flat scenario and even enjoyed visiting my flat, but with regard to living

together, we kept that a secret from the family for a while –
or tried to, because it is quite challenging 'removing' another
person's presence from your flat in five minutes when relatives
turn up uninvited. That's when you forget the biggest giveaway –
his toothbrush cuddling up to your toothbrush in the bathroom!

During the '60s, ways of thinking and living changed in a
major way and mostly for the better. One of those long overdue
changes happened in 1967 when a new act was introduced to
decriminalise homosexuality.

Remember, those were the days when we used the word
gay to describe someone who was generally quite a happy soul.
There were other words used but they were not very palatable,
and the term LGBT was a twinkle in the sky. In 50 years, we have
come a very long way.

The world of music, publishing, the arts and fashion
has always been less judgemental when it comes to sexual
preferences. Myself, I think this is because people who normally
frequent this path in life are usually of a creative nature, and
creativity is often associated with open- mindedness.

Like most late teenage, early twenty-somethings, my
friendships covered all groups. Without wishing to generalise,
heterosexual females usually rub along nicely with homosexual
men. We love the fact that they talk to us, listen, and tell us
truthfully how we are looking – good or otherwise. We feel 'safe'
in their company, not because sometimes we worry that straight
men will jump on us given the chance, we just feel comfortable
around gay men.

Being a female teenager in the late '60s was very liberating.
Of course, bad things still happened but there wasn't the same
paranoia about being mugged, raped or randomly stabbed on
your way home from a night out as there is now. While I am not
so naïve as to think that life was a bowl of orchids back then, I
do feel that life was generally a lot simpler.

The lack of social media meant that we were never bullied by online trolls or risked being set up on chat rooms. Even images in fashion magazines were more realistic – heroin chic had not yet reared its ugly head – so it was not an impossible aim for young girls to aspire to resembling the models. And yes, of course we did resort to air brushing on the magazines but mostly to enhance and certainly not to chop chunks off bodies or remove ribs and other body parts to give the impression that it was normal to be a size 0.

However, back to schooldays. I never actually thought I was doing anything wrong when I skipped Cooking, Knitting and/or Sewing lessons so I could write my version of 'Lord of the Flies' about my class being marooned on a desert island. It was easy to bunk off those lessons because you appeared for your form class and then disappeared. That's not a recommendation for younger readers by the way!

Naturally, my antics attracted a lot of attention but not always in a beneficial way! Like the time I took my mum's pet poodle into school on the premise that Ongar (yes, my father bought her from a kennel in Ongar, Essex on his way back from a business trip) had been locked out – she caused chaos in the classroom, as you can well imagine.

Originally, I wanted to be a dancer and trained in classical ballet. I still love to dance today whenever I can – Irish hard shoe dancing is my forte. And for some strange reason I thought I would make a good secret agent, obviously encouraged by watching too many Bond movies but again circumstances at the crucial age of 11 decided the fate of the former and I can't boast that keeping secrets is a talent of mine.

I enjoy being a girl – clothes, make-up, perfume and a good gossip over a glass of wine – but running parallel to this is my desire to be accepted as 'one of the boys'. Being competitive hasn't always helped when it comes to the blossoming of successful romantic liaisons with members of the male sex, but that would take another book to explain in more detail. My father, a commando in WW11, admired my 'spunk' on a number of occasions – now that's a word we never use nowadays to describe someone with a bit of bottle.

My actual first job was when I was 14 selling shoes in True Form, one of a chain of shops that no longer exist which sold reasonably priced footwear at Hendon Central. For slogging my guts out all day on a Saturday, I received the princely sum of 15 shillings, plus one penny in the pound commission for every pair of shoes sold!

There were two of us Saturday girls but somehow I always got the job of climbing the ladder in the stockroom to retrieve the other shoe for trying on – and it seemed that every shoe requested was always on the top shelf.

And funnily enough the manager never offered to help but stood and watched me swaying about at the top of a ladder. The stockroom was extremely small and narrow so to be fair it was unlikely I would have done any permanent damage if I had fallen off the ladder.

Shoe shops in those days expected their staff to assist their customers with trying on a potential new pair of shoes, unlike now, where you are just left to get on with it. I also realised that many members of the British public knew very little when it came to foot hygiene. I certainly never contemplated a career in a shoe shop after my experience.

So, I was ever so pleased when I found a job advertised in the *Evening Standard* – always a good place to find jobs – for an editorial assistant (a posh name for a 'runner') on the *Daily Sketch*, a national newspaper based in Fleet Street. In July 1967, at the tender age of 15, I was allowed to leave school a month earlier than I was legally allowed to. I am sure my teachers all heaved a sigh of relief as they wished me good luck and escorted me off the premises. I joined the *Daily Sketch* on about a fiver per week.

PLUNGING INTO PUBLISHING

Dressed in a fashionable pink skinny knitted top and matching pink and green floral-patterned skater skirt, I headed off in plenty of time to take the Northern Line tube from our home in Brent Cross to Blackfriars tube station on the District Line. My parents had drummed into me and my siblings that it was very important to turn up on time, so much so that I am always usually ten minutes early for everything. I would love to be 'fashionably late' once in a while but it's never going to happen.

The *Sketch* was part of Associated Newspapers and housed in Carmelite House, situated at the bottom of Carmelite Street just off Fleet Street. The offices faced the Embankment, although from the Editorial floor you couldn't see very much of the River Thames because the windows were too high, or maybe it was because I am quite small in stature.

Nearby were the offices of the *Evening Standard*. At least five editions of the paper were published six days per week. When the editions came off the presses, there was a great theatrical show of organised chaos as the editions were delivered by van all over London. To be honest, *Standard* drivers were a unique bunch and a bit like Marmite – you either liked or loathed them. Normally, their jobs were handed down from their fathers and their fathers' fathers. Now, of course, *ES* is a freesheet with only one edition 5 days a week. How times change.

My brother, who worked on the *ES* for a few years, had 'threatened' to take a party of friends and relatives to see the action on the editorial floor on a Saturday when results of the sporting fixtures were coming through. Deadlines were not just tight but nigh on impossible, tempers taut and the air more purple than blue from the blasphemies. It was not for the fainthearted.

There was a definite demarcation between the journalists and the printers, and they very rarely agreed with each other despite the fact that they couldn't exist without each other. SOGAT, one of the main printing unions, was very militant to say the least, and it didn't take very much to start a strike. I very nearly caused one myself – unwittingly, of course – and all down to my naivety.

A package had to be delivered to the print room and I was accompanied by an older, more experienced editorial assistant down to the ground floor. It was a fascinating place and I was transfixed, and especially by the typesetting equipment. I decided to pick up a piece and have a closer look, as you do, and you would have thought I had set off a bomb.

I was quickly ushered out by my knowledgeable companion and then tutored by my elders as to how not to anger the print unions in the future. Strikes cost money for the newspapers and I was now aware how easily they could be set off!

But I digress, so let's get back to that first day when I discovered I was the only girl in a team of about five boys led by a Mr Barnes – never did find out his first name and certainly even if we knew, we would never have dared call him by that name to his face.

This is where I learnt to swear, not from Mr Barnes but the eclectic mix of journalists that I rubbed shoulders with every day. When the pressure was on, the swear words flowed and so I followed because it seemed the right thing to do. Apart from delivering messages, packages and other information all over London, I also worked with the legendary Jean Rook, who was fashion editor at the time. I decided to produce the 'Scaily Detch' newspaper and wrote my little news stories and gave them to the reporters so they could give me feedback.

One job I had to do every month or so for the Fashion department was to return the rails of clothes we borrowed for fashion shoots from designers and showrooms in the West End. However, not all the clothes borrowed appeared in the newspaper. The fashion industry has always been highly competitive and from a designer's point of view, one week you are in vogue and the next struggling to get anyone to even look at your designs for a fashion shoot.

Eric, one of the drivers, used to collect me from the main reception hidden under a big bundle of clothes, and then we worked as a team to return them to their rightful owners. The idea was to get a signature as proof of return and then run in case they spotted any damage to the clothes. Eric would be sitting in the car with the engine running so we could make a speedy escape!

When I first joined the *Sketch*, outside of work I was a 'weekend flower power girl'. After work, we donned fur waistcoats, floral kaftans, beads around our necks and flowers in our hair, but I drew the line at walking around in bare feet on London's dirty streets.

To all intents and purposes, our message to one and all was love and peace, until the time when I was handing out flowers in the West End and this person told me to 'f*** off' to which I replied in similar vernacular and so... it was time to move on.

But during this halcyon period I experienced an unforgettable moment where I and a few others sat in a big circle in Hyde Park with the iconic Marc Bolan singing 'Deborah'. At the time I never

Embracing the flower power era... but not for long.

imagined that within a couple of years I would be interviewing him on *Mirabelle* magazine.

While I was on the *Sketch,* my father accepted a job offer in Yorkshire. He was very supportive of my ambition so when he told me of his plans – and before I had time to object – he said I would not be going with them but that he would find 'digs' for me in London so I could stay and pursue my quest for a career in journalism. I was extremely grateful to him for this opportunity, so when they departed, I moved in with a nice couple in Colindale, north London as their lodger.

So here I was at 15 effectively on my own in London! In 1967, life even in a big city was very different to how it is now! I was streetwise so was more than capable of surviving the temptations of living in London during the swinging sixties. Indeed, I did survive but there were times when it was borderline. I am no angel after all…!

There was a hierarchy running through our team of messenger boys and girls. The editor's boy (we shall call him John) was higher up in the pecking order than the rest of us and he was also someone I was attracted to almost immediately. The feeling was mutual, I am glad to say.

Aloof from his contemporaries, but in a pleasant way, he was witty, clever and funny and so 'in the moment' of the late '60s. With his shiny, floppy, blondish hair and aquiline nose, he had almost an aristocratic look, although he was a boy born and bred in mainstream Essex.

He was also irresponsible and quite reckless, but I wasn't aware of those character traits in the initial stages of our budding relationship. However, a strong bond developed between us, basically because we were different form the other messengers as we both yearned for careers within the media (we never used that terminology in those days), while the others were just using the job as a stopgap before moving on to more lucrative work.

Hit with the entrepreneurial stick, John's head continually brimmed with ideas. Early on in our liaison, he had this vision of turning me into a photographic model. I was certainly not catwalk material, I hasten to add, as I am only 5' 3" small and – some would say – blessed with an ample bosom which is not such a good look for the catwalk.

Some of the so-called agencies we visited were seedier than others, and all of them filled me with dread before we even ventured through the door. My height, or lack of it, was mentioned quite a lot; one man called me 'dinky', another booker 'cute' or 'interesting'. To be honest, my heart wasn't in it anyhow.

The thought of spending hours in front of a camera while the photographer and their assistants, the fashion and beauty editors and anybody else who happened to be around, discussed and criticised your bad points was not my idea of a fulfilling career. But, to please John, I allowed his brother to take a selection of photographs over a weekend and then one Saturday we trailed around the model agencies, which were not in the same league as they are today. Now, in the main, they are professionally run and aim to take into account the welfare of their models first and foremost.

However, through my contacts at IPC Magazines via the *Daily Sketch,* I was asked to attend a couple of photo sessions for which I was paid, including the *Fab 208* session pictured here but it didn't change my mind about abandoning writing in favour of selling images of my face or body. And finally it dawned on John that I wasn't interested and so he moved on to another project.

I continually reminded my big bosses about my ambition, and those who suffered this included the very distinguished Howard French, editor-in-chief of the *Sketch* (John's boss), Louis Kirby and Peter Bostock, who in different ways all took me under their wing to guide me on my path to write professionally.

Modelling for Fab 208/Future Publishing Ltd.

It was Peter Bostock's wife, Ann Beveridge, fashion editor of *Woman's Own* magazine, who presented me with the opportunity to enter magazine life. They were in need of an office junior and so I applied for the job and thankfully got it! Although a step up from being a messenger girl, it was still low in the pecking order.

MAGAZINE WORLD, HERE I COME!

It was sad leaving the *Daily Sketch* even though I had only been there just short of a year, but in that space of time I had learnt a lot. I said goodbye to a lot of colleagues I would never ever forget and was thankful for their help and support that set me up for my career.

The move to *Woman's Own* was to be used as a way to learn my craft and indeed I did under the tutelage of Jane Reed, who was assistant editor at the time. It was never my intention to stay in the fashion world, but at last I would begin learning the finer elements of my craft from highly respected journalists.

Under supervision, I would learn to write captions (not as easy as it sounds), sub-edit and precis. I was also encouraged to come up with story ideas in between carrying out the more mundane jobs such as looking after the 'cupboard', ensuring clothes from the fashion houses were booked in and out, returning the clothes after photo sessions, keeping the cupboard in as good a condition as possible and fetching endless cups of tea, coffee, packets of cigarettes and sandwiches to keep everyone going when the heat was on, especially during the spring/summer and autumn/winter collections and shows.

Working on a women's magazine was entirely different from a newspaper office – less profanities for a start. There were far more women than men, although the editor at the time was a man.

Emotions ran high, which I found quite

Caught in the middle of the Woman's Own *fashion team.*

uncomfortable, and I was surprised by the lack of camaraderie between women in competitive jobs. At this stage in my career, I was no serious threat to my team as they were all well-established journos who had fought hard to reach their positions in a predominantly male world. I was treated well and indulged like a younger sister by the majority of my female colleagues.

They loaned me money when I had overspent, and that was often, offered advice on my love life, which I usually ignored, and most importantly provided me with cast-offs from the Fashion department cupboard.

Diane Knight was the assistant fashion editor and I found her a very intriguing character. Unfortunately, she died in an accident at home at quite a young age. She was what we would call now 'her own woman'. She dated Louie Brown, playboy and owner of La Valbonne club in Kingly Street, which attracted all the beautiful people of the moment. She was quite tough but always looked very feminine.

I coveted her wardrobe of angora dresses and coats in just about every colour of the spectrum by the knitwear designer Mary Farrin. They were soft and warm and incredibly sensuous and very expensive, even with a press discount. I did manage to acquire a pale pink angora number, thanks to Diane, and I loved wearing it.

Occasionally, while working on *Woman's Own*, I was allowed to arrange interviews and write mini features in order to gain experience of writing at a professional level. During that time, I interviewed The Nashville Teens, best known for their 1964 hit 'Tobacco Road', and I couldn't have hoped for a more well-mannered, genuinely nice and courteous bunch of men.

Woman's Own introduced me to lavish press receptions for launching perfumes, skin products and the budding career of an actor or singer, but most of the time was spent running around collecting and delivering rails of frocks. It's also when I first met fellow Magazine Girl Penny in the lifts at Tower House in Southampton Street, just off the Strand. Normally, we were huffing and puffing under a very large bundle of clothes, either bringing them up to be scrutinised by our bosses or taking them down to reception to be collected by the fashion house courier.

We always said hello and had the occasional moan about the lowliness of our respective jobs and our transportation chores of the fashionable frocks and outfits that probably cost about ten times our salary at the time.

I don't think for one moment during those brief episodes travelling in the lifts in Tower House that we thought we were going to still be friends catching up regularly over *vino* and pasta 50 years later, even less writing a book together.

TWO

A Brief Departure from Publishing (1969–1972)

At sweet 16, just when I thought I was on a steady professional path, an economic blip hit which meant I had to go and live with my parents who were residing in Yorkshire. I knew in my heart that it would only be temporary, as once things were settled I seriously hoped I would be returning to London to rekindle my career.

Mum and Dad had enjoyed having me back under their roof for those few months but once the blip was resolved they actively encouraged my return to London. I had tried to procure jobs locally, one being on the *Yorkshire Post,* the celebrated and award-winning provincial newspaper based in Leeds with a satellite office in London. It was more of a mentoring meeting and certainly boosted my confidence. However, there were no jobs available at the time applicable to my current experience.

I have always been 'a glass half full kind of gal', so I was pretty certain that with my contacts I would be able to find the right job. One of the main reasons was because at just 17 I had two years' valuable experience behind me on the *Daily Sketch* and *Woman's Own,* plus had written a few freelance articles which had already been published.

My romantic liaison with John had continued despite my absence, so once I had made up my mind to return, I phoned him to divulge my plans. We had kept in contact by the occasional letter and by phone (landline, of course) and seen each other once or twice. Even by '60s standards, I would describe our relationship as fairly open with no real jealousy on either side.

He was very glad that I was returning to London, more for my career than any personal wishes on his part and echoed my positivity. Such a pity that the relationship would not survive, and I never dreamt how final it would be, but more about that later.

Even more convenient was the fact that John was now working for a news agency in north London as a junior reporter and sharing a flat with two of his colleagues in Highgate. According to John, there was plenty of room at the flat and I could stay and help with the rent. I just needed to find the job of my dreams, which was a hell of a lot easier in 1969 than it is now, thank goodness.

I left Yorkshire by coach at 9am on Monday, 23 June 1969 and arrived back at London's iconic Victoria Coach Station at 4pm. Although it took three times longer to arrive at your destination, travelling by coach was the cheapest form of travel. Passing driving tests and owning cars at the age of 17 was quite unusual at that time – so very different from now.

My son passed his test by the time he was 17 and owned a Mini, albeit an older model. Anyhow, I was saving my pennies, as I didn't know how long I would have to exist before getting a permanent job.

I turned up in North Hill, Highgate and met my new flatmates – fellow like-minded young journalists a couple of years older than me who I would share my life with for two years – and boy, did we have fun! It was manic and frenetic but we also did our best to support each other when things were not going so well in our private or professional lives.

Now it's quite common to share a mixed gender flat but in 1969 it was considered very risqué. I always preferred to be different from the crowd so no one in my circle was very surprised. My parents, when they returned from Harrogate to London, found the whole scenario quite amusing, but they were not normal parents and allowed me a lot of freedom to pursue my path in life.

I had also been fortunate enough to arrange with my former employer, *Woman's Own*, to come back and work for a couple of weeks but this time with the Features department. The one lesson I had learnt even at that young age was always try to leave an employer on a high note because you never know when you will need them in the future. I have been proved right at least twice in my career.

I turned up at *Woman's Own* the following day and it was as if I had never left. I resumed similar duties but running alongside this was my hunger to find a job, so I reminded all and sundry about my long-term aspirations, and I am pretty sure that behind the scenes they had a number of conversations with their friends and contacts in the business.

Getting a job during the '60s and up to nearly the '80s in the private sector was relatively easy. A prospective employer either liked you and was impressed with your CV and previous work or was not interested and it ended up in the dustbin. Either way, you knew immediately. And that was the bottom line. None of this waiting around for weeks for an answer – and then probably not the one you wanted to hear. Of course, this way of recruiting staff works both ways. You could be hired immediately but you could also be fired just as suddenly if not sooner!

The next morning, I went in and was called directly into my ex-boss' office, who told me that a Scottish chap called Bill Williamson over in IPC Magazines' Young Magazine Group had a vacancy on *Mirabelle* magazine. I remember standing looking at her and waiting for her to continue when she said to me, "Well, what are you waiting for? Phone him now and arrange an interview!"

I had very little time to prepare as it was arranged for the following day. Yes, it was the world of the media, but even outside of the publishing industry jobs were purloined or lost on a very immediate basis. Winging it has become a popular saying these days, and that is really what I did for this interview. My *Woman's Own* colleagues carried out a mock interview and soon-to-be new flatmates ran through a few questions that they thought I was more than likely to be asked. I prepared a brief resume of my career to date and scrabbled around to find what press cuttings I had acquired in that short time, one of which was 'Talking to the Tortoiseshell Cat', which was my first-ever published article in *Fab 208*.

I was wearing a striped red and yellow shirt dress, but I don't remember too much about the finer details of the interview because it was a long time ago. But one thing I do remember saying to him was the following – and that was the clincher:

"I can write about anything you want me to write about and for that reason I think you should hire me. I won't let you down."

So he did and another chapter began in my quest to write professionally.

Popping into the Pop Phenomena

I turned up at Fleetway House in Farringdon Street just round the corner from Fleet Street, so back to my old haunting ground. Fleetway House was home to IPC's Young Magazines Group, previously owned by George Newnes, and I was a fully fledged employee on a starting salary of £20+ a week. I felt like I was a millionaire because I had almost tripled my wages in less than six months. What can you buy for £20 in this day and age?

The set-up at that time centred around Bill Williamson, the editor of *Mirabelle* who had interviewed me. I was going to be working alongside Pat Bostock-Smith, previously a local newspaper news editor/reporter who was very experienced. I am sure she must have thought that I was some little upstart who knew it all.

Pat was married to Colin Bostock-Smith, who was the editor of Rave and other magazines within IPC. With them being ten years older than me, I kind of looked up to Colin and Pat.

I think Pat went back into newspapers and Colin later went on to write comedy programmes for the BBC such as 'Metal Mickey', 'Not the Nine O'Clock News' and the sitcom 'Me and My Girl'.

Also working with me at the beginning of my time with *Mirabelle* was a lovely *avant-garde* lady called Helen Hooper. Again, she was quite a bit older than me and wore lots of brightly coloured scarves and large hooped earrings. She was very funny, witty and cynical at the same time, especially of senior management and the pop world.

But that set-up changed quite quickly with the demise of *Rave* magazine. Bill Williamson became editor-in-chief, Paul Raven became our very young editor and that's when I met Linda Newman, who at 19 was the senior features writer and pop reporter to my junior features writer and pop reporter at 17. Linda, of course, is now a fellow Magazine Girl too!

We were one of about six publications in the Young Magazines Group of IPC Magazines. The stable encompassed titles such as *Loving, Valentine, Love Affair, Fab 208* and latterly *Petticoat* and *19* magazine. There was also an Art department and a production editor, and we shared an Accounts and Customer Services department with the other mags.

Jackie magazine was *Mirabelle's* main rival with a circulation of around a hefty 600,000 readers per week, while Mirabelle hovered around the 500,000 mark. Our editor's mood swings mirrored the circulation figures when they were released by the publishing trade magazines – pure elation or sheer desperation. I know it probably should have done, but it never worried me one way or another.

In the main, the staff on *Jackie* operated out of Dundee in Scotland, but they did share the facilities of a room or two at the very ornate London offices of the DC Thompson publishing house of the *Dundee Courier* and *People's Friend* in Fleet Street. We used to bump into some of the *Jackie* staff and freelancers at press dos, and being young and immature, I would always be quite cocky. We always got better pop star interviews than they did anyhow!

We were NOT screamers, Linda and I! If we had been star-struck and prone to this rather cringeworthy habit, we would never have been able to carry out our jobs with professional aplomb on a pop magazine with easy access to all those sensual pop and rock stars.

Linda and I listening intently.

Linda and I had to carry ourselves with an air of nonchalance and act like we were a bit bored by the whole thing. When we turned up for interviews or at press receptions, we had to give off this aura that they didn't impress us that much.

That's not to say we didn't like music – we loved it – or didn't respect the groups and bands that we would meet in the three years we were in this role, but it would have been very uncool if we had acted like slavering dolts around them. I for one would never have allowed myself to behave like that in front of any man. Sometimes, however, our blasé attitudes got us into trouble with our superiors.

One Monday morning, the editor-in-chief called Linda and I into his office.

"Would you two like to trot off to the Isle of Wight Festival next weekend?"

It's a pity there wasn't one of our photographers around to capture the expression on our faces – a combined look of horror. We just didn't get it, wallowing around in mud and the toilet scenario, or rather the lack of toilets that put us off, not being able to wash our hair and just feeling dirty for the whole weekend. Besides, we could see all the bands that would be there in London!

Despite the ed.'s protests that it couldn't be that bad if all who were great in the music world at that time were attending, Linda and I could not be moved on our decision, so a freelancer went instead. Our punishment was to stay in town and think up some new and innovative ideas for features.

So did we miss much? Well, 150,000 turned up on 29 August 1969 to see acts including Bob Dylan, his first public appearance since a serious motorbike accident three years earlier, The Who, Free, Joe Cocker, The Moody Blues, The Pretty Things, King Crimson and more.

The event was well managed and trouble-free in comparison

to the recent Woodstock Festival in America, which Bob Dylan had snubbed even though it was virtually on his doorstop in favour of the Isle of Wight. He had surfaced from semi-retirement and he and his family travelled on the QE2 to Britain and nearly missed the gig completely when his son was hit by a cabin door and had to be hospitalised. Dylan ended up finishing the journey going by plane.

And, of course, we did miss one or two of The Beatles line-up who turned up to watch Bob Dylan, as did Eric Clapton and Keith Richards. And The Who included in their set some of their hits from their rock opera, 'Tommy'.

Since then, I have broken my refusal to attend festivals when in 2016 I trotted off to Reading with one of my old PR friends who could not believe that I had worked in the pop world and never been to a music festival.

However, I still wrestled with the toilets situation, especially the female urinals that had just been introduced the year before. Please tell me, what's that all about, especially if you are wearing a playsuit?

Despite enjoying Biffy Clyro's finale, I don't think I'll be attending any other festival. I was also amazed at some very young girls taking a pee – while their friends recorded their antics on their iPhones – in front of everyone in one of the tents while a band was playing. Maybe it's my age, but that certainly takes the 'r' out of romance.

Also, I would be the first one to admit that I do have a 'potty' mouth but at the Reading Festival there were lots of Biffy fans walking around wearing t-shirts that proclaimed Biffy 'F****** Clyro'. My friend and I decided that they probably weren't wearing official t-shirts. How wrong could we be? As soon as the very lovely lead singer, Simon Neil, introduced them as, "We are Biffy 'F****** Clyro'," we just looked at each other and laughed. What did we know?

BACK TO 1969 AND THE FUN BEGINS

This is the time when the nucleus of us Magazine Girls began. We worked hard and played hard and in the main enjoyed every minute. We were very aware that we were privileged and extremely lucky to have had the opportunity to forge our careers in the publishing world.

It still amazes me to think that we Magazine Girls only really worked together for around three years, yet we have forged a friendship with each other that has spanned 50 years. It has encompassed all the many good things that have happened throughout our lives and, of course, the not-so-good things that have befallen us, such as changes to our careers, ill health, marriages, divorces, births and sadly, although inevitable, deaths of family members and friends – indeed the whole gamut of all that can be thrown at you during a lifetime.

In 1970, a young man from Pinner quietly appeared on the music scene with 'Your Song', a lilting love song he co-wrote with his lyricist, Bernie Taupin. His name was Elton John and I am happy to say that I was one of the first – and the youngest people – to interview him.

I am sure that Elton would not mind anyone saying this, but Bernie, a stellar lyricist who has written the lyrics for most of Elton's songs and who to this day still collaborates with him, looked more the part of the pop god against Elton's persona of thick-rimmed spectacles, a well-built frame and gingery hair which was neither short nor long, as was the fashion at that time.

The story goes that Bernie answered an advertisement that was placed in *NME* by Liberty Records and coincidentally Elton John answered the same ad. Neither passed the audition, however, but Elton informed the man behind the desk that he couldn't write lyrics, so the man handed a sealed envelope from the pile of people who had submitted lyrics and that is how their story began. The rest is history as they say.

We all thought that 'Your Song' was destined to be a big chart stomper and also that if the duo continued to write music and lyrics as good as their first they would make it into the realms of super stardom.

I predicted that 'Elton is bordering on great' in my first

ELTON JOHN has that rather overpowering look that makes you want to run up and cuddle him. Needless to say he's not as helpless as one would like to imagine. If you've heard *Border Song*—and I daresay you have, then you'll know why.

Indeed Elton is a brilliant pianist and has a lovely deep singing voice. He was born to be an entertainer and no-one can argue about that statement! And some people think he could well be The Songwriter Of The Seventies!

It was over a pineapple juice and baked potato with a couple of bangers, that I talked to Elton. Mind you, he seemed to be very involved with his food!

Who do you think has influenced you most with your career? I asked him.

"I couldn't say just one particular person because really quite a lot of people have influenced me. I would say Bob Dylan's band and Neil Young have had the strongest effects on me.

"Tamla Motown music could even influence me sometimes—it all depends on what sort of mood I'm in! Even reggae could. I liked 'Young, Gifted and Black' but I suppose you couldn't really class that as reggae music!"

Elton seems to have a style of his own. Did it take him long to adopt it?

"Not really. I didn't even realise that I was adopting a certain style. It's just me—naturally! Bernie Taupin writes the lyrics and I write the melody, so I suppose by doing it that way, we've achieved a certain style without really trying!

"I don't know that I'm much of an authority on the music scene today. I would say it's much more healthier than it ever was before. There are so many good things going on around us that I find it quite hard to get bored with it all.

"Everyone is far more broad-minded about music today. They are listening to songs that they might never have bothered to listen to three years ago and there's more decent records in the charts.

"I hope I will appeal to all audiences. I don't want to be tied down to a certain type of music because it just becomes a drag after a while. And if you do something different then people will start saying that you've changed, when all the time you haven't really!

"At the moment, I probably appeal more to the underground type rather than the young ones because

ELTON JOHN

he's bordering on being great says Mirabelle's Sandie Robbie...

they can't really dance or rave to my songs—they have to listen to them.

"We don't sit down and compose for any particular type of people. You could call us unpretentious. We just do what we want to do and hope that everyone will listen."

At Elton John's press reception a couple of months ago, Birds Of A Feather, the sister duo act who released a record called 'The Blacksmith Blues', sang the backing with him. Elton told me that they won't be accompanying him all the time but he will eventually get a band together for himself.

"I played in a group about two years ago but it's a very insecure life. It didn't hold much future at all and then I met Bernie and we decided to write songs together and of course I joined up with Dick James. I feel much more

secure now. The group I was in was called Bluesology!

"For the future I hope to be doing a European tour with Sergio Mendes. They aren't exactly my scene so I just hope the audiences will accept us both. On the Continent, though, they are inclined to mix up the bills. It's quite a good experience, I suppose. I hope to be going to the States in June. I'd really love to go there."

To prove to you just how talented Elton is, his 'Lady Samantha' was recorded by Three Dog Night, one of America's top groups, on their last album and they have a million advance orders for their new LP, which included Elton's 'Your Song' as well as their own material, of course!

Silver Metre chose 'Ballad Of A Well Known Gun' as their 'A' side and also have three other Elton songs on their first album!

To go to show just how Elton's style of music appeals to everyone, both John Peel and Tony Blackburn have played his records on their programmes.

Elton learnt to play the piano by himself and only once in his life did he sway from singing and playing and that was when he had the idea to become a footballer, but he says that he was too fat! I don't believe it—he's just being modest again!

interview with Elton, and it was included in the record company's promo for record chains such as HMV alongside interviews published in *New Musical Express, Rolling Stone* and *Melody Maker* by some revered music writers at the time, so I was well chuffed!

During that period, I saw Elton John quite a number of times and he would try and provide me with tickets for concerts. We were convinced that we were in the presence of a rock genius who would be around for a very long time. And we were correct.

At the beginning of his career, I and the rest of the *Mirabelle* gang were always invited to events at Dick James Music, his publishing company, and it was at a Christmas party that I first realised that Elton John was not interested in female company in a sexual way. There was a girl who worked at the company who would have done anything for Elton, or Reggie, but her love was not reciprocated.

In those days, if budding superstars like Elton were not interested in girls, they had to keep their sexual preferences a secret. "Not good for the punters," the A &R people would say. They wanted their pop idols macho and heterosexual in order to encourage their teenage female fans to buy their records and swoon and scream at their concerts. And even if you were straight, if you had a wife and family or a steady girlfriend, it was a bit of a no-no in the pop world. Thankfully, all that appears to have vanished without a trace. In fact, it may even be a bonus if you are not straight – after all, being bisexual keeps everyone on their toes!

Me and the guys in my flat made friends with a couple of sisters who liked to have a good time. They rented a very large ground-floor flat which was perfect for parties. They lived not far from us in Highgate and on the night that Armstrong and Aldrin reached the moon, we and some others watched the whole programme from start to finish on TV. We were lucky to

Brighton Belles on location with Kenny Everett, Mirabelle © Rebellion Publishing IP Ltd.
All rights reserved

watch it in colour. It had only just caught on a few years before. Like most of the world who had access to a TV, we stayed up all night to watch this historic occasion and to hear the now infamous words, "That's one small step for man, one giant leap for mankind."

And actually most of us were in time for work the next day despite having no sleep and drinking far too much, but I expect we were on a high, as it seemed to enforce what we felt then: that we were invincible and things could only get better.

It was a wild time for me, hobnobbing with pop idols and rock gods, going to parties – some posh, others not so posh – volunteering as a dare to be hung out of a top-floor window by my ankles, chasing – and in turn being chased by – celebrated male journalists around my flat with giant wooden salad servers.

Interview with David Essex during Godspell, Mirabelle © Rebellion Publishing IP Ltd.
All rights reserved.

In case you ask, they were all the rage then – the spoons that is and not the journalists!

One time, we had such a mammoth water fight that we flooded our flat. The landlords lived downstairs but were very fond of us so made us clean it all up, shrugged and put it down to high spirits!

Meanwhile Planet Sandie Continues

I was invited to the première of 'Twinky', known as 'Lola', up in Leicester Square, starring Susan George and Charles Bronson. I was not dating at that particular time so it always came in handy to have a male flatmate on hand who could act as an escort, and because they were journalists and not star-struck, they knew how to 'behave' in front of celebrities.

It felt a bit strange walking along the red carpet with all the flashlights popping but quite a nice feeling at the same time to be in the spotlight. I was wearing a powder pink dress with a pink angora coat to match. I was invited because I was working on a teenage magazine and not much older than the part Susan George was playing as a 16-year-old schoolgirl falling in love with someone old enough to be her father, but the film seriously bombed.

Although there was a popular song around this time about roaring off on trains, boats and planes, not that many people had regular annual holidays abroad unless they were quite well heeled. In 1970, when I was 17, some of my school friends and I soared off on a Monarch plane to Benidorm for a dose of sun, sea and sand.

Before we departed, we were recommended to grab a pot of coconut butter which was selling like hotcakes to slap on before we hit the beach. I won't tell you what a couple of us looked like after an hour or so in the sun. Needless to say I have not let even a smear of coconut butter come anywhere near my skin, whether going out in the sun or not. A sharp contrast to the advice we are given today about going out in the midday sun!

I am an animal lover and have always been extremely sensitive when it comes to the cruelty – intentional or otherwise – subjected to animals.

While we were in Benidorm, the enigmatic El Cordobes was staging a bull fight at the local bullring. Bull fighting is a traditional spectacle that in many areas of Spain is considered a cultural event. Not surprisingly, there is a lot of controversy surrounding the 'sport' and in some areas it has been banned. Cordobes with his pop star good looks and flamboyant lifestyle, encouraged a new wave of supporters, as he had introduced an acrobatic and theatrical style to his performance.

I refused at first when my friends suggested attending but

at the last minute I decided to witness whether it was as cruel as I had imagined. Everyone is entitled to their own opinion, but it didn't change mine, and I nearly caused WW3 within the bullring once the blood fest was over. After the bull is dead and the judge deems that the matador has despatched the bull skilfully, he or she is then allowed to cut off the ears and/or tail to be preserved on a plaque.

Well, Cordobes must have had loads of them, so on this particular occasion he decided to throw the bull's body part into the audience as a present for some delighted fan. And guess where it landed?

At my feet! Of all the hundreds of people that were in attendance, why the trajectory of the ear had to pick me I have absolutely no idea.

I made the impulsive decision to throw it back into the arena, and it landed at the feet of the matador. My best shot ever! Obviously, that was considered an insult. How my friends and I got out of there unscathed I will never know, except that our nationality and youth were probably on our side. It was one of those 'it could only happen to me' moments.

On a completely different tack, editor Paul and I took a short but memorable trip to Amsterdam with a photographer we knew as Frank Murphy (now Francis Murphy and based in New York), who as well as being a talented photographer had the Irish gift of the gab and a great sense of humour. We also took along a pop star called Richard Barnes, who was fairly religious and in a relationship with Cindy Kent of The Settlers (also religious and who is now a reverend). They joined us for a day on this trip. Both were very friendly with Cliff Richard, who was the only person that didn't turn up.

As soon as we landed, we were taken off to a private room to be searched and interviewed because we were from a teenage magazine and were in the company of a pop star and a trendy photographer. None of us were carrying anything untoward, and I had to laugh when they asked the pop star to open up his case and on the top was a bible. No further questions were asked after that.

Our hostess from the Dutch tourist board was a real treasure and drove us around Amsterdam at about 90 mph at all times. She took no notice of speed restrictions and we were amazed when she overtook a police car and gave them the finger salute because they were driving too slowly in her opinion!

We visited the red light district where we had a lot of fun visiting the sex shops and being mesmerised by the ladies of the night who advertised their wares in shop windows. Obviously, those exploits were not published for *Mirabelle* readers. We saw some sights that really made us laugh, and it was where I first tasted chips with mayonnaise. In the UK, we were still into Heinz Salad Cream.

One of my personal faves of all time next to Led Zeppelin was The Who. I loved most of their music and had been a fan since I was 13 years old. I could hardly believe it when I had the opportunity to meet all of them, and on a fairly regular basis as well.

Despite their 'bad boy' image, I found most of them in the main to be friendly, courteous, well mannered and generally nice to be around. However, Keith Moon, whose nickname was 'Moon the Loon' due to his eccentric and often destructive behaviour, became another statistic of the drugs culture when he died at the age of 32 in 1978.

Despite his sometimes irrational behaviour, Moon was posthumously inducted into the Modern Drummer Hall of Fame in 1982, becoming only the second rock drummer to be chosen. In 2011, he was voted the second greatest drummer in history by a *Rolling Stones* readers' poll.

But rewind back to November 1971 when I was given four

Interview with John Peel. Mirabelle © Rebellion Publishing IP Ltd. All rights reserved.

tickets personally by The Who to see them perform at the first concert to be held at the Finsbury Park Astoria, renamed the Rainbow, and all of the guys were in their prime and on top form.

I took Linda and Richard, an artist from our Art department who would go on to be a well-respected cartoonist, not forgetting Linda's soon-to-be husband, in addition to my soon-to-be hubby. The four of us were treated to a backstage visit as well as much sought-after front-row seats. It was a tumultuous gig and we were treated to the full pelt of The Who's performance when they turned the megawatt spotlights on all of us and trashed all their equipment (Keith Moon went ballistic with his major drum kit), and the volume was deafening. To this day, I have never watched a performance as mind-blowing as that was, but neither have I been as ill.

It was an experience worth having despite the fact that next day all four of us suffered from sound sickness and had to take to our beds. I never realised that sound combined with light could ever make you feel that sick.

STORMY WEATHER AHEAD

Marie Stopes, a campaigner for women's rights, founded the first birth control clinic in Britain in 1925. She never advocated abortion but believed that the prevention of conception was the way to help bring only wanted babies into the world – obviously at that time there was neither a simple pill nor the 'morning-after' pill.

In the late '60s and '70s, many girls were on the pill. They took trips to their local family planning clinics to ensure – provided they remembered to take one on a daily basis – that they would be protected from becoming pregnant.

Even at that time, to fall pregnant out of wedlock was not considered the right thing to do and certainly not by the religious factions purporting that it was the worst sin in the world. Indeed, earlier in the decade, girls had been locked away in asylums and their babies cruelly torn from them at around six months, when they had bonded, then put up for adoption. If you came from a religious background, giving birth to an illegitimate baby could be life-changing. Fortunately, neither I nor my family were of a religious persuasion.

When it came to family planning issues, I have to admit I was a bit negligent about it all. This was mainly due to the fact I suffered either a medical or psychological problem – or a bit of both – which prevented me from losing my virginity. So by the time I was 18 and began living with my first husband before we married, I had foolishly forgotten to put a visit to the family planning clinic at the top of my action list. I fell pregnant almost immediately, but even when the expected monthly visit did not arrive, I was in denial. I couldn't possibly be pregnant.

I think most of my friends thought that because I lived quite a lively life they presumed that I was sexually aware and already on the pill. Most were surprised about my mistake because they thought that I would be a tad more savvy when it came to gynaecological matters. It was a very convincing act but resulted in a traumatic time for me.

My soon-to-be hubby and I were sharing a flat in Muswell Hill with a photographer friend. One night, I had a pain and – being forever the optimist – I thought it was my period arriving at long last. However, when I went to the toilet, I realised that I was actually giving birth to a dead foetus.

The two men in my flat were at a loss as to what to do. I reassured them I was okay and would see about it in the morning. After all, I could hardly just phone the female members of my family and tell them what was happening. They were unaware that I was living with anyone, so it would have been a double shock to the system. I decided it would be best to go into work and seek the help of older female colleagues – they would know what to do if indeed I needed to do anything at all. I was in blissful ignorance that one just had a miscarriage and then got on with it.

However, after bleeding all night, I padded myself up with as many sanitary towels as I could find. I left the flat but unfortunately bumped into my downstairs neighbour, who was extremely religious, and because I didn't tell her what had happened during the night she expected me to run for the bus that took us to Highgate tube station. This, of course, didn't exactly help the 'bleeding' issue.

On arrival at the offices of *Mirabelle*, I was completely white in stark contrast to the lining of my beautiful purple velvet maxi coat which had done a great job of hiding to all and sundry what was happening to me down below – it was completely saturated with blood. Paul took one look and discreetly made his exit, while Linda took me off to Charing Cross Hospital in a black cab – as you did in those days!

At some time during the examination, a police officer arrived, as they suspected I had visited a backstreet abortionist to get rid of the baby illegally. I was also asked if I had personally taken anything to damage the foetus. As I had never accepted the fact that I was pregnant in the first place, I had nothing to do with either of those accusations and the examination proved this was the case. The police then left the building, confident that I was innocent of any crime against the foetus.

I had to stay in hospital for a couple of days to have an operation to remove the rest of the baby, and also to ensure that the bleeding had stopped. I was told to visit the Margaret Pyke Family Clinic near Oxford Circus ASAP to pick up a supply of birth pills, which I did once I was back on my feet.

While it was a sobering thought that I had a miscarriage when I didn't even know I was pregnant, there was also a sense of profound relief, not only for me but for hubby-to-be. But one thing I was unaware of before I married was that my husband never wanted any children, which I only found out not long after we tied the knot. Shortly after this episode in my life, I heard some bad news from an ex-flatmate who informed me that John at 18 had been killed in a car accident near where his family lived in Essex. As far as I remember, the car had been full of people and most were quite drunk but unsure whether the driver was under the influence.

The UK drink driving laws were introduced in 1967 but not taken that seriously until a few years later. John apparently went right through the windscreen – few of us wore seat belts, the law not being passed until 1983. So sad because John with his entrepreneurial skills had so much potential for going a long way but alas it was just not to be.

Back to first hubby-to-be. It was his parents who actually

proposed to me. We had finally alerted our respective family members to the fact that we were living together, and both camps seemed happy with the arrangement and had indeed been around for dinner on a number of occasions.

On one visit with his parents, we were talking about life in general and his mother casually suggested we should get married, so we did, making me the first of the Magazine Girls to tie the knot.

I was married at the age of 19 and when I think about it now it makes me shudder. Although I had crammed quite a lot into my formative years, I just wasn't mature enough to make that commitment. And neither was my husband.

Strange as it seems, by 1971, life on a teenage magazine had become a little restrictive and monotonous, and as we were all at the beginning of our careers, it was time to move on and expand our experience in other areas, but we were all extremely thankful for the opportunities that IPC had given us.

In my personal life, our aim was to buy a house but we could not afford to buy in London. We took a week off work and managed to put in an offer on a delightful 2-up 2-down terraced cottage in a village outside Faversham, Kent.

It was on the market at around £7.5k – a lot of money in those days.

Meanwhile, I was hankering after a job with a local newspaper to hone up my general reporting skills, and coincidentally a job as a news reporter and woman's page editor (the latter now thankfully outdated) came up on the *Kent Messenger Group*, which I duly accepted.

As it transpired, Linda in addition to our production editor and I all left *Mirabelle* at the same time. Other Magazine Girls were also moving on to other publishing companies and jobs, so it was definitely the end of an era.

The first year or so of our marriage had not been particularly easy. He had to commute to London and although I was learning to drive, I had not yet passed my test and, consequently, had to suffer a tortuous journey to Ashford every day. Yes, I should have thought about all of this and prepared myself better, but I don't think any of it was meant to be.

The job sounded good on paper but after working on national publications, I found working for a provincial newspaper a bit limiting and, sadly, my heart was just not in it. I also found it odd that they expected me to bring in my own typewriter to the office, which was my brother's old portable and in need of a good overhaul.

After less than a year, the city girl had already decided that going down the provincial route had been the wrong decision, but at least I tried, tasted and tested and it was found wanting! Meanwhile, hubby was still in the music business and worked long hours as an A&R man for EMI. The fact that we were now working in two totally different worlds did not enhance our marital relationship. I felt marooned and far away from family and friends. We decided we should move back to London and I began to look for other jobs, but this time I was concentrating on jobs within PR and promotions.

THREE

MIXED BAGS AND ALL CHANGE
1973–1978

I left the *Kent Messenger* during the lead-up to the festivities in December 1972, knowing that I had some work to tide me over if I didn't immediately acquire a job in PR. I had befriended the advertising manager of the *Kent Messenger*, who was also leaving to set up his own group of freesheet newspapers in Canterbury, and he was keen that I submit features and news stories in addition to me helping to sell ad space in return for column inches of PR.

The job that suited my CV to a tee turned up at a Fleet Street-based PR agency. I literally attended an interview on 2 January 1973 and began my new job the next day on the 3 January. We also managed to sell our cottage for a maisonette in Chingford with a London postcode – things were on the up, or so I thought. Little did I know that within less than a year of moving back to London, our marriage would be over, with the marital home sold.

The PR agency was housed in the magnificent Grade II listed Mary Queen of Scots House which was also home to the Western Morning News Group of newspapers. Down below was Le Bistingo, a French restaurant, and we were next door to the

King and Keys pub. Sadly, both establishments are no longer in business.

However, Ye Olde Cheshire Cheese in the next-door back alley where we entertained many of our clients is still going strong and indeed I visited it with some friends recently when we also took a tour of Samuel Johnson's house. Well worth the visit, dear readers.

There was another similar establishment to the 'Cheese' called Mother Bunch's, but it was more of a wine cellar with good food, which has hysterically funny memories for me. We visited this place often, especially with our clients.

Every table was adorned with wax-encrusted wine bottles with a lit candle. I agree that's a bit of a tacky design feature now but very *avant-garde* in the early '70s. When my boss and I took a prospective VIP client to lunch, as I took my seat, my long hair swished into the candle, setting my hair alight. I was oblivious to all of this and smiling away at all the growing faces of horror when my boss started bashing my head in order to dampen the flames. I think the would-be client thought it was a pre-arranged publicity stunt, because we secured the contract, so that was a result, and my hair was relatively unharmed with the exception of a few frazzled ends.

I don't mind admitting that I took to PR like a duck to water as the saying goes. Back in those days, being successful in the world of public relations demanded having to be very creative with an eye for a good story to ensure your clients' new inventions or products received as much print or air space as possible, and I became an expert in matching the product with a theme that captured the media's attention.

My new boss was a red-headed (well, what was left of it!) and bearded Scotsman, tenacious and ambitious in his quest to bring in reputable clients who would make him a lot of money for his pile out in Wiltshire. And I have to admit that I probably helped contribute quite substantially to his quest, although I earned a lot less than he did.

However, he did have his good moments when, after my split-up from hubby, he rescued me from a less-than-perfect flat-sharing situation in north London complete with my two beautiful half-feral cats Evenstar and Aragorn (from 'Lord of the Rings' in case you were wondering!). You can imagine the chaos that caused to a small office in Fleet Street with the account director literally sleeping 'on the job' and two cats who were not allowed out, but it only lasted for about three days.

He hired and fired when he wanted – we were too small an agency to have a 'personnel' team – and anyhow those were the days when bosses in the private sector could do almost what they felt like, providing it didn't involve murder... and even then... I managed to avoid being in the firing line because in his own way he was 'fond' of me and admired the way I worked, as my ideas achieved positive column inches for his clients.

At various points in my son's life, I have informed him of what I was doing when I was the same age as him. For example, at 15 working on a national newspaper, at 17 living in a flat, at 19 getting married for the first time and at 22 divorced for the first time. The only comparison he blanched at was me getting married at 19! I am very glad that he has not followed me in any of those particular footsteps but has certainly inherited my work ethic and outgoing, caring personality.

We cited 'irretrievable breakdown of marriage' for the divorce papers. Fortunately, we were living at a time when you no longer had to remain in a marriage without love or respect for each other.

There were many reasons why it just never worked, and it wasn't down to anything in particular. But, anyhow, hubby had already found another person to share his life with which he did. Despite the fact that when I took my marriage vows I expected our union would last forever, I now realise that the relationship had run its course.

After the 'sleeping in the office with two feline companions' episode, I found a flat in Wimbledon – my first foray into south London and the only accommodation available that would accept two cats. It was a decision I immediately regretted. It was like a cabin stuck onto a house and certainly didn't make me feel secure as a young woman living there on her own.

We basically lived in one room with lounge and bedroom and an add-on kitchen – it really was the pits and for my own sanity I had to get out.

The big downside of all of this was that I had no alternative but to ask a work associate if they could permanently look after my cats or find people who could. I had no way of knowing when I was going to be in a stable situation to take them back. The worst part of it was they had to be separated. The handing-over of my two furry friends, knowing I would never see them again, is a feeling of loss that I have never forgotten. I was relieved to find out that the cats survived and led very happy lives, albeit separately, but nonetheless I still have guilt trips about it.

I got out of Wimbledon as soon I could and lived with my parents in Welwyn Garden City on a temporary basis at the time. And then one evening on the train home there was an advertisement in the *Evening Standard* to share a large flat in South Woodford, London with three journalists.

Those were the days when you could actually specify who you were looking for in a potential flatmate, and they wanted someone who was a journalist and/or in PR. As I fell into both camps, I was pretty positive that they would offer it to me – which they did.

I moved in with all my belongings, which included some pieces of furniture, clothes and cuttings/photo albums, with three journalists who worked for the Florida-based *National*

Enquirer tabloid in the London office. They were all a fair bit older – and more mature – than me, so I was regarded in a fond way as the 'wild child' of their social group. They were also earning about four times the amount of money I did and were very generous, so I fell into a hedonistic *c'est la vie* lifestyle in addition to a relationship that would not be beneficial for me, but I was blissfully unaware of this when I trotted over to see them one night after work.

My new flatmates were a mixed bag, which is probably why I fitted in. There were three journalists I permanently shared with but there was also a hilarious devil-may-care Scottish stringer (as all the *NE* staff called freelancers) who occasionally used the flat as a base if he wasn't going home to Scotland, where he had a wife and young family. I was very fond of him, mainly because he was funny, generous, reckless at times and just had a great zest for life. He was also a hotshot journo, but I have no idea what happened to him – hopefully all good. Then there was an esteemed international journalist – old enough to be my father – who had very close connections to Aristotle Onassis and Jacqueline Kennedy. I hadn't long been ensconced in South Woodford when Onassis died, so our flat became the East London media hub. My working life paled in comparison during this time.

There was another female who I looked up to as my flat 'mum'. She also worked for the *Enquirer*. I had taken the place of her best friend, who had moved out to the Florida office of the *Enquirer* in her new position as what they called an articles editor.

Last but not least was an interesting and unconventional character who was what I would describe as a force of nature. Not my usual type at all, as he wasn't the owner of too much hair, but he did have a beard. He enjoyed a drink and was quite volatile but excruciatingly funny when reciting stories.

He was a contradiction in terms of his reputation as a supremo journo. At times, he was all too aware of this, but sometimes his self-esteem took a big hit and he was not so sure. He was also generous to a fault – I had never been bought such beautiful and thoughtful presents up until then or since by any man. He was also an excellent cook.

About two to three months after I moved into the flat, we entered into a relationship.

I enjoyed entertaining and hosting dinner parties myself, so to avoid any arguments, we cut a deal that I would create the starters and desserts and let him take over the main course. Many was the time that he had drunk so much sampling the wine during the preparation of the meal that he fell asleep after he had served up his culinary delight!

It's the only time I had both a dressing room and a bedroom at my disposal, as we didn't rent out my room. But my happiness was short-lived when he suddenly announced after about five to six months of us being together that he wanted to go off to America on his own and wasn't sure whether he would return or not. So he went. And to be fair, after the initial disappointment, I decided just to get on with my life and enjoy myself.

One night my friends and I had been uptown for a meal and decided to head over West London way to a bar that someone had recommended for a nightcap. We hailed a cab and off we went but as we were nearing the location I spotted an abundance of police and the area was cordoned off. I told the cabbie to stop, jumped out and ran to a policeman, holding my press card aloft, to ask him what was going on. I don't think he was supposed to tell me as much as he did but anyhow he divulged that it was a siege at the Knightsbridge Spaghetti House which had just begun.

After gathering all the details, I raced to the nearest telephone box and rang the *Daily Mirror* news desk and I actually said those infamous words, "Hold the front page," and they did.

I made a fair bit of money for this tip-off, but it was a complete coincidence that I was even in the area at that crucial time. The added bonus was that it was all resolved within about three days and thankfully none of the hostages were hurt.

It was late 1975 and all of a sudden we received news that the prodigal son was planning on returning from America and was interested in coming back to the flat. We all agreed that it was okay, and so we resumed our relationship where we left off.

As a couple, we eventually left South Woodford for a rather unusual basement flat in Little Venice off the Edgware Road in February 1976, but it wasn't long before we were making plans for us to both go to America on an extended working holiday.

Scooting Over to the U S of A

And so another adventure begins!

We flew out from Heathrow on a Jumbo 747 to Seattle on 28 September 1976. I remember feeling homesick even before I got on the plane as, even to this day and contrary to my unconventional personality, I am not happy being away from my family and friends for too long.

It had not been an easy experience gaining visas for us to work legally in the US – and I believe it is still difficult – but we finally got the all-clear. As recommended, we both had our own letters of reference from the UK magazines and newspapers to substantiate that we would be providing features and stories for them, thus ensuring our main source of income was coming from the UK and not the US.

We had more than enough of the relevant paperwork in hand and so thought there would be no problem. However, we did inadvertently cause consternation at the Immigration desk because as we were living together in the UK our suitcases were deemed as 'co-mingled' – their words not mine. Not to put too fine a point on it, they were not impressed that my underwear was mixed up with his because we were not married!

Anyhow, they couldn't have been that worried, because we were let through to catch a little plane to Spokane. Quite a contrast after spending hours on a massive Jumbo, and when we walked on the plane, the pilot, who was wearing a cowboy hat and boots and with his feet on the dashboard, enthusiastically waved at us as if we were his long-lost relatives.

The plan was to visit some of his American friends, a couple with an inquisitive six-year-old daughter, who were living an almost back-to-nature lifestyle in a log cabin in Idaho. The place where we resided was affectionately called 'St Maries in the Pines on the banks of the lazy St Joe River' by the locals – a bit of a mouthful by anyone's standards. The locals just called it St Maries or St Joe for ease. It is also home to the Nez Perce native American Indians who have lived there for thousands of years.

In return for the friends' hospitality for a six-week stay, we would assist them and their neighbours within the bartering system they employed when it came to sharing each other's DIY chores such as roof rebuilding, gathering wood for the winter and bringing in the hay. Winters are harsh in this rural retreat, with households sometimes being cut off for a month or two. Being born and bred a city girl, this was a whole new experience for me but I thoroughly enjoyed it as I knew I wasn't going to be there on a permanent basis.

At night when in bed in the log cabin, bears would come right up to the veranda and throw the garbage bins around, which was disconcerting at first but we soon got used to it. It was the same with the coyote screaming, again worrying until I was reassured that no one was being murdered, well, at least not humans – just animals going about their nightly business.

We always took a shotgun when we went for a walk in the

woods, even within the near vicinity of the cabin, because you never knew when you might come face to face with a bear. If you were caught in the middle of Mummy bear and the cubs then it was curtains if you didn't have a gun. Not that I wanted to shoot any bears but needs must in that case.

We grew very fond of the friends' nearest neighbours and found them quite hysterical. The wife wore curlers in her hair during the day but it turned into an elaborate beehive do when she was going out.

She always had a handgun tucked into her pants (trousers in our language) which was very disconcerting as it wasn't an everyday occurrence that you passed the time of day with a woman in curlers sporting a gun on her waistband. However, on our first meeting, she reassured me that it wasn't for protection against me but for any two-legged intruders wishing to cause harm, as no one could hear you scream out there!

Marge was quite incredible. One night in thick snow she was on her way to a ten-pin bowling game when she skidded and drove her pickup off the side of maybe not a mountain but certainly a substantial hill. She CB'd (radio) her neighbours to come and give her a hand to get her back on the road, brushed herself down and resumed her journey. Oh and won the game too!

Frank was another one of the local characters, an ex-rabies cop (rodent officer) who owned just about every type of gun you could imagine. In fact, when he gave us a lift in his pickup truck, you had to make sure you weren't actually sitting on one! I had quite enjoyed a couple of clay pigeon shooting bouts previously and done quite well at 'despatching the clay', but at the same time I am under no illusions as to what damage a gun can do in the wrong hands.

We did some salmon fishing in the rivers and I caught a few which we took back to the log cabin for the friends to eat, of course. We helped with gathering in the hay and attended the

Ice Cream Social as they called it to celebrate this event. A good excuse for a party and I always approve of that.

And although the men and women of Idaho seemed to be equal – it's a tough life out in those lands so chores are shared – most of the women chose to stay inside the barn eating the ice cream and catching up on all the gossip, although there might have been a few hip flasks in use. I chose to do both and being from the UK I got away with it!

After about six weeks or so, we realised we needed to start earning money again. In 1976 there were no mobile phones or laptops so working from Idaho was out of the question. Besides, our hosts had university and school commitments so were heading into the city. It was time to head off to Florida to make our presence known in the area, rent a condo and set up our workstations.

Even though we landed in the evening after the sun had gone down, when we embarked I found the intense heat stultifying and it felt like my lungs had given up working – not even a whisper of any air. But, like anything, you get used to it and your body adapts.

We arrived at our journalistic friends' house in Palm Beach where we would be staying until we could find somewhere to live. By contrast, where we ended up living was West Palm Beach, still nice but not quite Palm Beach. Anyhow, I diverse, that night I just wanted to go to the beach and take a swim. Oh yes, everyone had warned me not to go into the sea in the dark due to sharks coming in close to nibble whatever they could find. I, of course, didn't listen, but the gods must have been on my side because, thankfully, it was a Jaws-free experience for me. However, after being severely told off for my recklessness by my older and wiser friends, I did not go into the sea at night again during my stay there.

Not long after we had arrived, friends took us out for a meal and coming back I noticed in the distance what I first thought was a party of fancy dress revellers until we got closer. To my horror, I realised they were the Ku Klux Klan. I couldn't believe that this abhorrent organisation was still walking along the highways of Florida even in 1976. I pleaded with my friend to stop the car so I could get out and berate them, whereupon she speeded up and informed me in a tone that suggested she was not joking – she would not be stopping, as if I confronted them I would probably be hurt, if not shot!

"Where are the police then?" I shouted, not really expecting an answer, to which she retorted that some of the members under those white cloaks may indeed have been the police.

That incident made me feel physically sick and even writing about it now after all these years still makes me very angry. I have been told that in some areas of America the KKK still operates, which is even worse.

A major story – well for me, anyhow – that I covered was the case of Sonia Jacobs otherwise known as Sunny, a 28-year-old mother of two who was accused of shooting two policemen along with her partner, Jesse Tafero, who was executed in 1990.

I interviewed her on Death Row in Florida, which was an experience in itself. In order to do this we had to first meet with her relatives – mainly her father and brother – who would arrange a visit with the correction facility. I would have to be vetted but that was not a problem.

Obviously, her family believed Sonia was innocent but after meeting and talking to her in the flesh, I must admit I was convinced she was innocent. She was slight and vulnerable in appearance and was also the mother of a nine-year- old and ten-month-old baby from whom she had been separated. However, my partner and colleagues thought I was being a touch naïve, but I wrote my story biased towards proving her innocence.

However, the newspaper had other ideas, so when they

finally printed the story the entire context of the copy was changed completely and made it look like I believed she should receive the death sentence along with her partner.

I then waited with bated breath to receive the unfriendly calls I knew I would receive from her family and even Sonia herself when they read the newspaper, which is exactly what happened. There were also letters written by both as well. I mitigated as much as I could by sending my original copy to her and the family and writing letters to assure them that this was not the outcome I had desired, and we parted on fairly amicable terms.

Years later, when I was doing some sort of laborious job with the telly on in the background, I realised it was showing a TV movie called 'In the Blink of an Eye' about Sonia Jacobs, with Diane Kruger playing the lead role. I was old enough at that time for the experiences of life to have taught me to always look at the bigger picture when coming to an opinion and the importance of sometimes remaining impartial. I learnt that in 1992, after 17 years in prison, Sonia Jacobs' case reversed on appeal and she took an Alford plea for second-degree murder.

I seemed to be a little too close to police during my staycation in America. We had bought a nippy little Toyota not long after we arrived in Florida and on a dark night when we were returning from yet another job, I was stopped by the cops. Again, I think the gods must have been looking out for me because when they told us to get out of the car and put our hands up on the roof, they asked for my licence, which was in the glove box. Not thinking, I immediately reached in to retrieve the licence, but something made me turn round to tell them I was going to do that and, of course, they then realised I was not from those parts.

Their attitude changed to being very friendly and warning me to check in future that all my lights were working before setting off on a drive. Before sending us on our way, he reminded

The Magazine Girls 1960s–1980s

My one and only poem and special artwork by Richard Brookes, Valentine
© Rebellion Publishing IP Ltd. All rights reserved.

Interview with 'Cha Cha' Muldowney, 19/Future Publishing Ltd

me that, "This is America after all." Words from the horse's mouth indeed!

We covered so many wild and wonderful stories, like the nun who drank beer and wore skimpy shorts for our photo session but declined to answer the question as to whether there were any other men in her life apart from Jesus, drove miles to the Everglades to catch up with Joan Collins pre-'Dynasty' on the set of a 'B' movie called 'Empire of the Ants'. Also managed to fit in an interview at some lavish celebrity bash with Davy Jones, the only English member of The Monkees, whose creators probably helped to put reality TV on the map.

I also went for a ride with Shirley 'Cha Cha' Muldowney, a very fast and impressive lady who drove a dragster in a predominantly man's world, winning a number of prestigious titles that she had battled out with many men. Little did I realise that less than ten years later I myself would be racing cars, driving an MG Midget, initially as a publicity stunt but then I became hooked.

Unfortunately, I was not as successful as Shirley and spent more time crashing the car than racing! People gave up telling me, 'to keep it on the black stuff'! My racing was either 'on' or 'off' but I did meet the father of my son in the motor racing fraternity.

But the story that really made a big impression on me during my time in the US was when we were given the job, along with a well-respected national newspaper photographer who we had teamed up with, of interviewing Jimmy Carter's inner circle in White Plains, Georgia. Carter had just been made president-elect but he was ensconced in preparation for his big role in Washington and had temporarily 'left behind' his wife, Rosalynn Carter, and also his imperious mother, Miss Lillian, both of whom I was tasked with the job of interviewing. Also included in that list were many family add-ons such as his brothers, uncles, cousins *et al*.

In the fast lane.

We drove from West Palm Beach to Plains, Georgia along the boring, very straight highways – the only excitement was listening and responding to the CB (Citizen's Band) radio. This assisted us with going a little bit faster than the speed limit, which at the time was the equivalent to our 50 mph and meant we could cover the 600 plus miles in a speedier manner. I really enjoyed speaking on the radio and informing my audience, mostly truck drivers, with the greeting, "Breaker 1/9 for a good buddy – this here is The Limey and we got the front door with a bear in the air and an angry kangaroo," or words to that effect.

Admittedly, I didn't sound as cool as they did, as this language was second nature to them. Coincidentally to what was going on in my world, the hit record 'Convoy' by CW McCall was released in 1976 about trucks and automobiles using CB radio to get to their destinations faster than was allowed. It meant that when

I did return to old Blighty, I was able to regale my family and friends with my own stories about my CB experiences.

Before we embarked on the journey, we were vetted and screened by security but also my two male companions were told on no uncertain terms, "Do not let Sandie go anywhere on her own." That made me wonder where on earth we were going. As I recall, White Plains was a 'one- horse' town but it was nearly 45 years ago.

Appearances can be deceptive and I soon realised during our interview that Rosalynn Carter's nickname of 'The Steel Magnolia' was very apt. She came across as being shy and unassuming, but I think she was the power behind the White House and I genuinely liked her. I managed to sell the story to *Woman's Own* but when it was published, my by-line had been misspelt. As we say nowadays – LOL!

I didn't feel the same way about her powerful, and very

Interview with Rosalyn Carter, Woman's Own/Future Publishing Ltd

southern mother-in-law, Miss Lillian as she was known to locals. She sat in state on a rocking chair in a converted railway carriage that had been the pre-election HQ. There were no other chairs around, so I had to kneel on the floor trying to write my notes (I don't think she was keen on journalists) and meanwhile she would shake hands with everyone walking by as if she was more famous than her son... but I did notice that she was quite picky about who she actually did shake hands with!

Some of my good memories of Florida would be celebrating Thanksgiving; spending New Year's Eve on a beach with a BBQ; the occasional swim (not in the dark) not forgetting halloween.

Also toasting the Scottish poet with red wine at a Burns Night 'do' and the most exotic wearing of tartan I have ever seen and travelling down to Key West through the Florida Quays!

We stayed in Florida for six months. Our visas were running out and to be honest I was quite homesick, so we made our plans to return to the UK. However, I am very glad I had the opportunity to experience life-forming adventures, experiences and situations during our stay.

Thankfully, we both managed to secure our old jobs so decided to fly back via New York for a short break. I am in love with most big cities, especially London, and a sucker for those that come with a buzz – and the Big Apple did not disappoint either.

We moved into a rented modern farmhand house in a hamlet just outside Epping. Not my preferred choice of a place to stay but it served its purpose for a couple of years until our relationship became far too toxic to handle and so I left.

I have always been a firm believer in the adage, 'A picture is worth a thousand words'. While in America, I worked closely with photographers and was complimented on quite a few occasions that I had a good eye for a photo. So one of my first major purchases when we returned to the UK was a second-hand Canon camera. I suppose it was a natural progression from writing stories.

And then it seemed that just about every story I touched at that time had a 'big cat' connection.

One of our PR accounts was a petcare company who produced Lactol milk for animals which were unable to feed from their natural mothers. I had befriended the owner of Leamington Spa Zoo. The majority of his animals were rescued or were unable to go back into the wild and so had no choice at that time but to be kept in captivity.

They had reared a *pantig*, which was a cross between a panther and tiger – yes, don't ask who did what to whom here, please, because I didn't enquire at the time. Obviously, he was not being fed by his mother, who I think was the panther. I have been fairly close to feeding a tiger and they are very impressive, so I am not sure how the biological side worked, suffice to say that when I went armed with my Canon, the six-month-old pantig was more like a fully grown tiger than a panther, and very playful!

Cubbing around with a pantig.

I was in awe when they brought in the majestic cub who immediately decided that he rather liked me, so while I was aiming to get a good shot of him, he thought it would be more fun to jump up at me and then drag his claws down my legs. Bless – he was just playing. Oh, and another pair of tights gone!

This zoo was full of celebrity animals and I got very close to a cross-eyed, lazy but loveable lion. I could literally have sat on him, as he would not have reacted. I then said to the owner that I would really love to kiss a lioness and he agreed that it would not be a problem.

So off we went to see the lioness and he told me to listen carefully and do everything he said. I had no insurance for walking into the lion's den but I thought, *What could go wrong?* The kiss was not as nice as expected, as the lioness is the hunter and not 'cuddly' like the lion. However, I did what I needed to do and then he said, "Now get out," as he suspected that she may have picked up on my female pheromones so could have pounced at any time

Meanwhile, on the other side of the camera I was kissing baby cougars. Before I go any further with this story, I love animals and I am well aware of the anti-feelings regarding animals being used for commercial gain, which is why I went back to Leamington Spa Zoo because I was confident that the owner always considered the welfare of his animals as top priority.

I handled the PR for Red Kooga (a health food supplement so wanted to play on the name) for a PR stunt at an exhibition in Brighton. I thought that a couple of real cougars may cause a bit of a stir, which it did in PR terms.

So Daddy cougar was on a lead and I carried in baby cougar. The cougar and cub were literally on the stand for no more than 15 minutes. It was cut short because the owner was concerned about the father becoming distressed. The cub loved all the attention!

Swinging into my seventies.

The photographer who took the photo for the local newspaper wanted me to get up close and personal with the baby cougar, who had no qualms about this so it was difficult to extricate her from my clutches. She did a fair job of playfully scratching my chest and neck and as I was getting married a week or so later to my second husband, that actually proved to be a bit inconvenient with the wedding dress. At least I had proof as to where the scratches came from. Not long after, I stroked a python at London Zoo! Did I have a death wish?

But even after all this excitement, having my son is by far the best thing I have ever done in my life, but I suppose that is how most mothers feel. And, dear reader, this is where my part of the book ends.

And Then...

Linda Newman

After leaving *19*, Linda freelanced regularly for a host of women's magazines, also contributing to *Ideal Home, The Sunday Times Magazine* and national newspapers. She then worked full time for *Hello!* magazine as a writer, then assistant editor (commissioning). As a mature student, Linda finally gained the university degree she'd longed for as a young girl, followed by a Masters in Creative Writing from the Open University. Linda taught magazine journalism at college until grandmotherly retirement. Linda has two sons, three grandchildren and lives near Epping Forest with her Magazine Boy husband Richard Brookes.

Janice Collier

Janice (known as Jan) enjoyed the flexibility of freelance for many years, working with titles including *Good Housekeeping, Hello!* and *The Sunday Times* and regularly contributed to *Yours* magazine, the *Daily Mail* and the *Daily Mirror*. For the past ten years, she's worked with a team of volunteers producing the *Epsom & Ewell Talking Newspaper* (EETN) a local audio news and magazine service for people who are blind or visually impaired. Her interviews with celebrated local residents have included former cabinet minister the Rt Hon Chris Grayling MP. Enjoying their many interests, Jan and husband Rob Taylor love specially spending time with their family, who live in Scotland with their two cherished grandsons George and Freddie.

SHIRLEY DUNMALL

When Shirley gave up her full-time job working with *Hair & Good Looks* magazine, she forged a successful career in public relations, where her skills in journalism, and all the valuable experience she had garnered over those exciting years, held her in good stead. She still works in PR, with selected clients, and enjoys every moment.

Sadly, after 50 years together, her husband Eric Dunmall died of COVID in 2021. Shirley now lives in Southsea, Hampshire, close to her daughter Amy and grandson Michael. Son James and his partner Emma visit regularly. Son Michael is married and lives in Germany with wife Carina, who Shirley sees as often as she can.

JAN ILES-KALUZA

In 1992, Jan moved with her husband and young family to Montreal, Canada for a year, which turned into 30. She took up a new career writing, researching and associate producing for TV. Today, she gets her music fix following Montreal's flourishing grass-roots rock scene, and her eleven-year-old grandson's self-composed electro music on *Soundcloud*. Jan also gamely made a cameo appearance as the 'mad lady in the shed' on her son Alex's music video. Her guilty fashion pleasures are thrifting for old men's pants in size 10 petite for two bucks, and upcycling a treasured collection of her daughter's '80s baby clothes to pass on to her new granddaughter, Biba.

ANN CARPENTER

After going freelance, Ann worked in many different fields of publishing including editing business journals and a Quaker journal on animal rights. A committed advocate of lifelong learning, she gained a Diploma in Arts Foundation Studies and an Open University degree in Literature and Arts. She is particularly proud of a book on grief and grieving after loss, written with her husband Geoffrey Johnson, a former therapist and NHS hospital chaplain. The couple now live in rural Herefordshire with canine companions Archie and Jess and near their extended blended family. Ann continues working as a professional painter under her married name Ann Johnson.

PENNY SAUNDERS

Penny lives in Surrey and continues her love for fashion and beauty, working in the beauty industry as a consultant for premium brands, including YSL and Clarins. She enjoys socialising and travel and one day hopes to visit Hawaii. Sadly, she lost her husband Dave in 2022, but remains very close to her sisters and her family and enjoys spending time with them. Penny dedicates her story to her beloved brother Barrie and late husband Dave.

SANDIE ROBBIE

After a brief sojourn into the fashion PR world with the international Lynne Franks agency, Sandie Robbie went on to put Courtaulds on the media map within her own PR set-up SandiCo Promotions. From June 1987, she took up the position of account director at Stransky Thompson Public Relations, responsible for a number of key accounts such as Alcan Bacofoil and Alcan Recycling, Sellotape, Ronseal, Loctite, Wickes and MY Sports & Games. After the birth of her son, she joined Transport for London in 2000 where she has remained to this day in an operational communications role.

The Magazine Girls today:
Top row standing – left to right: Janice, Ann, Sandie and Linda.
Front row sitting – left to right: Jan, Penny, Shirley.

CREDITS

Boylston, H.D. (1939) *Sue Barton – Student Nurse*, The Bodley Head

Bowie, A. (1992) *Backstage Passes*, Orion Publishing

Carpenter, A., Johnson G. (1984) *Why Am I Afraid to Grieve?* Harper Collins

Collier, J. (1985) *Supersoft Hair Care Book*, Ward Lock Ltd

Caroll, A (Ed). (1984) *The Sweater Book, 50 Original Handknits by Top Designers*, Dorling Kindersley

Coleridge, N. (2019) *The Glossy Years*, Fig Tree/Penguin

Comfort, A. (1972) *The Joy of Sex*, Crown

Goddard, S. (2013) *A Brief History of Ziggy Stardust*, Ebury Press

Johnson, A. (2016) *Wild Margins*, Drawings and Inspirations, Amazon

Kent, N. (1994) The Dark Stuff, *Selected Writings on Rock Music 1972–1993*, Faber

Marius Pope, journalist, (2010) The Times

Murray, J. (1996) *The Woman's Hour: 50 Years of Women in Britain*, BBC Books

Pitt, K. (1983) *David Bowie The Pitt Report*, Design Music Ltd.

Polan, B. (1979) *The toughie at the top*, Guardian

Swannell, J. (2022) *Forty Years On*, Clarendon, Fine Art.

ACKNOWLEDGEMENTS

Photograph of Bill Cunningham: Melanie Tinnelly, collection of photographs of or by Bill Cunningham and Toni 'Suzette' Cimino, PR 329, Department of Prints, Photographs, and Architectural Collections, The New York Historical Society. Donated by Melanie Tinnelly in memory of Toni L. Cimino, known as Suzette.

mynewhair: Founded by Trevor Sorbie MBE, the charity provides help and support for those with medical hair loss. www.mynewhair.org

Epsom & Ewell Talking Newspaper is a volunteer-run charity, providing a free, regular audio local news and magazine service to blind and visually impaired local residents and those in neighbouring boroughs. www.eetn.org.uk

Sharon Reid, Editor *Retro* and *Yours* specials
http://www.yours.co.uk

Charlene Taylor, Rebellion Publishing
http://rebelliionpublishing.com

Time Magazine, April 1966, Issue: 'London Swinging City'
www.time.com

James Zanotto, AusReprints https://ausreprints.net

Our Thanks To

Members of Paula Beard Book Club, Tosh Berman,
Richard, Michael & David Brookes, Mick Brown,
Roger Charity, Kelly Coombs, Barbara Daly,
James, Amy and Myk Dunmall, Lynda Fitzgerald,
Jeremy Fletcher (1942-2022), Albert Gayol, Mark Glover,
David Hancock, Annmarie Hawes, Barbara Hulanicki,
Jeff Iles, Petsa Kaffens, Maggie Koumi,
Andy, Alex, Lara & Jackson Kaluza, Dame Joanna Lumley,
Alf Martin, Gillian McCain, Sally Morris, Grant Mudford,
Dr Gillian Murphy, Sir George Newnes,
Karen Okpala (née Clark), Ken Pitt (1922-2019),
Zandra Rhodes, Patty Roach, Barbara Rowlands,
Phil Rudge, Rosalind Russell, Dom Schunker,
Trevor Sorbie MBE, Nicola Stow, John Swannell,
Charlene Taylor, Rob Taylor, Cathy Tidiman,
Dr Melanie Waters, John Wheble, Ronnie Whelan,
And the readers of our magazines.

The Magazine Girls would like to thank Linda Brookes
(née Newman) for her endless patience and encouragement
in steering us through this project.

LAST WORD

The idea of putting our collective stories into a book came up during one raucous Magazine Girls' lunchtime – one of many such lunches over the years – in restaurant Joe Allen just round the corner from the publishing house in the Strand where we all met over 50 years ago.

Since that time, the world of magazine publishing has become an unrecognisable universe from the one we worked in – from the hugely popular women's weekly titles with their mega sales of millions back in the day to the proliferation of teen titles bursting forth to satisfy the baby boomers who'd come of age. The number of titles – though still a force to be reckoned with – have shrunk from those heady days, as have readerships.

Competition from online media has affected all traditional print media. However, being the chameleon-like creatures magazines have always been, new business models have been created, subscription sales pushed and some say combined print and digital circulation figures have been very positive – an indication that some readers like to read their magazines in both print and online versions.

So what does the future hold?

Magazine Girl Shirley, who set up a successful PR business, Shirley Dunmall P.R, when she left magazine publishing, has seen first-hand how the world of magazines has changed:

"With the introduction of bloggers, influencers, online

magazines, YouTube and IGTV (Instagram TV), the way we sourced information and entertainment changed dramatically. No need to buy a physical newspaper or magazine to get the latest news, beauty info, fashion trends and gossip, just log onto Google, Instagram, Facebook or Twitter – everything you need at the press of a few computer keys. Once the rush of the online presence started, which was about seven or eight years ago, it snowballed.

"However, I don't think print magazines will ever disappear completely, and who knows, they may very well have a huge resurgence, like so many things we feel nostalgic about. I hope so," says Shirley, echoing our thoughts.

The very last word in our book goes to the publications we worked on during 'The Glory Years', those closed and those alive and kicking.

LINDA NEWMAN

PUBLICATIONS WHICH ARE NO MORE

Boyfriend (1959–1966*)*
Daily Sketch (1909–1971)
Fabulous, re-named *Fab 208* (1964–1980)
Hair and Good Looks (1984–1988)
Hers (1966–1984)
London Evening News (1881–1980)
Loving (1970–1979)
Mirabelle (1956–1977)
Model Girl (1967–1969)
National Rock Star (1976–1977)
Paul Raymond Publications (sold in 2012)
Petticoat (1966–1975)

Popswop (1972–1974)
Rave (1964–1973)
Record Mirror (1954–1991)
Valentine (1957–1974)
19 (1968–2004)

PUBLICATIONS ALIVE AND KICKING

Evening Standard (1827– relaunched as a free newspaper in 2009)
Good Housekeeping (1922–)
HELLO! (1988–)
National Enquirer (USA) (1926–)
NME (1952– became online only in 2018)
Woman and Home (1926–)
Woman's Own (1932–)
Woman (1937–)

Follow us on Instagram for more stories and anecdotes
@thevintagemagazinegirls